FIELD MARSHAL
EARL HAIG

FIELD MARSHAL EARL HAIG

PHILIP WARNER

CASSELL&CO

Cassell Military Paperbacks

Cassell & Co
Wellington House, 125 Strand
London WC2R 0BB

A CIP catalogue record for this book is available from the
British Library

ISBN 0-304-35645-X

Printed and bound in Great Britain by
Cox & Wyman Ltd., Reading, Berks.

Contents

Acknowledgements

I AM DEEPLY grateful to many people for their generous assistance to me while I was writing this book.

Earl Haig, the son of the Field Marshal, has directed my attention to many sources from which I received valuable information, and in addition lent me books, photographs and documents from his own collection. Lady Dacre of Glanton, the Field Marshal's daughter, provided valuable insight into her father's character and career. Lord Blake very kindly gave me permission to quote from his book *The Private Diaries of Sir Douglas Haig 1914–19*. Lord Windlesham, Principal of Brasenose College, Oxford, provided me with material from the College archives, and drew my attention to essential points. General Sir Michael Gow very kindly sent me copies of Haig's speeches.

The curator and staff of the National Library of Scotland gave me every possible assistance in my study of the Haig archives in their care. Mr Derek Winterbottom, Head of History and Archivist at Clifton College, sent me valuable Haig material, showed me round the school and provided the answers to many questions which had previously baffled me.

Mr Roderick Suddaby, Keeper of the Documents at the Imperial War Museum, gave me his customary guidance, help and advice, all of which were invaluable. Mr Andrew Orgil, Librarian at the Royal Military Academy Sandhurst, and his patient staff gave me unlimited help in tracing sources of information. Mr John Terraine generously gave me help and guidance on Haig,

vii

of whom his knowledge is unlikely to be equalled, let alone surpassed. Mr Leo Cooper was, once more, a source of essential advice, guidance and encouragement. Dr John Sweetman, Head of Defence and International Affairs at the RMA Sandhurst, assisted me greatly in free-ranging discussions of military policy in the First World War. Mr John Hussey very kindly lent me his carefully and fully researched paper on Haig's loan to Sir John French.

These are but a few of the many people who, over the years, have helped in the preparation of the book, and though there is not space to list them all, this does not mean that my debt to them is any the less.

Introduction:
The Haig Enigma

DOUGLAS HAIG IS probably the most controversial figure in British military history, perhaps in all military history. It fell to Haig to command the largest army Britain had ever put into the field, a total of over two million men. No previous military commander had ever held such a powerful position. Before Haig, the fate of nations had been settled by battles between a few thousand men; to control armies of one hundred thousand or more had been considered impossible for any single man – although, of course, armies had occasionally reached and exceeded that figure. During the Second World War vast numbers were again put into the field, but by that time there had been a revolution in communications and the Commander-in-Chief could be better aware of what was happening in the front line than if he had actually been in it himself. Between 1914 and 1918, however, such communications were unimaginable. Winston Churchill said of Haig: 'He might be, he surely was, unequal to the prodigious scale of events; but no one else was discerned as his equal or his better.'

This book is therefore neither a eulogy nor a condemnation of Haig. It is an attempt to assess his task objectively and to decide whether he was better or worse at it than he might have been. His life story is interesting because it shows how he evolved from Haig the apparently undistinguished, industrious junior officer into the man who presided over the army which won the most gruelling war in history. If the criterion of a successful general is to win wars, Haig must be judged a success. The cost of victory was appalling, but it needs to be remembered that Haig's military operations were in accordance with the ideas of the time, when attrition was the method by which all the belligerents hoped and planned to achieve the desired result. The Germans fought a war of attrition, and so did the French until the casualties of the 1916 and 1917 battles became more than they could sustain. The Russians, too, planned a war of attrition: unfortunately for them, their military organisation was so incompetent than their armies collapsed at the front and their munitions and supply systems failed behind the lines. These are matters which will be examined in greater detail later.

Inevitably a number of books have been written about Haig, but nevertheless they are fewer than might have been expected. The writers have varied considerably in their opinions and their approaches. A number of them have denounced him as 'Butcher' Haig, finding ample proof for their views in the horrific casualty figures of the Western Front – figures only too clearly supported by the rows of headstones in the cemeteries of northern France. Some explain these casualties as being due to Haig's obstinacy and incompetence; some see a darker side and attribute them to a selfish indifference to the size of the sacrifice. Other writers, often military ones, have decided that Haig was incompetent because he had been promoted far beyond the rank he should properly have held. This ingenious argument makes Haig a victim of circumstances. Yet others have taken the opposite view, finding many examples of Haig's efficiency and suitability for his exacting role. And there are military writers who take an almost romantic view, seeing Haig as a man who did astonishingly well when faced with a virtually impossible task.

There have been good books on Haig and bad books on Haig. There have been books by writers who knew about soldiering but not about writing biographies, and there have been their opposites who knew something, but not a lot, about biographies, but had nothing in the way of balanced military knowledge. Some inaccuracies about his life have been repeated in volume after volume, obviously accepted uncritically.

Time does not blur the stark realities of the First World War – the 'Great War', as it was known until the Second came along. No one who walks among the graves in northern France, on the Somme, at Passchendaele or at Loos, to mention only a few locations, can clear his or her mind of emotion. Nor should they. The German cemeteries are equally moving. Among the vast losses and sufferings certain reminders still evoke almost unbearable anguish. War memorials which record the loss of all the sons in one family, or occasions when entire districts lost their young men in battalions such as the Bradford Pals, the Leeds Pals or the Manchester Pals, have a special poignancy. Even the replica trenches which are now beginning to appear in museums in Britain and France convey something which is so far removed from ordinary experience that the visitor can scarcely comprehend it.

The full realisation that the war was horrific for both sides came when Erich Maria Remarque published his chilling account *All Quiet on the Western Front* in 1929. There was a concept of mutual suffering in many other books about the war, although it was often implied rather than stated. Robert Graves's *Goodbye to All That*, Edmund Blunden's *Undertones of War*, Cecil Roberts's *Spears Against Us*, and the poems of Siegfried Sassoon, Wilfred Owen and Isaac Rosenberg convey something of it.

The fact that the horrors of the First World War still stun the imagination makes it difficult for the ordinary reader to reach a calm appraisal of Haig, the man who presided over it all and therefore, it is thought, must presumably have approved of it. A sizeable body of general readers and even some informed critics of Haig seem to assume that it was he and not the Germans who invaded France and established the trench system. Those who grudgingly admit that he had the responsibility of pushing a well dug-in enemy back off French soil criticise the cost of the way he did so without offering alternative methods. It is true that he made certain tactical mistakes, but these are easier to identify in hindsight, with all the German papers available, than they would have been at the time. In some situations there is no substitute for brute force and high casualties. Haig was faced with a task which was more difficult than Montgomery's of ejecting the Germans from

North Africa in the Second World War, or of fighting the North-West Europe campaign, neither of which was accomplished without heavy casualties. Only in the Burma campaign was a British general presented with a challenge as difficult as Haig's; there General Slim had to eject armies of fanatical Japanese who would die rather than retreat. His difficulties were increased by the ruggedness of the terrain, the exhausting climate and the endemic diseases which greatly reduced the fighting strength of his army.

The principal error of armchair strategists is to make an incomplete survey of the Second World War when comparing it with the First. Hitler's armies were not ejected from the Soviet Union without terrible casualties and hardships on both sides which bear comparison with those of the Western Front in 1916. Strategic bombing by the Allies in the Second World War was enormously costly in lives: the number of aircrew killed over Europe exceeded that of junior officers killed on the Western Front in the previous war. Losses in merchant shipping during 1939–45 were appalling, but no one believed that the Allies should stop trying to bring supplies across the Atlantic.

It has been suggested by many critics that Haig did not know what was going on, nor realise the conditions under which trench warfare was fought. It is true that Kiggell, his Chief of Staff, was reported to have wept when eventually he saw the edge of the Passchendaele battlefield and to have said, 'Did we really send men to fight in this?' – but Kiggell had never been anything but a staff officer. As such, he was probably too busy with reports and maps and figures to have taken in the true meaning of the conditions in Flanders. But Haig often came close enough to the front to see the troops coming out of battle and could not have failed to notice their condition, even if his generals had not already made the brutal facts clear to him; on the Somme, for example, Charles Carrington tells us that Haig reconnoitred Carrington's section of the front personally before deciding not to make an attack.

It was highly unlikely that Haig would be criticised by the average soldier during the war. The vast majority of them never set eyes on him: to them, he was a figure so remote in rank and personality as to be almost unimaginable. Soldiers have no time for detached thought about the Higher Command. In France and Belgium their immediate concerns were German shells, mud, food, work, NCOs, junior officers and lack of sleep. Their basic needs were cigarettes, sleep, food, drink (not necessarily alcoholic) and women, in that order. The merits or otherwise of the Commander-in-Chief are unlikely to have intruded into their pattern of thought. Many would have been perplexed if asked to name him: Kitchener was a more familiar name and face.

On the other hand, those who knew Haig well through having worked with him at various stages of his career were anything but inarticulate. They expressed themselves freely and clearly and, no doubt, honestly, but without knowing the background to their personal relationship with Haig it is difficult for the modern reader to know how to assess their opinions. Thus the views of William Robertson, Haig's Chief of Staff, who achieved the miracle of rising from the rank of trooper to field marshal, fall into the category of admiration, and those of Lloyd George, who had emerged from a poverty-stricken Welsh Baptist family to become Prime Minister of Britain, represent the reverse.

Adding to the difficulty of assessing the truth about Haig is the vast mass of papers he left. They comprise literally millions of words: his diary alone contains three-quarters of a million.

Simple though he may at first seem as a character, Haig was clearly anything but that. Although not intellectual in the conventional sense, he clearly had a form of high intelligence which is difficult to analyse or quantify. On the surface he appears to have been a conventional, highly motivated and decisive character. In the course of this book we may find he was no more and no less than that. But from what has been said already it is clear that finding the true Haig is going to be a far from simple task.

Inherited characteristics and upbringing combined to make Haig what is nowadays called 'a private person'. Although there had been signs of a violent temper and unruly disposition in his early boyhood, these characteristics had either disappeared or been placed firmly under control once he was an adult. Being a member of a large family soon develops self-discipline, for brothers and sisters are exacting teachers; an only child may grow up with faults uncorrected and mannerisms unnoticed, and may later find some difficulty living in a community, but a member of a large family will be made only too well aware of any weakness of character or oddity of behaviour.

Failure to pass the Staff College examination might have caused a less dedicated man to abandon a military career altogether (as it often does), but Haig's reaction was different. Although greatly mortified by not qualifying, and smarting from a sense of injustice at having failed an unexpected eyesight test as well, he exercised remarkable forbearance, returned to his unit and served with good grace in a subordinate position. He made light of his misfortunes and earned the admiration of his contemporaries by proving that he neither wanted nor expected sympathy.

When he later reached the Staff College, through a special nomination, he applied himself to his studies with a determination which impressed those around him. The general assumption was that, because he was less intelligent than his contemporaries, he needed to work harder. It seems, however, that his industry was due not only to ambition but also to the fact that he had an enquiring mind: he saw virtue in learning for its own sake. The late Victorian period was, of course, an inspiring time to be alive. There were new ideas, new philosophies, new branches of knowledge. Haig was well aware of this. Although he was a talented games player, he scorned the 'philistines' who thought of nothing else.

In the following pages I shall try to identify the stages at which Haig realised he had the qualities and opportunities to progress to the supreme post of Commander-in-Chief. Although he possessed certain social advantages, they were not sufficient in themselves to take him to the top. To achieve his ambition he needed to plan and to use influence; he was a realist and knew that to wait for his qualities to be recognised would probably be futile. There seems to come a stage in the careers of many ambitious people, particularly in the armed forces, when they assume that what is good for their personal advancement is good for the community in which find themselves. Generals like Montgomery are not troubled by self-doubt. Haig was an entirely different character from Montgomery, but at a certain stage in his career he decided – perhaps rightly – that he was the only general on the Western Front who could win the war for the Allies. It became his duty to continue.

This devotion to duty extended into his retirement when, although exhausted by the strains of the previous decade, he never spared himself in his efforts to improve the lot of ex-servicemen. Undoubtedly he shortened his life by his work for that particular cause.

Many people are surprised to learn that this symbol of blinkered militarism was musical, could draw and paint, and had a talent for design. At Bemersyde he set out and built with his own hands an impressive sunken garden.

Perhaps this book should carry the title 'The Mystery of Earl Haig'.

I
Early Life

DOUGLAS HAIG WAS born on 8 June 1861 at 24 Charlotte Square, Edinburgh, the last of a family of eleven. Haig forebears can be traced back to the twelfth century, their name then being De Haga. They appear to have come from Cape de la Hague in Normandy, and formed part of a settlement on the Borders which was encouraged by King David I of Scotland. The countryside which they acquired has been described by contemporaries as 'primeval forest' in which clearings were being made. However, since the arrival of William the Conqueror in 1066 Norman settlers had shown that they could tame and develop wild stretches of territory, provide soldiers for their feudal overlords when required, and foster trade and agriculture which were valuable and taxable. Only the most resolute could survive, for in addition to the difficulties of establishing a viable homestead there was the ever-present danger of raids by predatory neighbours. No doubt the Haigs could be as ferocious as their contemporaries when an opportunity presented; it was part of the price of survival.

The history of the Haig family, *The Haigs of Bemersyde*, was researched and written by John Russell, and published by Blackwood in 1881. Russell was a scrupulous researcher: confronted with many fascinating but unauthenticated stories, he rejected them all as 'unverifiable'.

By the thirteenth century, Russell tells us, the Haigs had become rich and powerful: the fourth Petrus de Haga endowed Dryburgh Abbey with a portion of forest named Flatwode.

8

However, at the time of making this and other bequests, de Haga signed a deed in which he agreed to pay the convent of Old Melrose ten salmon a year. Ten salmon appears to have been a mere token for one whose lands adjoined the Tweed, and it is assumed that ten salmon were probably a nominal penalty for some misdemeanour committed by de Haga against Melrose – the presence of nearby unprotected but valuable abbey lands, rich in cattle and game, could sometimes prove a strong temptation to medieval lairds.

The family motto:

> Tyde what may, whate'er betide
> Haig will be Haig of Bemersyde

dates from the thirteenth century. This was a time of great turbulence and trouble for Scotland, and it is said that Thomas the Rhymer, a noted local seer, used the words when speaking to Johannes de Haga (1280–1326), who was looking gloomily at lands devastated by the English, probably under Edward I. However, the couplet seems to have been refined into the present form at a later date: the name Haig in place of De Haga did not occur until over a hundred years later. But whatever its date and original form, it would be difficult to think of a more memorable and inspiring family motto.

The dispute with the Abbot of Melrose, once resolved for ten salmon a year, came to a head again in the fifteenth century and led to the excommunication of the entire Haig family 'and others, their advisors and abettors', who were all named in the abbey records. Most people would have been over-awed by excommunication but the Haigs paid scant attention, preferring the ownership of the disputed lands to eternal bliss. However, three years later a civil court awarded the lands to the abbey and the excommunication was therefore lifted.

Century after century the Border families made fighting a way of life. Sometimes the Scots fought against the English, but at other times they fought against their fellow Scots. It was the same on the English side of the border; often there was a better reason to fight near neighbours, who might be encroaching on land, or stealing cattle, or merely being quarrelsome, than to campaign against more distant foes – though the name Haig also occurs regularly in records of military expeditions which set out from Scotland. Over the centuries such conditions produced dour, stubborn characters who were not accustomed to deviate from the path they had chosen. It has often been observed that Douglas Haig's branch of the family was not in the direct line but only a collateral. The point is immaterial: a member of a Scottish Border family would have been steeled in the art of survival whatever his place in the hierarchy.

Younger sons of landed families in Britain usually have to make their own fortunes, for the bulk of the inheritance goes to the eldest son. Some try to do so by military means, others by venturing into commerce. Douglas Haig's immediate ancestors had prospered in the distilling and marketing of whisky, and in consequence his father was wealthy. However, in the strange world of Victorian, or perhaps feudal, values, being prosperous in 'trade' did nothing for one's social standing: members of the upper echelons of society who made money by commercial ventures were thought to have lowered their status. But the social stigma of commercial prosperity did not prevent impecunious heirs of ancient titles or land seeking brides among heiresses, whose dowries could pay for urgently needed repairs to crumbling family homes and fortunes.

At the age of thirty-seven, John Haig had reversed the usual pattern when he acquired for his bride Rachel Veitch, aged eighteen, daughter of a family who thought themselves socially superior to the Haigs but were too poor to endow their daughter. Nevertheless, when Rachel married John she discounted any social pretensions and became an excellent wife and mother. Her position cannot have been easy. John Haig had the ill-health which usually goes with heavy drinking, and it was alcoholism which eventually killed him. However, he was able to look after his business and was apparently a considerate employer.

The task of bringing up his family was left to Rachel, who wore down her health in domestic responsibilities nearly as rapidly as John Haig did with over-indulgence. She would get up at four every morning and from then on would supervise her large family until she attended their prayers at bedtime. She was deeply religious and ensured that they conformed, even if they did not share her zeal. John Haig does not seem to have been particularly interested in his children, of whom nine survived. Their disparity in ages was considerable, and Douglas's eldest brother was twenty years older than he was. Apart from his mother, the most influential person in his upbringing and life was his elder sister Henrietta. According to one of his early biographers, Duff Cooper, who knew him well, it was Henrietta who directed Douglas's attention to making a career in the Army; there was actually no need for him to work at all, for he had sufficient money to spend his time in idleness. Although Henrietta married William Jameson, another well-known whisky distiller, she continued to be Douglas's confidante and adviser until his death, and only survived him by a few months.

After Haig's death, his widow, Countess Haig, who was greatly concerned by some of the criticisms of her husband, wrote a book entitled *The Man I Knew*. In her research she questioned Haig's surviving brothers and sisters, and the correspondence which ensued is now in the Haig Papers at the National Library of Scotland in Edinburgh. There are 425 items in the collection and some contain numerous letters. Perhaps the most informative of the correspondents is Haig's eldest brother John.

From the correspondence it is clear that John Haig senior was extremely rich, earning £10,000 a year from his business before it was sold to Distillers Ltd in 1876. That sum in the mid-nineteenth century would probably be the equivalent of £500,000 today; small wonder that there was no shortage of money in the Haig household. The prosperous businessman was also a Freemason and took a prominent part in local and charitable affairs. Although he was quick-tempered, his outbursts were so brief that his children were never frightened of him. He was a lifelong sufferer from asthma, an illness to which Douglas too was initially prone, though later he grew out of it. Looking after her husband's physical health and her children's spiritual welfare clearly wore out Rachel Haig, for she died in 1879 at the age of fifty-eight; her husband had died the previous year, aged seventy-six.

Although Douglas had been born in Edinburgh at his parents' home, his early upbringing took place in Fifeshire, where they had a country house; there he never had a pram but was conveyed around in a little chair on the back of a small pony. Like many children of the day he had long golden curls, much admired by his mother but less by his brothers and sisters, who forcibly cut them off one day. His mother saved them, and two survive in Edinburgh: one in the National Library and another in the Huntly Museum. Angelic though he may have been in appearance, Douglas was very different in his behaviour: he appears to have been a remarkably stubborn and unruly small boy. At the age of four he flatly refused to be photographed in a family group: he was eventually persuaded to comply the following day by being allowed to hold his favourite pistol. During another tantrum he refused to cross a bridge and screamed so violently that a passer-by tried to intervene under the impression that he was being ill-treated, only to realise his mistake quickly. His mother gave him a drum and wrote on it: 'Douglas Haig – sometimes a good boy', an inscription that seems to have been written in a spirit of optimism rather than expectation.

Rachel Haig's fervent wish to make her son religious did not, as might perhaps have been expected, make him rebel violently against all religion but eventually made him almost as devout as she was. Possibly her early death, when he was at the impressionable age of eighteen – an age when many of his contemporaries would be having doubts and expressing them freely – confirmed her early influence. Undoubtedly Haig the Field Marshal saw himself as a man with a mission. In 1916 he wrote to his brother John, 'I feel sure *we are meant to win*', and attended church service every Sunday all through the First World War. His father had been in the habit of swearing in front of his family, but in January 1915 Douglas Haig went to the other extreme when he wrote to his brother saying how bad conditions were for 'the poor d---ls in the trenches'. His mother had never missed an opportunity of letting him know how much he depended on his Maker: all her numerous letters concluded by commending him to God's loving care and protection. When he was at school and deliberating whether he should try for Oxford or Cambridge, she wrote hoping that he was earnestly seeking for 'direction in this matter that you may be led to choose what is best for you and that God's blessing may go with you which has never failed'. Here we begin to see the foundation of Haig's eventual steely sense of purpose.

Accounts of Haig's education vary somewhat. Like any boy of his background at the time he began with local day schools and then went to a preparatory school as a boarder; the preparatory school was Orwell House at Clifton-on-Dunsmoor (as it was then spelt). Its headmaster was David Hanbury, a former Rugby boy, a Cambridge MA and barrister, who had formerly been an assistant master at Tonbridge. Orwell House was probably typical of many other similar establishments of the time, kept either by retired schoolmasters or by well-qualified vicars. They were sometimes many miles from the boys' homes; there were no half-terms or exeats, and their main purpose was to instruct and keep their pupils out of mischief by giving them plenty of work to do. Some schools had pupils whose parents lived and worked abroad and therefore never saw their offspring for years on end. Such establishments did not encourage self-pity.

Clifton-on-Dunsmoor was two and a half miles from Rugby, and no doubt Mr Hanbury was closely in touch with the academic requirements of his old school. The Haigs wished to send Douglas on to Rugby, where it was felt that the influence of the late Thomas Arnold would ensure that he was brought up as a Christian gentleman; moreover, other members of the family had already been at the school. Unfortunately for the family plans, Mr Hanbury had to point out that Douglas fell well short of the educational standard required for entrance to Rugby, particularly in Greek. However, the disappointment was only temporary. John Percival, headmaster of the relatively new public school at Bristol, Clifton College, was also a former Rugby master and the school prospectus made it clear that Clifton was based on the Rugby model, with the boys having studies rather than common rooms. Clifton, which had been founded in 1862 and was thus a year younger than Douglas Haig himself, was a Proprietary Institution owned by four hundred shareholders with a stake of £25 each, and each shareholder had the right to nominate a boy for a place in the school. Firmly established, with the academic level steadily moving upwards, Clifton seems to have suited Haig well: it did not push him to attain standards beyond his powers, though six years after he had left it was at the top of the list of schools winning scholarships to Oxford and Cambridge, beating Eton, Winchester, Rugby and many others in the process. However, there was no question of Haig being a late starter intellectually: he was well aware that academic study would never be easy for him, and accepted without rancour that the only way he would ever gain success was by plodding hard work. Interestingly, he never adopted the defiant, resentful attitude which is encountered frequently among those whose mental attainments are below average. This says a lot for his character, even though it put a question mark against his suitability for certain appointments. Haig was no anti-intellectual snob, nor a snob of any other kind either, although many factors in his life might have made him one. His family background was scarcely conducive to a democratic outlook, while his membership of the most fashionable clubs in Oxford might have given him a high opinion of his social qualities; and his commission in an élite cavalry regiment, combined with his prowess at polo, could have made him insufferable.

Clifton imbued Haig with all the qualities which public schools tried then to inculcate. He believed in loyalty, in working for a team, in not blaming others when matters went wrong, and above all in serving his country. Henry Newbolt, a Clifton contemporary, expressed the attitude which Haig undoubtedly shared, and though much of his verse may seem absurdly naïve today the feeling behind it is sound enough:

> To set the cause above renown
> To love the game beyond the prize . . .

While still a schoolboy Haig had already decided on the Army as a career, and it is noteworthy that, inarticulate though he was later alleged to be, he should have been the proposer of a controversial motion for the school debating society: 'The Army has done the country more service than the Navy.' In the West Country, with the beat of Drake's drum almost ringing in his ears, that was an emotive proposition. The fact that his speech was recorded by his brother John, who was also at Clifton, suggests that it stirred the audience. The story is confirmed by the Countess Haig.

Having played rugby football for his house Haig was awarded a school cap, which meant that he was one of the twenty best players in the school. Although Clifton had had regular cricket fixtures with Sherborne, Radley and Cheltenham since 1865, its only rugby football fixture had been against Marlborough in 1864. There was some confusion during that game as Clifton had to refrain from what was known as hacking, which Marlborough had already abolished. The game of rugby football at that time did not bear any comparison with its modern namesake. There were twenty players on each side, and points could only be scored by kicking goals. However, in order to be allowed a kick at goal a player had to force his way over the opposing line, which allowed a 'try' (at kicking a goal); otherwise the try was valueless, unlike today when it counts for more points than a goal. Until 1871, in order to obtain the ball players indulged, legally, in hacking. Good hackers kicked a way through a bunch of opponents, no doubt inflicting many painful and perhaps lasting injuries. Hacking was made illegal in 1871, but the ball was still obtained by methods which would promptly be disallowed by modern referees. The House XX was no place for the timid. Haig was variously described both as a forward and as a half-back: 'full of guts and by no means lacking in fun . . . a dour fighter, active as a cat, brave as a lion', were some of the comments by unnamed Clifton contemporaries quoted by the Countess Haig in her book.

On arrival at Clifton Haig had been placed in the Lower Fourth; two years later he was promoted to the Lower Fifth, in which he remained for the rest of his time at the school. His worst subject was Latin, but it appears that in his last term he came top of his form in that subject. Aptitude at Latin is usually considered a test of intellectual ability, but in the earlier stages, when pupils work over prescribed translations, it is possible to achieve a reasonable level by sheer industry. A standard textbook in those days was the *Via Latina*, which contained such helpful rhymes as:

> A woman, island, country, tree,
> And city, feminine we see . . .

Victorian pupils, whatever schools they attended, acquired much of their learning by 'repetition'. Repetition applied to mathematical tables and formulae, English and Latin poetry, and divinity, for which 'portions of the Bible are committed to memory', according to one school prospectus. The range of subjects also included history, drawing and natural science, but the emphasis was on the classics.

The key to Haig's adult character and much of his subsequent attitude to life seems to lie in the influence of his headmaster, John Percival. When Haig entered School House at Clifton in 1875, Percival had been headmaster for thirteen years, the entire period of the school's existence. He had begun with 76 boys: when he left in 1879 there were 680. Derek Winterbottom, the present Head of History and Archivist at Clifton, describes Percival as a 'phenomenon'. When appointed he was just twenty-eight, and although he had had a brilliant academic career at Oxford, his experience of teaching boys was limited to two years at Rugby. The founders of Clifton had taken a great risk in appointing one so young and inexperienced to the headmastership, but the risk was soon shown by the results to have been a decision of great wisdom and foresight. The headmaster was also housemaster of School House and would therefore have known Haig well. He wanted Haig to return for a further year during which he could have been in the Sixth Form, and this extra year might have made a considerable difference to Haig academically.

Percival was a moral, religious idealist, but he was also a practical and forthright organiser and businessman. Apart from his two years at Rugby he had no experience of the public school ethos with its ritualised standards. He would not have discouraged what others might have branded as 'sneaking', and he encouraged boys to come to him with their problems, even if these included unfair treatment by seniors or masters. There was, and still is, of course, widespread disapproval of a boy who 'sneaks', and over the years there have been innumerable cases where bullies and other anti-social characters have been able to make the lives of their juniors intolerable because they knew the latter would never report them. Nowadays one rarely hears of severe bullying in schools, though there are often cases in the services. After years at Clifton, where Percival would expect to know what was going on in the school, Haig would not have found himself in a dilemma later in life when Sir Evelyn Wood, the Adjutant General, asked him to write letters full of frank opinions of his seniors and their operational skills. His more traditionally educated brother officers might not have approved if they had known.

In spite of his enthusiasm for the Army as a career, Haig knew very well that his chances of passing the entrance examination to Sandhurst were minimal. Although not as demanding as the entrance to the Royal Military Academy at Woolwich, Sandhurst★ still required high marks in Latin, Greek, mathematics, modern languages, history, natural science (mineralogy and geology), chemistry, heat, electricity, magnetism, and geometrical and freehand drawing. Passing into Sandhurst or Woolwich was regarded, not surprisingly, as an achievement, and was often recorded on honours boards in schools.

Haig found an easier way. At this time, and even into the 1930s, many colleges at Oxford and Cambridge had no entrance examination for the ordinary undergraduate. This meant that a young man could be accepted by a college and when in residence work for the comparatively simple university entrance examinations, known as 'Responsions' at Oxford and 'Previous' at Cambridge (and known to undergraduates, not inappropriately, as 'smalls' or 'little-go'). Crammers or, as they preferred to call themselves, 'tutorial establishments', had these examinations expertly assessed

★ The two establishments, Sandhurst and Woolwich, have since merged.

and an undergraduate would need to be exceptionally idle or stupid if he failed after their ministrations. Before the two examinations were abolished midway through the present century, most undergraduates were excused them by virtue of having obtained matriculation in School Certificate. Having attended a crammer, Haig passed Responsions without difficulty, and was accepted by Brasenose College in 1880.

The advantage of this system for Haig was that, although Sandhurst stipulated a high standard in the entrance examination for ordinary candidates, it was waived altogether for university men who had passed Responsions or Previous. All Haig had to do now was study at Oxford and then enter Sandhurst any time up to the age of twenty-three. He would not need a degree – although the university would require him to study for one during his nine terms of residence. The more intelligent undergraduates read for an honours degree, which was limited to a single subject such as classics or history. The less gifted, like Haig, opted for a pass degree which encompassed a miscellany of subjects but at a much lower level. They included English, French, history, basic economics and aspects of classical literature. Haig's studies in these subjects were supervised by different college tutors. A tutorial would include discussing an essay or paper Haig had written and some conversation, possibly about the college prospects on the river or playing fields; the termly examination would be anticipated in the papers set, and the final exam itself would be little more than a formality. Nevertheless at the end of this the undergraduate would be the possessor of a BA degree, provided he had also completed the nine obligatory eight-week terms in residence. In the event, Haig had to miss a term through a bad bout of influenza and he failed to obtain a degree. Many years later, when he was elected to an honorary fellowship of his college and also awarded an honorary doctorate of civil law, he enquired with a rare display of humour of the Brasenose Principal, 'Have I passed enough exams for this?'

A later Principal of Brasenose, Mr Sampson, told the Countess Haig that Douglas acquired his English style from the essayist Walter Pater, who was his tutor in that subject. In fact there is no trace of Pater's peculiarly artificial style in Haig's unadorned writings. It is also reported that Haig was exceptionally conscientious in his studies and would leave a social gathering without hesitation when he had work to complete, though this is frequently a necessity when an essay has to be written and the allotted time has already been wasted. In an article written for *The Oxford Magazine* in 1928 Haig's Brasenose contemporary, Lord Askwith, says: 'For the Schools he read French Literature and the Elements of Political Economy, under Sir Richard Lodge and in other subjects, such as Homer, dealt with Walter Pater.' However, at a dinner for old Brasenose members held in London in 1909, Askwith reports that Haig mentioned recalling his delight in having nothing to do for two years after passing smalls. Much of the information about Haig's Oxford career comes from this article: Askwith's memory seemed remarkably clear, forty-seven years later.

Brasenose prided itself on its sporting prowess; it did not, however, neglect the academic side. The Principal at that time was Dr Cradock, an eccentric in his twenty-seventh year in the post. On his first interview with Haig he said, 'Ride, sir, ride – I like to see the gentlemen of Brasenose in top boots.' Perhaps he had sized up Haig as a potential cavalryman. Askwith was given even more startling advice: 'Drink plenty of port, sir, you want plenty of port in this damp climate.' Doubtless Cradock would have approved of the eccentric John Mytton who, intending to become an under-graduate, sent a pipe (745 bottles) of port ahead to ease his arrival, though he never took the opportunity to come into residence and drink it. However, Cradock's views on the proper conduct of undergraduate life were not typical of the university as a whole, as Haig was no doubt aware. At Christ Church, which had the distinction of providing ten prime ministers in the nineteenth century, academic work took precedence over sport. When attending compulsory chapel at 8 a.m., all the undergraduates were required to wear white surplices, but these had to be left open at the front. Undergraduates who planned to spend the rest of the day in the hunting field instead of lecture rooms were thus thwarted.

Haig took a full part in the university activities of his day. In his first year, in spite of Dr Cradock's advice, he took up rowing. In a reply dated 1 January 1909 to the then Principal of Brasenose, who had requested information from former students for use in the college register, Haig added a footnote: 'By the way I have two pewter cups which I value greatly as they record the fact that I rowed "2" in the winning boat of the only two rowing races in which I competed, viz "Coxed College Fours 1880" and "Brasenose and Trinity Scratch Fours 1880".' Haig's cup for the latter event is now in the Huntly Museum in Edinburgh.

Askwith says Haig gave up rowing because he was too light in build and in addition found the training and coaching boring. He then played golf, hunted with the Bicester, and took up polo. Polo had been introduced to England by the 11th Hussars only ten years earlier, and had very few supporters in Haig's day. Then, as now, one needed to be wealthy to play the game. When a few enthusiasts decided they wanted to bring it to Oxford, they requested permission to use the Parks for the purpose. It is said that, on that occasion, they claimed the game was of great antiquity and had been introduced to Europe by Marco Polo. A game against Cambridge was soon arranged and Haig scored the only Oxford goal. He was introduced to the game, according to Askwith, by an American fellow undergraduate: 'His principal friend was "Tommy" Hitchcock, of BNC [Brasenose College], from America, himself a great polo player and father of a great polo player; and by him Haig was started on polo, worked hard at the game with strenuous energy, and, with Hitchcock, played polo for the university in 1882 and 1883.' Haig went on to become a very good polo player, frequently representing his regiment and also England.

Although naturally abstemious he belonged to several dining clubs, as well as the two élite ones, the Bullingdon and Vincent's. The Bullingdon was, and still is, a club for the hunting fraternity and tends to include a number of members of the aristocracy. Vincent's is principally a sporting club for the leading university games players and athletes, though in Haig's day many fewer games were played at universities than today. At that time

Vincent's was probably in the pocket of Brasenose, for Haig and other members of the college were on the committee, while most of the members of the Bullingdon probably came from Christ Church where Haig had several friends. Although Haig seems to have taken a full part in university life he is said by Duff Cooper to have found it casual and purposeless. No doubt it made a sharp contrast to Percival's reign at Clifton.

Haig began keeping a diary at Oxford but, like most under-graduates' diaries, it contains little but observations of people around him and nothing of his own philosophy; however, it shows that his and his contemporaries' interests were not entirely limited to Oxford. In a discussion it was decided that the Church was both narrow-minded and hypocritical. A Channel tunnel was discussed in 1882; the verdict was that its only practical advantage was that fruit and vegetables from the continent would reach the London markets more quickly.

When the Prince of Wales – the future Edward VII – visited Oxford, Haig and his colleagues resolved to decorate Vincent's in his honour. The club premises are above a shop (now Shepherd and Woodward) on the corner of King Edward Street and the High, as High Street is invariably known. The Prince was staying with Dean Liddell of Christ Church, and when the pair drove down the High at 9.15 p.m. on their way to a concert the streets were crowded with a set of roughs such as were only to be found in Oxford. Haig, who observed the scene from the windows of Vincent's, wrote, 'From one end of the High to another there was a free fight going on . . . There was one seething mass in front of the windows which hustled and swayed to and fro . . . at length they took to throwing stones.'

Haig's upbringing made him somewhat impatient with many Oxford attitudes. He felt that all work should have a purpose, and the Oxford view that research was an end in itself and that there was nothing immoral about idleness irritated him. Askwith men-tioned that Haig in fact rarely visited Vincent's; his particular circle consisted of undergraduates from Brasenose and Christ Church, although he was courteous in his behaviour towards everyone else.

He never (as far as I am aware) entertained any woman, though I have seen his face set, in a silent but obstinate protest, against any loose jokes about women. My impression was that he disliked any remarks derogatory to women, and showed it, without speaking, so clearly that any would-be raconteur 'dried up'.

Haig had grown to his full height when he came up. His shoulders stooped more, and also his head, but to the end his head, with a pushed-out chin and marked jaw, had the effect of peering forward, as if he was short-sighted, which he was not.

For his first two terms Haig had been allotted rooms in the college, which he did not like. They had been built – as temporary structures – during the Peninsular War, so were already seventy years old, and consisted of no more than lath, plaster and a few coats of wallpaper. They were still being used thirty years after Haig had left, but were later demolished. According to Askwith:

Haig spent much of his time working in his rooms but attended the big college lunches which were occasionally held. He knew and was pleasant to everyone, not minding with whom he sat but by no means courting popularity. He liked to talk quietly to his neighbour about a subject interesting to his neighbour or affecting the life or athletics of the college rather than his own interests. He loved a quiet joke but I never heard him make one. To Hall [dinner] he seldom went but dined out, always returning early, and hating to sit up at night.

He was ever loyal to Oxford and to those whom he knew there . . . The glamour of Oxford caught him and the University and the city of Oxford may both claim and honour him with justice as one of their very faithful sons.

Although there was no need for Haig to pass another examination for Sandhurst entry, he was well aware that he was completely ignorant of many of the subjects in which his future colleagues would already be proficient. He therefore spent the next six months, over the autumn and winter of 1883–4, at a

crammer named Litchfield near Hampton Court. It was an interesting decision, and showed he was already capable of assessing a
situation and acting prudently. Owing to the lost summer term,
when influenza had prevented him from being in residence, Haig
was short of the eight weeks still required for his pass degree. He
now decided that the degree was of no immediate value to him
and that the time would be better spent looking to the future
rather than making up lost time in the past.

It has been asserted by some of his biographers that after leaving
Oxford Haig paid no attention to his old university until he came
back to receive honorary degrees after the First World War. Like a
number of other statements made about Haig, this is quite untrue.
In a letter to the Bursar of BNC, dated 25 August 1889, he
enquired how long he would need to take an MA provided he
completed his residence for his BA. He explained that he had
passed all the exams for the BA but was short of one term's
residence, missed because 'I was seedy.' He continued:

> Up to date I have not been able to keep this term, owing to my
> having joined the Army, but I hope some day to make the term
> good, and take my MA. Having been to Oxford for three years
> it is just as well to have a degree, to show one went thro' the
> place fairly creditably, for it seems that a fair proportion of
> those who go to the university now return without one.
>
> I shall probably be able to keep the term in two or three
> years' time, but probably the College authorities have other
> views on the subject.

Haig entered Sandhurst on 12 February 1884. His military
education thus began at a time when the British Army had
recently experienced a number of traumatic reverses. The expedition to Abyssinia in 1867–8 had been a brilliant success, as had
Wolseley's campaign against the Ashanti in West Africa in
1873–4; but these had been offset by the Isandhlwana massacre of
1879 and the death of the Prince Imperial, son of the exiled French
Emperor Napoleon III, in the Zulu War, even though that
campaign had eventually culminated in success. The 1st Boer War

of 1881–2 had ended in defeat, which the Liberal government of the day was willing to accept, unaware that it was storing up trouble for itself later. There had been two spectacular victories against a rebel army in Egypt at Tel-el-Kebir and Kassassin, but even as Haig was entering Sandhurst there were disturbing reports from the Sudan: the Hicks expedition of 1883 had been massacred, Gordon was isolated in Khartoum and there was a dangerous guerrilla leader near Suakin; soon the unthinkable would happen and a British infantry square would be 'broken' at El Teb. The message which all these events conveyed was that the British Army would have no easy victories in Africa.

In the present century it has been fashionable to denigrate these small colonial campaigns as unfair contests in which the unfortunate natives, armed with spears or equally primitive weapons, had no chance against the modern weapons of the British soldiers. In fact, many of the so-called 'savages' had a considerable quantity of rifles and some heavier guns; if they did not use them effectively it was because of lack of fire discipline rather than opportunity. The basic lesson which would have been drilled into Haig was that successful campaigning in remote territories required training, planning, logistical support, hygienic practices and flexibility. Within a few years he would be engaged in similar campaigns himself and putting these rules into practice.

2

From Sandhurst to Staff College

WHEN HAIG ARRIVED at Sandhurst he was already twenty-two years old and was in the invidious position of being older and more experienced than cadets who had been able to pass the examination he would inevitably have failed. On average they were three to four years younger than he was, and no doubt seemed to him extremely immature. Haig was not the type to unbend and form friendships among people so much junior to him in age; at the same time he was well aware that whatever progress he himself made could only come through hard and continuous work. Unfortunately the course at Sandhurst was theoretical, rather than practical. Once again he found himself having to spend long periods 'swotting' – the word originated at Sandhurst and was apparently a modification of 'sweating'. Although there was riding, and a chance to show his abilities at polo, there was no musketry or revolver shooting, but instead the study of tactics, fortifications, topography (map reading), military law and military administration, together with drill and gymnastics. Military history was not taught at all, although there was a library in which cadets could study if they had the time or the inclination.

Haig is said to have awed his fellow cadets and impressed his instructors with his industry. No doubt this, his popularity with the instructors and his aloofness with his fellow cadets made him disliked rather than admired. He was appointed a Senior Under Officer in his company and in that capacity was responsible for seeing that the Company Commander's wishes were quickly and conscientiously observed, working closely with the instructors, both commissioned and non-commissioned. SUOs, as they were called, undoubtedly had more power than was good for them or for their juniors and some became bullies and tyrants, supported by the system. Haig was neither a bully nor a sadist but was undoubtedly a perfectionist – respected, but avoided when possible. There is a story quoted by John Terraine, Haig's biographer, that one of the instructors described him as the best of his intake, 'top in everything' and likely to become head of the British Army. It sounds like the remark of an NCO of limited intelligence: similar prophecies are regularly made by such characters about members of various intakes as they pass through Sandhurst.

Haig did not win the Sword of Honour, as has often been claimed for him: there was no Sword of Honour, awarded to the best cadet of each intake, at that time. He did, however, win the Anson Memorial Award, which has now ceased to be a sword and become a prize for the cadet judged best in military subjects: in Haig's day the Anson Sword seems to have been an award for the best SUO. Examination of the results over the years at Sandhurst and Woolwich suggests that winning the Sword of Honour or a prize is a poor guide to predicting future high rank. Some winners have later reached the top, but others have eventually been lucky to rise as high as brigadier. Kitchener, who was eleven years older than Haig, had studied so hard at Woolwich that he had actually made himself ill by overwork, it was said, but came nowhere near the top of the order of merit. Nevertheless both men were desperately anxious to be successful in the Army and spared no effort to achieve their ambition. Later, neither hesitated to try to bypass a superior officer if by doing so they could further their own careers, though neither did so with the panache that Montgomery subsequently showed in this art. No doubt all three would have claimed that any apparently unscrupulous steps they took were really in the best interests of the Army, and for that reason justifiable.

On looking back over Haig's career prior to his being commissioned in 1885, it seems obvious that there was nothing in his upbringing and no visible character traits that made him particularly suitable or unsuitable for exercising the enormous power which he eventually held. Some of the attempts, like those of a recent biographer, Gerard De Groot, which have been made to infer from his early life that he was dominated by his mother's religious views are ridiculous. He grew up with eight brothers and sisters and, however hard his mother might have tried to influence a lively, healthy, naughty boy like Douglas Haig, she would have found the task difficult, though undoubtedly he admired her and respected her religious convictions.

His school life, at preparatory school and Clifton, would have drummed into him the necessity for hard work, unselfishness, keeping one's temper, being modest and showing consideration to others. School life would also have given him the ability to endure boredom and humiliation: backward boys are not treated kindly at school; they tend to be mocked by masters and fellow pupils alike. In Victorian schools there was little scope for an enlightened master who could open a boy's eyes to the beauties of literature, or influence his imagination to make him wish to acquire knowledge for its own sake. For Haig, at Clifton and Oxford, being a bookworm was simply a means to an end, and a very dull and uninspiring means at that. But drudgery had worked: it took him into Clifton and through Clifton; it ensured his survival at Oxford, and now it had taken him through Sandhurst. By 1885 Haig knew that there was no quick way to success for him. Popularity achieved nothing by itself; but work could achieve everything.

He would find plenty of sympathy for his views in the Army of the day. It tended to be distrustful of 'brainy' officers, although it acknowledged that they could sometimes clear the way to victory. There had been brilliant generals in the past, like Wolfe, but the important victories had been won by the workers, like Wellington, who knew how to slog it out when necessary, or Marlborough, whose inspired strategy was always accompanied by lengthy and meticulous planning and preparation.

Haig's regiment, the 7th (Queen's Own) Hussars, which he joined in 1885, was of some antiquity, having been formed in 1690 as Cunningham's Dragoons. It became the Queen's Own Dragoons in 1727, the Queen being Queen Caroline, wife of George II, the last British monarch to lead a regiment in battle. In 1805 there was another change of name when it became the 7th (Queen's Own) Hussars, and in 1958 it was amalgamated with the 3rd Hussars to form the Queen's Own Hussars. Efficient in battle, but rather dandified in peacetime, in Haig's day it became known as 'The Saucy Seventh'.

Cavalry regiments are noted for justifiable pride in their appearance, courage, dash and a slight contempt for other branches of the Army. Other arms respond with remarks such as 'There was once a cavalry officer so stupid that even his brother officers noticed it.' In Haig's day there would be no point in being an officer in a cavalry regiment unless a man had a substantial private income; an officer without means would not be excluded from being commissioned into a fashionable regiment, but he would be unable to take part in any of its expensive recreations. The cavalry officer would appear on parade occasionally and would take part in exercises, but otherwise would have no real work to do. Occupying his leisure was a serious task in itself, for the day's 'work' was over by mid-morning, and much of the rest of his time would be taken up by hunting or equestrian competitions. It was a different story for the troopers, of course, for they had to feed, groom, exercise and generally see that the horses and stables were immaculate, and then make themselves and their equipment immaculate too.

Much of Haig's leisure time was now occupied by polo and preparations for it. He visited America in April 1886 as a member of the England polo team: the team played two matches and won by large margins in each.

Three months later his regiment embarked for India on the troopship *Euphrates*. On board were several married women accompanying their husbands, and Haig noted that there were occasional quarrels caused by outsiders being too attentive to not unappreciative wives. He commented in a letter home that 'women are at the bottom of all quarrels'. Troopships and other ocean-going vessels are well known for the destabilising effect they can have on marital harmony, but this voyage must have been exceptionally turbulent to have drawn a comment from Haig. As a rich, handsome, athletic officer in a fashionable cavalry regiment, he must have received plenty of invitations from young women or their parents, but he does not seem to have been particularly interested. The impression that Victorian upper-class society was extremely moral and strait-laced is of course a fallacy, and 'middle-class morality' was considered something of a joke by many people in the circles in which Haig moved. However, there was never any hint that he himself was anything but moral, and it was then perfectly possible to live in a male group, such as a regiment or the staff of a school, without being suspected of being either a heterosexual philanderer or a homosexual.

Two years after embarking for India, and after a bout of typhoid, Haig became Adjutant and therefore found himself with more to do. In that appointment he was responsible for ensuring that the discipline of the regiment was up to the required standard, and that its activities were properly co-ordinated and at the expected level of efficiency. He would note whether any squadron or troop was becoming less ardent than it might have been. A good adjutant has an instinct for sensing any potential disaster before it occurs, and with the paraphernalia of a cavalry regiment, its horses, its weapons and ammunition, and its supplies of every variety, there is considerable scope for administrative break-downs, particularly in a climate such as that of India. In 1891 he was selected by the Inspector General of the Cavalry to be the Brigade Major at the Cavalry Camp at Aligarh.

The 7th Hussars would have been moved from one training ground to another, apart from the main cavalry base at Secunderabad. However, Haig was often away from his regiment, for he had two periods of leave in London, spent some time in Paris, visited Monte Carlo, where he tried his luck at the casino, and went to the North-West Frontier, Ceylon and Australia. All the overseas trips involved lengthy sea voyages.

In India, whatever his position in the regiment, whether a senior subaltern or adjutant, he never forgot his ambition to rise to higher levels. The essential step on that road was to qualify at the Staff College back in England. Accordingly he took leave of his regiment, knowing that perhaps it would be the final one if he eventually achieved a staff job, and sailed to England in 1892. He arrived in September and spent the next nine months grinding away in preparation for the examination the following June: he stayed in his sister Henrietta's flat in London and attended a crammer daily. As German was one of the subjects in which he was to be examined, he also stayed with a German family in Düsseldorf in order to acquire some fluency. It was all to no avail: the Staff College entrance examination was not particularly onerous then but it was too much for Haig. He failed the paper in mathematics. However, even if he had passed the written exam he would have been rejected on physical grounds, for the Staff College required its entrants to pass a medical and Haig was adjudged colour-blind.

The disappointment of failing the written examination was considerable, but to be judged colour-blind as well was mortifying in the extreme. He might perhaps have another try at the exam and pass it, but nothing was going to change his colour-blindness. Any other man might have decided that was the end of the road for his military ambitions: but Haig would not accept failure. Perhaps his dour Scottish ancestry and certainly the memory that he had overcome other setbacks in the past made him resolve to carry on against all odds. Friends and family were sympathetic, but he did not want sympathy: he wanted success. Just as he had manoeuvred himself into Sandhurst by the lengthy strategy of going through Oxford, he decided there must be a way round this obstacle too.

His German friends told him of an excellent oculist who was an expert on colour-blindness. Whether the German specialist claimed to be able to cure colour-blindness we do not know, but he certainly gave Haig a document asserting that the colour-blindness no longer existed, even if it ever had. Haig found this dubious document extremely useful, for the specialist was apparently a name to conjure with; at the same time Haig also protested that the Staff College had exceeded its brief when testing him for colour-blindness. Nevertheless, according to Duff Cooper there was no doubt at all that the medical report had been correct. He says that Haig's colour-blindness always prevented him from distinguishing brown from pink or red, and that there is absolutely no question of the fact that it existed, in spite of Haig's attempts to pretend otherwise.

In the meantime, though, short of resigning his commission, there was no alternative to returning to his regiment, which Haig did with good grace. Unfortunately the position he might have expected, that of squadron commander, had been filled in his absence and he now had to become second-in-command of a squadron. The experience showed him at his best – neither resentful nor self-pitying, but giving his superior all the support he could have wished for. When he left, a year later, his CO wrote to him, addressing him as 'My dear Douglas' and saying, 'I cannot say how much you will be missed by all of us, officers, NCOs and men. Your example in the regiment has been worth everything to the boys.'

Haig's next appointment was back in England as ADC to General Sir Keith Fraser, the Inspector General of Cavalry, for the period of the autumn manoeuvres in 1893. Manoeuvres, of course, are not primarily for the training of troops but for the benefit of generals, who thereby learn how to handle large bodies of men. Although far short of being a general, Haig was becoming an acknowledged expert on cavalry and the experience of riding with the Inspector General on this important occasion confirmed him in his view that, in spite of the setback over the Staff College, he could still find a future and an outlet for his ambitions in the Army in this particular field. It is of some interest, therefore, to examine the theories of warfare that he was formulating.

Haig read widely during his military career and in consequence knew how most battles had been won. He learned that on many occasions the decisive stroke had come from the cavalry. At Hastings in 1066 William I had used cavalry to defeat Harold's foot soldiers; the knight on horseback had then dominated the battlefield until the longbow and pike restricted his activities a hundred years later. The whole concept of medieval chivalry had been based on the *chevalier* – the horseman. In more recent times there had been the cavalry victories of the English Civil War. Cromwell had been a regicide, but he had also been a brilliant cavalry commander: a cavalry charge won the vital battle of Naseby. Marlborough had used his cavalry to devastating effect, and so had Wellington with those famous cavalry charges at Waterloo. And then there had been the charge of the Heavy Brigade in the Crimean War, less well known than the ill-advised charge of the Light Brigade but far more effective. The cavalry was capable of doing almost everything on a battlefield: it could conduct the reconnaissance, protect the flanks, safeguard the rear, consolidate victory into a rout with devastating charges, even turn defeat into victory by disrupting the enemy's line of communications. If cavalry fought as mounted infantry, as the 7th Hussars had done when they were dragoons, it could dismount and hold recently captured ground. To a young man brought up, as Haig was, in the sure conviction that the course of British history had been shaped by the cavalry, it would have seemed extraordinary that other arms of the services, particularly the infantry, should refuse to recognise the fact, even when it stared them in the face.

Absurd though this line of thought may seem to modern tacticians who can see, with the virtue of hindsight, that the reign of the horse on the battlefield was drawing to its close with the arrival of modern weaponry, it was not quite so misguided as might be imagined. As we shall see later, Haig still believed that after the costly victories of the battles of the Somme and Passchendaele the cavalry would be able to come up and exploit the breakthrough. He envisaged cavalry turning defeat into rout and sweeping through miles of thinly defended, or even open, countryside into Germany itself. This was the way victories had always been consolidated, even back in the days of pre-Christian warfare. In the nineteenth century the commanders of every army in Europe – French, German, Italian, Spanish, Austrian, Polish – would have agreed with this orthodox view. It would last until barbed wire and the machine gun brought the realisation that what had always been true would not necessarily always continue to be so.

Before leaping to condemn Haig for holding a view of warfare in which he had been brought up, we might perhaps look a little further ahead. He died in 1928 when theories of tank warfare were only just beginning to be voiced. Early tanks were scorned by the older generation of army officers in Britain, France and Germany because they were too slow to do more than smooth the passage of the infantry. At that time there seemed no prospect that the lumbering ironclads could ever move at a faster pace than a horse or man could walk, but if Haig and his contemporaries could have lived another twenty years they would have found all their theories of warfare vindicated. The German tank divisions which carved a slice through France in May 1940 used shock and surprise to make an unexpected breakthrough in a weakly defended portion of the French line, and by doing so probed deeply into the heart of, and behind, the Allied positions. It was a traditional cavalry tactic. Haig would have been surprised at the speed of the 1940 tanks, which could maintain twenty miles per hour over considerable distances. In fact their average speed would make them faster than the traditional cavalry 'charge', for which the orders were: walk, march, trot. Sometimes the cavalry would gallop over the last hundred yards or so, if the 'Charge' was sounded, but sometimes it was not: it was never sounded in the charge of the Light Brigade, for example, and in fact the brigade maintained a steady pace throughout.

Warfare in the Western Desert was even more closely akin to the cavalry tactics of Haig's day. Rommel used what were called 'hook tactics', or wide sweeps, by which he often turned the Allied flank, and which were possible in the desert where the room for manoeuvre was vast. Not surprisingly, when British cavalry regiments were mechanised they adapted themselves very quickly to desert styles of fighting which tended to produce the tactics of former light cavalry, such as hussars; while in other areas tanks were used to smash a way through defended positions in the style of the former heavy dragoon regiments. If Haig had been fighting a war fifty years later, he would have adapted easily to tank warfare.

In the nineteenth century there were reasons for placing a high value on cavalry, quite apart from the record of success from ancient to modern times. The cavalry had 'style': its victories were won with dash and courage. The sight of a cavalry regiment drawn up on parade, or going through its exercises, was stirring and impressive. For a man like Haig who knew and understood horses, as a capable polo player must do, the cavalry acquired a mystique. Somehow, no victory could be complete if it did not involve cavalry at the critical phase. This deeply held conviction would be disturbed by the experiences of the Boer War, but never sufficiently damaged to prevent Haig keeping large forces of cavalry in reserve in the First World War; there they were, in readiness to exploit the breach in the enemy front which the gunners, or the infantry, or even the tanks, would make sooner or later. The cavalry regiments were not, of course, kept in complete isolation and idleness when murderous trench warfare was going on ahead of them: the troopers took their turn as infantry of the line just as their predecessors in the dragoons would have done; if they survived, they resumed their cavalry duties in reserve.

After performing his duties as ADC in the cavalry manoeuvres of 1893, Haig took leave in France and managed to get himself invited to attend the cavalry manoeuvres of the French Army in Touraine. He was an excellent, appreciative and well-informed guest, and made himself so agreeable that he was invited to attend other exercises the following year. On both occasions he submitted lengthy reports to the War Office. He found the French cavalry in excellent shape but somewhat handicapped by having too many elderly generals. Napoleon, he commented, had observed that the best generals were the young ones. This must have made very acceptable reading for the younger generals in the War Office, who considered their own army was in a similar plight; it was also noted with interest by more elderly generals who considered that they themselves had just the right blend of age and experience.

Having observed and reported on the French cavalry, it was obvious that Haig should now do the same for the German, with whom Britain's relationship at this time was extremely cordial.

German officers were not yet drinking toasts in their messes to *Der Tag*, when they would go to war against Britain and deprive her of the leadership of the world. Haig was received with great courtesy in Berlin, where he had many friends and saw all he wanted to see. The only discordant note was struck by the British military attaché, Colonel Swaine, who clearly resented the presence of this young and ambitious cavalry officer who was intruding in an area where he himself had been settled comfortably for nine years. However, Haig had taken the precaution of obtaining a letter of introduction to the Governor of Berlin from the British Inspector of Cavalry, Sir Keith Fraser, whom he now knew well having been his ADC. The Governor proved particularly affable, took Haig everywhere and gave him more introductions, while Swaine was left to grind his teeth in fury. To crown it all, Haig was invited to a dinner at which he sat opposite the Kaiser. The Kaiser politely drank Haig's health and afterwards chatted to him. After this visit Haig sent a series of letters to people whom he thought might be interested in his observations on the German Army: many were.

His next assignment was another cavalry exercise, during which he met Sir Evelyn Wood, who had commanded the army which had defeated the Zulus and was now Quartermaster General. Wood was interested in Haig's experiences in Germany and marked him as a promising and enterprising young officer. Although there was no reason why Haig should not have been attracting the attention of his seniors at this time, it is difficult to avoid the impression that he was playing his cards with quite remarkable skill.

During this cavalry exercise Haig also met the Duke of Cambridge, who was just completing his thirty-ninth year as Commander-in-Chief of the British Army and was about to retire. The Duke, who was Queen Victoria's cousin, was said to have been an ineffective figurehead, and had been strongly attacked in *The Times*. Nevertheless he was a man of enormous influence while he still held the post, and in consequence Sir Evelyn Wood and Sir Keith Fraser both appealed to him to nominate Haig for entry to the Staff College without taking a further written or medical examination. The Duke promptly agreed. Haig was no doubt as deserving an entrant as any of the others – probably much more than most – but these tactics would not have been admired by his contemporaries.

Accelerated promotion in the Army is usually a mystery to those who do not receive it, and sometimes to those who do. There are three classes of ambitious officers. There are those of outstanding merit who should obviously be promoted quickly, though this does not always happen. Then there are those whose claims are good but not exceptional, but who achieve their ends because by luck or judgement they get to know the right people or are in the right place at the right time. There are also those who are almost as good but do not know how to make the correct moves to achieve their ambitions. Anyone with experience of the services will be familiar with all three types.

One of the most effective ways of drawing attention to oneself is to write reports on visits and events. By the time they are written they will have all the benefit of hindsight and may well contain some judicious flattery. Another method is to ask complicated questions at the end of lectures, or when one is introduced to a very senior officer. Officers who use such tactics may be regarded with some dislike and contempt by their fellows, but this will not worry the ambitious promotion-seeker who knows that, if he is successful, others will soon be adopting the same tactics with him.

In 1895 the German staff was happy to establish good relations with potentially influential British officers for, behind strict security, a master plan had just been drafted. This was the brainchild of General Graf von Schlieffen, Chief of the German General Staff. Schlieffen and his colleagues were well aware that Germany's expansionist policies were likely to involve the country in a war on its eastern and western frontiers simultaneously. Of the two potential opponents France was probably the more dangerous initially, but Russia, with its vast territories and harsh climate, was ultimately the most formidable. The most hazardous policy for Germany was one which involved fighting on two fronts at the same time. Schlieffen and his colleagues had therefore devised a strategy by which France could be knocked out by a two-pronged surprise invasion. The war which was being planned was considered to be no concern of Britain's at this point, for Britain was a colonial sea power which had always tried to avoid entanglements in Europe. Besides, the Kaiser was the grandson of Queen Victoria of England and this made hostilities between the two countries inconceivable.

The German Army was very strong in cavalry, as it had shown when defeating the French in the Franco-Prussian War of 1870–1, but, less obviously, was also well equipped with highly disciplined infantry. Eventually it would be the German infantry, and the German readiness to adopt that most deadly of anti-cavalry weapons, the machine gun, which would give the Allied generals problems in the unforeseeable war of attrition which would last from 1914 to 1918.

Sir Evelyn Wood would have liked to have learned more about the German infantry, but unfortunately Haig was in no position to supply information. He wrote to Wood from Germany:

Dear Sir Evelyn,

I was greatly delighted to receive your kind letter and thank you very much for what you say about me. I shall always remember with more than pleasure the kindly way you spoke to me during the staff tour.

I now enclose a few notes in answer to that question you asked me about the share taken by NCOs in polishing up the young soldier in Germany.

I wish I could have given more *detailed* information about the work done by NCOs in the infantry. To tell you the truth my time at Berlin was devoted entirely to cavalry work, tho' what I have put down regarding the infantry I know to be *the fact*. I hope however to find out in more detail the work of the company before I return.

I am drinking the waters here as I had not got over the effects of fever which I used to get in India, but when this course is finished I shall return to England via Berlin, where I know plenty of officers in the infantry.

There is an officer (cavalry) Lieut von Bülow* of the General Staff (in Berlin) coming to England *on leave* for the month of August. He is anxious to see something of the manoeuvres in the New Forest, and the Cavalry Division which is to be formed at Aldershot. I take the liberty of asking whether you would get him permission to go to the New Forest. I am, I understand, to be Brigade Major at the Aldershot drills so I can look after him and give him one of my horses to ride when he comes there.

Please forgive the liberty I have taken in asking this for Bülow but I have received so much assistance and kindness from German officers of all ranks that I feel sure you won't mind. It was from Bülow that I got two accounts of how cavalry staff tours (*Ubungsreisen*) are carried out in Germany. I translated them and gave them to Colonel French with a request (if he thought fit) to ask you to look at them. The papers are not in the least confidential but these Germans are so peculiar in some things that I should not like it known how the papers came into my possession.

Again thanking you for your kindness and hoping the notes I now send may in some measure answer the question you asked me.

> I beg to remain
> Yours very truly
> Douglas Haig

To modern eyes this letter seems a little over-effusive, a little too anxious to please, though in view of the fact that James Marshall-Cornwall, who served on Haig's staff in 1916 and 1917 and got to know him well, described Haig as a man of integrity we may accept that this letter to Sir Evelyn Wood is naïve rather than dishonest. Haig has, in fact, performed brilliantly. He has established a rapport with the Germans, brought back useful reports and presumably done nothing to arouse German suspicions

---

* A cousin of the general who later commanded the German 2nd Army in France.

over his intentions. However, he has been unable to obtain information about the German NCOs which could have been invaluable later. And he has already sent the papers to Colonel French, his superior officer, whom later he will criticise and then replace.

For the remainder of 1895 Haig was busy completing the new cavalry drill book, which French had begun but had left unfinished owing to his promotion to Assistant Adjutant General. The Army has been accustomed to 'go by the book' as it has learnt its lessons over the centuries. There is a book for everything from hygiene in the field to controlling troops in battle. Officers will occasionally diverge slightly from 'the book'; NCOs, if they are wise, never. Army books, or manuals, are the distilled results of experience. One can, of course, encounter disaster through following the book too closely and unimaginatively in unorthodox situations, but one would be unlikely to be blamed for it if one survived. It was a considerable accolade for Haig to be allotted the task of completing the cavalry drill book while still a captain, for he was taking over from a colonel. However, he was well qualified for the task.

In Haig's time the Staff College course lasted two years. As with other establishments of further education, much of its value came from discussions and arguments with fellow students. A group of approximately thirty entered every year, so every student was in turn a junior and a senior. In Haig's year there were E. H. Allenby, who later commanded the victorious army in Palestine; J. E. Edmonds, who became the official historian of the First World War; T. Capper, an extremely promising officer who was killed at the battle of Loos in 1915; and W. Robertson, the ex-trooper who became Chief of the Imperial General Staff at the time when Haig was Commander-in-Chief of the BEF (British Expeditionary Force). Several of Haig's contemporaries at the Staff College served under him during the 1914–18 war. One of his fellow students, the future General Sir G. de S. Barrow, thought that Haig and Allenby were the outstanding men of their year. He noted that they were two very different types of soldier: Haig was the dedicated professional whose mind was entirely occupied with the Army and his career in it; Allenby was no less professional in his skills but also had outside interests in ornithology, botany, literature and music, and was a Fellow of the Zoological Society.

Field Marshal Wavell made a comparison between the two men in later life and observed that Haig was so confident in the correctness of his own judgement that he never listened to the opinions of others; Allenby, by contrast, always listened even though he did not necessarily accept their views. Both men had quick tempers, but though Haig had learnt to control his feelings Allenby would sometimes burst out and send everyone scurrying: years later, in Palestine, Allenby was nicknamed 'The Bull', and when he was not pleased the word would go round: 'The Bull is loose.' However, in 1896 at the election of the Master of the Staff College Draghounds Allenby won easily. This was a mortifying experience for Haig, for there was little to choose between the two men in horsemanship. It was an accolade on which Haig had set his mind, though he took it well and did not allow it to influence his attitude towards Allenby. Their later paths diverged when, after a period on the Western Front, Allenby was given command of the army entrusted with the task of pushing the Turks out of Palestine. Later he was High Commissioner in Egypt for six years, during which time the country became a sovereign state.

Haig found the Staff College interesting, enjoyable and eminently worthwhile. In 1896 it had just emerged from a long period of mediocrity characterised by pedantry and uninspiring instruction, a change mainly due to the appointment of H. J. T. Hildyard as Commandant and G. F. R. Henderson as Professor of Military Art and History. Hildyard introduced much more practical work in place of written, formal instruction, and Henderson breathed new life into the teaching. The latter had distinguished himself in all his previous posts, which included being a company commander in the 1882 Egyptian campaign, but his outstanding achievement was his ability to write military history in a form which made it ideal for instruction. He had made a careful study of the American Civil War and in 1899 produced a classic study of the Confederate General Stonewall Jackson. Much of the value of the book lay in the lessons it drew from the strategy and tactics of what was generally acknowledged to be the first modern war. Field Marshal Lord Roberts was so impressed by *Stonewall Jackson* that he appointed Henderson as his Director of Military Intelligence when he himself was appointed Commander-in-Chief in South Africa at the end of 1899. Unfortunately Henderson, who was then forty-six, succumbed to malaria soon after arrival and had to be invalided home, where he died in 1903. The Staff College historian, Brian Bond, records that Henderson had once said in an informal discussion: 'There is a fellow in your batch who is going to be Commander-in-Chief one of these days. No, not any of you, Captain Haig.' This may have been because Haig spent more time on his studies than anyone else and would not have been sitting in the ante-room casually chatting. It might also be related to Haig's friendship with the Prince of Wales, later Edward VII.

Soon after Haig's arrival at the Staff College he had put an application in the leave book for three days' leave. There was nothing unusual in that, of course, but the reason aroused both irritation and amusement among his fellow students: he had written, 'To shoot and to meet the Prince of Wales.' Haig had in fact already met the Prince of Wales, for his brother-in-law, William Jameson, who was married to Haig's sister, Henrietta, owned a large estate in Suffolk and gave shooting parties which the Prince often attended. Haig never achieved quite the rapport with Edward VII that he had later with George V, but the fact of being close to the court was no disadvantage. He had already seen how royal patronage could work for him when the Duke of Cambridge nominated him for the Staff College and the handicap of being colour-blind was brushed aside and forgotten.

Haig preserved many of his Staff College papers and they reveal that, in spite of Henderson's pioneering work, the Army at that time was looking mainly to the distant past for lessons in warfare rather than trying to forecast future tactics in relation to developments in modern firepower. The battles of the Napoleonic Wars were studied in detail which seems almost obsessional. Brigadier General John Charteris mentions in his biography of Haig that

Haig made no attempt to ingratiate himself with his instructors, and if he thought a task was almost valueless he made no secret of it. This point was endorsed by Edmonds, who in the Official History recalled an occasion when the students had been instructed to make a road reconnaissance sketch. All the others produced elaborate drawings in which even letter-boxes and gateways into fields were marked. 'Haig handed in a sheet with a single brown chalkline down the centre, the cross roads shown and the endorsement "twenty miles long, good surface, wide enough for two columns with orderlies both ways."'

However, although there was a general opinion among the Staff College instructors that Haig was a worthy and industrious student and should go far, it was not shared by everyone. The future Field Marshal Lord Plumer, who examined him in the final exercise, considered in his report that Haig's concluding performance at the Staff College was mediocre.

Charteris wrote of Haig: 'From the Staff College he carried away with him a belief in the "educated soldier" which never afterwards faltered.' By this, of course, he meant 'professionally trained and widely read in his subject', but the phrase was later borrowed for the title of a biography by John Terraine and was assumed to have a wider connotation. Terraine has made an exhaustive study of Haig and the campaigns of the First World War but, in the opinion of some, tends to take an over-indulgent view of Haig's abilities. Haig was a man who absorbed a huge amount of information by massive and continuous industry. Whether he was intellectually capable of using that information to make the correct deductions and was thus deserving of the word 'educated' in its true sense may be open to question; but he must have been one of the most devout students at what were called 'Staff Rides'.

An essential part of officer training, Staff Rides were described by Brigadier General R. C. B. (later General Sir Richard) Haking, one of Haig's Staff College contemporaries, in a book published in 1908. They could vary from exercises for small units to combined operations with the Navy. Reading Haking's book over eighty years later, one is impressed by the common sense and practicality, even though weapons, tactics, skills and other attributes of war have changed. Haking observes that 'prior to the South African War there is little doubt that education was looked down upon'. He remarks that the guidance and information contained in a book could, if remembered by a student who took the trouble to read it, make all the difference between success and failure. However, he stresses that theory without practice in applying it was of limited value. He emphasises that in writing reports it was better to be clear and simple rather than clever and too comprehensive, but he warns of the dangers of omitting the dispositions of administrative units. Even so, Haking's examples were not for the muddle-headed. One of his paragraphs runs:

We can now ascertain the number of mules which will be required to accompany a division from the third to the fourth stage on June 4th. Two days' supplies must be carried for the division, one to be consumed on the evening of the 4th and one on the 5th. We have already discovered that 144,046.5 lb must be carried from the fourth to the fifth stage on June 5, and to this we must add 131,659 lb, one day's supplies for the division, to be consumed on the evening of June 4, a total of 275,705.5 lb; this we will call the initial weight to be carried forward from the third to the fourth stage on June 4. The number of mules required to carry this and also one day's forage for themselves amounts to 275,705.5 divided by 146.25 lb, that is 1886 mules. Add 10 per cent and we get 2074 mules. Of these we have seen that 991 must go on from the fourth to the fifth stage on June 5, and the remaining 1083 can return unloaded from the fourth to the third stage on June 5th. If we multiply 2074 by 12.5, the weight of a day's forage for a mule and a proportion of the driver's kit and rations, and add the 275,705 lb we shall get the total weight to be carried forward from the third to the fourth stage on June 4 – that is 301,630.5 lb.

This continues for several pages and gives an insight into some of the calculations required from Haig when he was serving as a staff officer later. Staff officers are not the most popular members of the Army, but the Army gibe 'Bread is the staff of life and the life of the Staff is one long loaf' seems to be a trifle harsh.

Haig's notebooks and Staff College papers are all in the National Library of Scotland. They show that, although the course paid more attention to the past than to the future, it also provided excellent guidance for the budding staff officer. It was emphasised that the most satisfactory literary style was that which 'renders it impossible to misunderstand the writer's meaning'. Later, when Adjutant, Haig wrote various instructional pamphlets for his regiment: they are all models of common sense and clarity.

The only glimpse into the future in the Staff College course concerned the next and inevitable war in South Africa. In the discussions on this it was anticipated that the Boers could raise a force of twenty thousand, but might reach thirty thousand; this was about half the eventual number they put in the field. It was thought they could be defeated by a combined frontal and flank attack. 'Once the Boer Army is defeated,' concluded the pundits at the Staff College in a syndicate paper which is still among the Haig Papers, 'the territory will be at our mercy.' Time would show how mistaken that view was.

3
Haig on Active Service

WHEN HAIG LEFT the Staff College as a captain at the age of thirty-six he had yet to experience active service. Nor, for the moment, did there seem to be any prospect of it. He took leave in the winter of 1898 at the end of his Staff College course and enjoyed himself hunting with the Warwickshire; his brother-in-law William Jameson, who owned a house at Radway, near Edgehill, had lent it to Haig as a hunting lodge. But soon after arriving he received a telegram from Sir Evelyn Wood, now Adjutant General at the War Office, informing him that his next posting was to the Egyptian Army and that he should report to the War Office forthwith for further details. There he was informed that he was to command a squadron in the campaign against the Dervishes in the Sudan. He could not have wished for better news.

The situation in the Sudan had been volatile and dangerous for most of the nineteenth century. In 1821 the northern part of the country had been conquered by a vigorous and active young general, Mehemet Ali, who had previously seized power in Egypt. From then onwards it became a valuable source of slaves and ivory: most of the former were bought from local chieftains, and there were said to be some fifteen hundred traders working in the country. The British government, which had abolished slavery in the British Empire in 1834 and had set the Royal Navy the task of hunting down slave traders operating off the west coast of Africa, strongly disapproved of the situation in the Sudan, but felt that little could be done about such a landlocked area. The Sudan was a vast country, sprawling over a million square miles of territory which was, to put it mildly, inhospitable. By the middle of the century Egyptian control had slackened, but the slave traders were as active as ever. Charles Gordon, then a colonel, had been sent out in 1874 with the mission of reporting on the slave trade and freeing any slaves he found, but nothing further was done after he returned. Then, in 1880, a young Muslim leader, claiming to be the Mahdi (the Messiah), raised an army and proceeded to win a series of victories against the Egyptian troops sent to suppress his revolt; even more seriously, he wiped out a British expeditionary force sent to retake the areas which the Mahdi's army, known as the Dervishes,★ now controlled. Gordon was sent out again, this time to withdraw the remaining Egyptian garrisons to Khartoum. There he was surrounded by Dervishes and murdered in 1885.

At that point the Prime Minister, Gladstone, and his cabinet decided to abandon the Sudan to its fate. The Mahdi died in June 1885 and his place as leader of the Dervishes was taken by the Khalifa. From stories emerging from the Sudan it soon became clear that the Khalifa's regime was a bloodthirsty tyranny and that sooner or later the British government would have to bestir itself and free the Sudan from his harsh rule.

The person eventually entrusted with this task was the future Field Marshal Lord Kitchener. In 1882, Kitchener decided that his career would be furthered by a period with the Egyptian Army which after the financial collapse of the Suez Canal in 1875 was under the dual control of the Egyptian and British authorities. He was well aware that the pay and rank structures were better than at home, and had accordingly manoeuvred himself to a posting as second-in-command of the Egyptian cavalry. Kitchener was just as ambitious and hard-working as Haig, but was a Royal Engineer, not a cavalryman. Nevertheless, when given his appointment in Egypt Kitchener soon proved that he was capable of learning

---

★ Dervishes were originally poor friars, but had developed various fanatical sects. The word was applied to the Mahdi's followers, although he preferred the term '*ansar*', meaning 'follower'.

the art of cavalry warfare and training Egyptian troops in it. Ten years later he had risen to the rank of major general and was Commander-in-Chief of the Egyptian Army. By 1895 he had brought it to a level of efficiency which no one could have anticipated.

Initially his brief was to retake the northern province of Dongola in 1896, but soon this was extended to defeating the Khalifa in his stronghold of Khartoum. Kitchener's campaign was a model of careful planning. Knowing the character of the country, he had built a railway to deal with any logistical problems which could not be solved by using the Nile, which had dangerous cataracts. By the time Haig was appointed to the expedition the campaign was reaching its final stages, but the critical battles were still to be fought. The Khalifa was known to be particularly strong in cavalry, of which he had some fifty thousand, and the Dervishes were not merely armed with spears but also had a good number of firearms. The greatest obstacle to defeating the Dervishes, however, was not so much their firepower as their numbers, which their leaders were prepared to sacrifice without hesitation. The decisive battle would take place in what is known as good cavalry country – that is to say, open plains. The British cavalry were well aware of the problems: one of them was that the Dervish infantry had the unusual and disconcerting habit of lying in the long grass until horses rode over them, and then slashing at the animals' legs, bringing down both horses and riders. The campaign was being fought in temperatures well over 100°F by an expeditionary force few of whom had had the opportunity to become acclimatised. The first important battle, at Atbara, was fought on 8 April 1898 in a temperature of 117°F, and involved twenty thousand Dervishes. Haig arrived just in time to take part in this battle.

Much had happened since he had received the telegram from Sir Evelyn Wood. On receipt of the news that he was to go to Egypt, he had decided to make the best use of his few remaining days of leisure by hunting in a temperate climate – in fact, staying in Warwickshire. But his plans were altered by a summons to join the Prince of Wales at Sandringham. The occasion could not have been more advantageous for him. Not only was the Prince there himself but so too were the Duke and Duchess of York, who in due course would become King George V and Queen Mary. Sir Evelyn Wood was also in the party. Both the Prince of Wales and Sir Evelyn asked Haig to write to them regularly about his experiences and opinions of the campaign in which he was shortly to be engaged.

Haig reached Cairo by 3 February 1898, acquired the distinctive headgear known as a tarbush which was worn by all ranks in the Egyptian Army (and in which he was photographed), continued his journey by train and Nile steamboat to Wadi Halfa, and there received a cordial welcome from Kitchener. He was given command of a squadron of cavalry in the brigade of 16th Lancers commanded by Colonel R. G. Broadwood and soon afterwards took his men into action in a minor skirmish. This enabled him to send a lengthy account to Sir Evelyn Wood, who had specially requested detailed descriptions of such actions. Having seen the determination of the Dervishes, Haig commented that the expedition needed more machine guns: fanatical troops, a category to which the Dervishes undoubtedly belonged, would not be stopped by the recognition that they were being defeated; they would continue to advance until no one was left to do so. It is interesting to observe that Haig had recognised the importance of the machine gun at this early stage. Later he would see only too clearly how effectively the Germans could use it.

Broadwood, who was older than Haig, had spent several years with the Egyptian Army and was pleased to have alongside him a person with as much cavalry knowledge as Haig clearly possessed. Haig immediately went up a rank to major (Bimbashi); soon afterwards he was selected by Broadwood to be his brigade major and thus responsible for the co-ordination of the squadrons in the brigade. Haig had no doubts about the difficulty of his task: the Egyptians did not lack courage but, man for man, he knew they did not match the fighting quality of the Dervishes.

His first experience of full-scale battle was Atbara, to which a brief reference has already been made. On that occasion the Khalifa had decided to check Kitchener's force by placing an obstacle firmly in its path, rather than by using sweeping cavalry attacks. The Dervish field commander, named Mahmoud, had therefore placed his infantry in trenches inside a *zareba* (enclosure) of prickly thorn. He could not have made a worse decision, for Kitchener was able to pound the *zareba* with his artillery and then send in his own infantry. Many of the Dervish infantry had been chained into their positions, making sure that they would stay there and fire their rifles. This left them almost helpless when the British infantry charged. However, many of the Dervishes in the rear and the flanks were able to get away. The casualty figures for the battle were said to be three thousand Dervishes killed, based on a body count, and two thousand taken prisoner. This meant that some fifteen thousand had ridden away to fight another day. Even so, the battle of Atbara had removed one of the Khalifa's best generals in Mahmoud, who had been taken prisoner, raised the morale of Kitchener's force and correspondingly diminished the manpower in the Khalifa's army. All this had been accomplished for a loss of 568, including 125 British casualties.

Three weeks after the battle Haig wrote a long report to Sir Evelyn Wood, in which he criticised Kitchener's conduct of the battle:

> For instance why was the attack frontal? It seemed to me from the very first day that we reconnoitred the place that an attack on the enemy's right offered great advantages. The enemy would have been forced to retreat across the open desert to the Nile without being allowed time to fill waterskins, etc. for the march. Our side says the guns did tremendous damage. As far as I can make out the artillery preparation frightened a good many of the spearmen and they bolted.

Presumably Haig had not examined the enemy trenches personally or he would have given a different account of the effectiveness of the artillery. It is easy to be wise after the event, and never more so than if the event is a battle. Kitchener would have been furious if he had known that Haig was writing to Sir Evelyn Wood, let alone casting disparaging remarks on the way he had handled the affair. Wood wrote an almost sycophantic reply to Haig, thanking him effusively and regretting that Haig had not had a free hand in the battle. Wood's behaviour in encouraging subordinate officers to criticise their commander seems extraordinary, but it was not only Haig who benefited from it. Kitchener himself had made use of Wood in order to get away from Cyprus and obtain his original posting to Egypt and he himself, though in general a man of integrity, was not above cutting a corner if he felt the occasion justified it. It has been suggested that Wood encouraged Haig to write frank accounts because in that way he obtained a better feeling of the battle than he would have done from the Commander-in-Chief's report. At the time such conduct might not have seemed dishonourable, and it is worth noting that Haig's contemporary, Churchill,* never hesitated to pull any strings he could grasp if they enabled him to pursue his career.

Haig had been impressed by the conduct of the Egyptian cavalry, which had acquitted themselves well and not run away as the British HQ had feared they would. He had rescued one Egyptian who had been wounded in the shoulder and was lying on the ground, expecting to be finished off by the Dervishes. Haig picked him up and, after putting him on the front of his saddle, carried him out of danger.

His health was standing up to the rigours of the climate very well. The food was not good, often consisting of tinned bully beef or sardines, but it was enlivened with claret mixed with filtered Nile water. In addition to the constant flow of letters he endeavoured to keep in touch with events elsewhere in the world, noting that the Spanish and the Americans were at war. He mentions, 'the *Spectator* is capital reading out here. The week's summary is always good in it.'

The next, and decisive, battle would be on the plain of Omdurman in front of Khartoum. Four months were allotted to

---

* Churchill had contrived to get himself attached to the 21st Lancers, although this was not his own regiment, in order to get more military experience and also to become a newspaper correspondent to bolster his finances at the same time.

reorganising and reinforcing Kitchener's army after the battle of Atbara, and then on 24 August he began the approach march to Omdurman. For this momentous occasion he had a force of twenty-five thousand: although this was less than half the strength of the Khalifa's army, the disparity was made up by Kitchener's advantage in artillery and automatic weapons. His guns included a 4 inch howitzer, eight 12-pounder quick-firers, several 6-pounders, three 9 cm Krupps and forty-eight Maxims. All these would be invaluable in the destruction of Khartoum itself if the Khalifa decided to defend the city – and, even if he did not, would be very effective if he chose to adopt close formations. However, this was mobile warfare and the mechanism of the guns was likely to be temperamental in that climate: under those conditions, the importance of the artillery could be over-rated.

The news of the Dervish advance towards the expeditionary force was brought to Kitchener by Churchill, who, as we shall see, had manoeuvred himself into the front line in spite of Kitchener's attempts to prevent him from doing so. The ensuing battle was heavily criticised afterwards by many who had not been in it, and by some who had – not least because Kitchener had taken over the tactical command at a critical moment and over ruled his subordinate commanders. Haig sent a long account to Sir Evelyn Wood, and found plenty about which to comment adversely. Not surprisingly, the charge of the 21st Lancers came high on the list. The 21st Lancers had had a chequered career since its formation in 1759, having been disbanded three times; in 1898 it was virtually a new regiment, anxious to prove itself in its first modern action. What happened to it can scarcely be blamed on Kitchener. He had ordered the regiment, 320 strong, to conduct a reconnaissance and report back on the strength of the Dervishes. The 21st set off briskly, full of spirit, and when they spotted some Dervishes half-concealed in a *khor* or dried-up watercourse were ordered by their commanding officer to charge and scatter them.

However, when the 21st reached the *khor*, they discovered to their consternation that there were not just a few Dervishes concealed in it but two thousand, who rose to their feet and received the cavalry with enthusiasm. The 21st had no option but to continue the charge and, having ridden through the *khor*, to re-form on the other side and ride back. In the course of this action the regiment suffered twenty-one killed and forty wounded. An unknown, but not very large, number of Dervishes were killed, and the action had absolutely no effect on the outcome of the main battle. Heroic though the charge was, it was also an act of folly which caused Colonel Martin to be removed from command of the regiment.

One of those riding with the 21st was Winston Churchill, whose regiment was the 4th Hussars but who had pulled strings with Lord Salisbury, the Prime Minister, and Sir Evelyn Wood, to get himself posted to the front. Kitchener regarded Churchill as a pushy interloper and had been incensed to see him; he would be even angrier later when he realised that Churchill had secured for himself a contract to send despatches from the front to the *Morning Post* at £15 per column. Kitchener had offered Churchill to Haig for his squadron, but Haig, who shared his superior's views of the man, had refused to accept him: it was an offer, not an order.

Haig's account of the battle is given below. Although he did not care for Churchill, he trusted him and therefore gave him letters to take back to England both for Wood and for his sister Henrietta. Churchill would be returning there immediately after the battle. Haig wrote:

> The officer in chief command (whether Kitchener or Hunter⋆) insisted on doing every detail himself instead of trusting a staff officer to allot the camping area to units. I had occasion to see this for on 24th August I covered the advance of the Egyptian army with my squadron, two maxims and one company of the Camel Corps.

He went on to criticise Kitchener's plan, which involved having themselves and the 21st Lancers out ahead of the army, doing much the same reconnaissance task.

⋆ General Hunter was Kitchener's deputy.

You will hear a lot of the charge made by the 21st Lancers. It took place at 9 a.m. south of Signal Hill, into an arm of the Khor Shambat. The Sirdar* was then meditating an advance on Omdurman, and the 21st were to precede the infantry. The regiment seems to have advanced without any patrols in front. Seeing a few men in front the Colonel thought it a good moment to charge. He seems to have marched parallel to the enemy in column of troops, then wheeled into line on the right and charged. While in column of troops they were under hot fire, so his suspicions ought to have been aroused, especially as Slatin† before had told him of the *nullah* (water-course).

Away the regiment went, four squadrons in line and came down in this *nullah* filled with rifles and spearmen. The result was scarcely as bad as might have been anticipated, for the two flank squadrons suffered little. Two troops of the centre squadron were, however, practically wiped out. A rally with their backs to the river followed, the enemy meantime going on to join the attack on McDonald. The loss inflicted on the enemy (judging by the corpses) was trifling, fourteen or fifteen at the most. We onlookers in the Egyptian cavalry have feared this all along, for the regiment was keen to do something and meant to charge something before the show was over. They got their charge . . . but at what a cost. I trust for the sake of the British cavalry that more tactical knowledge exists in the higher ranks of the *average* regiment than we have seen displayed in this one. Yet the commanding officer [Martin] had had his command extended. I wonder why? Is he a tactician? No. Is he a good disciplinarian? No. Is he a stud groom? His predecessor Hickman was, but alas the latter's mantle has not fallen on this man. Really I cannot think that the Promotion

---

* The title given in Egypt to the Commander-in-Chief – thus Kitchener.

† Rudolf Slatin, an Austrian, had served as an administrator in the Sudan but had been taken prisoner even before the fall of Khartoum. He described his experiences in *Fire and Sword in the Soudan*. He escaped from Omdurman in 1895 and in doing so crossed the Khor Shambat.

Board fully appreciate the responsibility which rests with them when they put duffers in command of regiments. I am writing to you just what I think, and now one word on the Battle as a whole.

I had ample time to 'appreciate' the situation on the 1st and 2nd morning. The enemy, halting as he did on the upper pools of the Khor Shambat on the night of 1–2 September, abandoned the key to his position, Signal Hill, to the Sirdar. The latter hill has long sloping shoulders and to my mind should have been occupied on evening of 1st. Why should the enemy not have taken it? And what losses would we not have suffered in turning him out? Lastly, occupied and used as a pivot, and keeping our army concealed to the east of it with gunboats and heavy guns in position protecting the flanks, we could anticipate any moves of this enemy. Then on morning of 2nd when the enemy had divided his forces, the Sirdar's left should have been thrown forward to this hill, and gradually drawing in his right and extending his left south-westwards, he might have cut the enemy off from Omdurman and really annihilated thousands and thousands of Dervishes. In place of this, altho' in possession of full information, and able to see with his own eyes the whole field, he spreads out his force, thereby risking the destruction of a Brigade. He seems to have had no plan or tactical idea for beating the enemy beyond allowing the latter to attack the camp. This the Dervishes would not do in force, having a wholesome fear of gunboat fire. Having six brigades is it tactics to fight a very superior enemy with one of them and keep the others beyond supporting distance? To me it seems truly fortunate that the *flower* of the Dervish army exhausted itself first in an attack and pursuit of the cavalry. Indeed the prisoners say: 'You would never have defeated us had you not *deceived* us.'

Again thanking you most sincerely for your kind letter, and hoping that you won't think me forward in criticising *this* successful General.

> Believe me yours most truly
> Douglas Haig

Haig was, of course, only doing what he had been asked to do by someone who had been a very good friend to him in the past and who was immensely interested in the battle. But it leaves the reader with a feeling of uneasiness. Haig knew as well as anyone that it is simpler to fight a battle in retrospect than on the day, that there is such a phenomenon as 'the fog of war' when confusion occurs, and that the Dervishes were a totally unpredictable enemy. He knew that his own future and that of Kitchener lay in the hands of Sir Evelyn Wood, the Adjutant General, and that Kitchener himself was well-disposed towards him – in the event Kitchener recommended him for promotion on the strength of his conduct in the campaign. No doubt Haig saw his writing confidential and frank letters to a very senior officer as being in the best interests of the Army as a whole. Possibly the two men had a slight contempt for each other. Haig saw Kitchener as the industrious, painstaking sapper who was excellent at administration but lacked the flair for command in battle; though he was perhaps unaware that Kitchener had commanded a brigade in the victory against Osman Digna in 1888. Kitchener saw Haig as the traditional cavalry officer with all the virtues and faults of his class. It would not have occurred to him that Haig could ever rise to be commander-in-chief of an army of millions – or, for that matter, that armies could ever reach that size.

The victory at Omdurman had effectively ended the brutal and tyrannical rule of the Khalifa, which had extended over seventeen years. Subsequently the Sudan was governed fairly and efficiently under the principle of trusteeship supervised by the Anglo-Egyptian Condominium (1899–1953) and prospered economically. As soon as Omdurman was over the seconded officers such as Haig were no longer required and mostly made their way home. Haig hoped to be posted to the Horse Guards, where he had been promised a position by Sir Evelyn Wood, but this did not materialise and instead he returned to his regiment, then at Norwich. Six months later he was appointed Brigade Major to the 1st Cavalry Brigade at Aldershot under Major General John French.

Although one might have thought Haig would have regarded

the Egyptian campaign as a very useful development in his career, Charteris, who must often have discussed it with him, put forward a very different view in his biography:

> Neither the brevet [provisional] rank of major, nor the new appointment satisfied him. He felt the Egyptian campaign had been a failure as far as he was concerned. He was thirty-eight years of age and still a regimental captain [his actual substantive rank]. There was no prospect of swift promotion. The goal of his ambition was still dim and distant. The war in Egypt was definitely over, and there seemed little probability of any further active service in the near future. His work at Aldershot did not absorb him, and the amusements of London entirely failed to attract him. He fell a victim to discontented ambition. Even his studies were in arrears and he became morose and brusque in manner. This was perhaps the least satisfactory year of Haig's military life: but it proved only a brief interval.

Charteris's statement skims lightly over the problems which concerned Haig at that moment. French, his new commander, had a lively imagination, a warm heart and compassionate nature and was as chatty and sociable as could be wished. In this latter respect he was a complete contrast to Haig, who could write fluently and clearly but was inarticulate to an embarrassing degree. On occasions Haig could give the impression that he was a fluent and witty public speaker, but that was when he had received considerable help with the content of his talk and had committed it to memory. Charteris mentions a more typical occasion, when Haig was presenting prizes to successful athletes at a sports meeting in Aldershot: 'I congratulate you on your running. You have run well. I hope you will run as well in the presence of the enemy.' Charteris also quotes an occasion when Haig had to make an important speech at Cambridge: 'He became totally unintelligible and unbearably dull.' But Charteris's tendency to exaggerate in order to make a good story may have come into play here.

In contrast to Haig, whose private life was almost puritan, French moved from one illicit liaison to another. One of his mistresses, the wife of a Foreign Office official, was over six feet tall. French, well under that height and later known as 'the little field marshal', was apparently accustomed to addressing her as 'my little darling'. Haig, as we know, was no intellectual but was sensible enough to remedy this with hard and continuous work. French was no intellectual either, but had risen in the Army through his ability to give the impression that he was a master of his profession.* The presence of a thorough, conscientious, knowledgeable officer like Haig as his brigade major was therefore of inestimable value to him.

A less savoury aspect of their relationship arose from the fact that French was so short of money that his Army career looked like being terminated at any moment by a financial scandal. He had endeavoured to improve his shaky finances by investing heavily in South African gold-mining shares in the 1890s. Fortunes were being made from South African gold mines, none more easily than by those selling speculative shares at inflated prices to gullible foreigners, of whom French was one. Knowing that Haig was wealthy, French did not find it in the least embarrassing to borrow money from him to check one of the more persistent of his creditors. The sum of £2000 was lent in 1899: four years later the debt was still owing, but Haig, who was then in India, left instructions that French should not be pressed to repay it. This matter must have been more embarrassing for Haig than for French, for it is well known that a borrower forgets a debt more easily than the lender. Even for a person as wealthy as Haig, £2000 in those days was a not inconsiderable sum. One may also hazard a guess that there were other, smaller, amounts which went the same way.

John Hussey, who has made a detailed study of the First World War and of Haig's career, finds many of the latter-day criticisms of Haig ill-founded and unbalanced. Among them is the implication that he furthered his career by astutely lending money to

---

* French had begun his service life as a midshipman in the Navy, but after four years had transferred to the Sussex Artillery Militia and thence to the 19th Hussars, with whom he had served on the Gordon relief expedition of 1884.

French, and by this means maintained a hold over his senior officer until he himself replaced him.

Hussey confirms that Haig lent French £2000 in 1899. In his account he says that the two men had known each other well for seven years and held certain ideas in common, though differing considerably in their lifestyle and members of different regiments. French was a spendthrift and had no business sense, but had a good grasp of cavalry warfare and the panache and experience to command troops in action. He was a vivacious, amiable friend, but Hussey points out that his history of disastrous relationships was unlikely to create a favourable impression with the Army authorities:

> As a young subaltern French had contracted an unsuitable (and apparently concealed) first marriage, which might have damaged his career; in 1878 his sister's lawyer husband, who had once *already* paid off Johnny's debts, arranged that a divorce should take place quietly and without fuss. Sometime later French again needed financial assistance and again turned to his brother-in-law, this time to be abruptly rebuffed. He married again, but while in India in the early '90s he went away with another officer's wife (on 'French leave', as it was jokingly said) and was cited as co-respondent in the ensuing divorce. While this did not wreck his career (or end his marriage), it led to several years on half-pay, which drained him financially and set back hopes of promotion.

Haig thought French was an asset to the Army and was appalled when he realised that his foolishness had created a situation in which he would be unable to pay his debts and therefore have to resign his commission. With a war in South Africa likely to break out at any moment, the disruption to the British cavalry which would be caused by the disgrace of French was too depressing to contemplate. He might well have feared that French would shoot himself, as many others in similar disastrous situations had done before him. There was no possibility at that point that Haig would replace French if he went.

In a letter to Henrietta on 16 May 1899, Haig wrote: 'It would be a terrible thing if French were made a Bankrupt – such a loss to the Army as well as to me personally. For of course we can do a lot here together towards improving things.' So the loan of £2000 was arranged by lawyers and paid over in two instalments. It was not meant to be more than temporary help, and French paid interest on it. It is perhaps worth noting that after this episode French managed to keep his business affairs on a more even keel, although he did not manage to repay Haig's loan until a few years before the First World War.

4

In Pursuit of the Boers

ALTHOUGH ACCORDING TO Charteris, Haig saw little prospect of further campaigning after the end of the Sudan war, there were numerous indications that the next conflict would be in South Africa and would occur soon. A major war in South Africa had been brewing for over seventy years, and in order to understand its course when it came it is necessary to take a brief glance at the events leading up to it.

South Africa consisted of four provinces: the Cape, the Orange Free State, Natal and the Transvaal. During the early 1600s the Cape had been used as a staging post by Dutch traders on their way to and from the East Indies, now Indonesia. In 1652 the Dutch had established a permanent settlement at the Cape, and by the end of the century had been joined by Protestant Huguenots from France; names from each source predominate in South Africa today.

However, when Napoleon set off to conquer Europe in the 1790s Holland was one of the first countries to be over-run. In the bitter naval conflict that characterised the first stage of the Napoleonic Wars it seemed improbable that the conquered Dutch would be allowed to retain their convenient trading post *en route* to the East: it appeared more than likely that the French would send a fleet south and take possession of it. In order to forestall such a dangerous possibility, which would in any case be against Holland's long-term interests, the Royal Navy arrived there first. In 1814, with the Napoleonic Wars apparently drawing to a close, it was decided in the negotiations for a peace settlement that Britain should retain the Cape, but pay the Dutch generous compensation.

At first this arrangement looked like a satisfactory outcome. However, as the years passed the Dutch settlers became increasingly incensed by two factors: one was the beginning of raids on their farms by the warlike Bantu who had now reached the Cape after a long migration southwards; the other was the British reaction to the treatment of the natives by the Dutch, who were usually known as Boers, from the Afrikaans word for farmer. The Boers had no inhibitions about capturing natives and employing them as slaves; this was, at the time, a worldwide practice. However in 1834, as mentioned earlier, the British abolished slavery in the British Empire. Although compensation was paid to the Boer farmers to enable them to hire labour to replace their own slaves, the amount was inadequate and alternative labour was difficult to acquire. Finally, disgusted by the restraints put on them by their British overlords, the Boers left the Cape in 1838 and set off 'up country' in what became known as the Great Trek. One party crossed the Vaal River and set up the state known as the Transvaal; another crossed the Orange River and established the Orange Free State.

However, in their new territories the Boers were still British subjects, and when they were in trouble with Bantu tribes who resented their presence the British had to send troops to protect them. The expense of maintaining troops for the purpose was more than the government in London was prepared to finance, and in the early 1850s both the Transvaal and the Orange Free State were given their independence, subject to safeguards.

All might have been well if rich diamond mines had not been discovered in the 1860s in an area claimed as their territory by both British and Dutch. An independent tribunal subsequently awarded it to the British, with compensation paid to the Boers, but the event confirmed the Boers in their view that the more they could keep away from the British and the inroads of settlers brought in by the diamond mines the better.

Unhappily the next big discovery was gold in 1884, in indisputably Boer territory – the Transvaal. But gold is not easily extracted from granite rock, and to exploit it the Boers had to let in British and Turkish engineers. The president of the Boer Republic was Paul Kruger, a man who was said never to have read any book but the Bible, whose attitudes had been settled for life when he was a boy on the Great Trek, and who was dedicated to retaining control over the Transvaal and exploiting its riches. He distrusted the motives of the British, for in 1877, following disturbing reports about Boer treatment of the Bantu, Britain had annexed the Transvaal and ruled it directly with a view to safeguarding the Africans' interests as much as those of the Boers. The annexation had been short-lived, for in 1880 the Boers had suddenly revolted, taken the British government by surprise and inflicted two severe defeats on the British forces sent to suppress the revolt. The British government of the day shrank from the expense of financing a war in a remote territory in which they had no interest – this was before the discovery of gold – and weakly handed the Transvaal back to Kruger and his friends. Ironically, the Boers would have had no chance of defeating the British in 1880 if a year earlier the British had not gone to considerable trouble to defeat the Zulu nation, who had posed a very serious threat to the Boers.

Kruger used the wealth which came from the gold mines to buy arms which the firm of Krupps in Germany obligingly supplied, as they did to most other countries. Meanwhile the immigrants – mainly British and Turkish – who were mining and refining the gold were treated nearly as badly as the Boers used to treat their slaves. The compulsory language in schools and courts was Afrikaans and the immigrants, though essential to Transvaal industry, were allowed no political rights whatever. In 1896 Britain suffered a further humiliation when Dr Starr Jameson, a hot-headed and ill-advised patriot, decided to lead a raid from the town of Mafeking into the Transvaal, overturn the Boer government and return the Transvaal to the British Empire. He failed ignominiously and served merely to convince Kruger that his policy was correct, that he must make no concessions and that his imports of arms must be increased.

The British authorities were now viewing the South African situation with increasing concern. The Transvaal government could only become more stubborn, and there were indications that Germany, whose Kaiser was now more belligerent and ambitious than in the days when he had drunk Haig's health, was planning closer relations with Kruger. This was a period when all European countries were trying to secure for themselves colonies in Africa, and Germany had been one of the less successful competitors. When Britain began to reinforce her Cape garrison in 1899, it was in the belief that she might soon find herself not merely in conflict with the Boers but also with her own increasingly bellicose European neighbour. During 1899 both sides were pressing ahead with preparations for the inevitable war. Realising that their best hope lay in first strike and mobility, the Boers made their commandos ready; the British initiated the despatch of forty-seven thousand men to supplement the fifteen thousand already in the country.

The Boers were well aware of the advantages they possessed: knowledge of the terrain, well-developed skills in fieldcraft, smokeless powder and strong motivation. They knew they could live off the country and be independent of cumbersome supply columns; if they wished to supplement their rations they would expect to do so by ambushing stores travelling along the vulnerable supply routes. With these thoughts in mind, Kruger wanted to begin the war before the British were properly organised. He therefore issued an ultimatum that Britain should withdraw all reinforcements despatched since the previous June and send in no more men or arms, though he himself had imported 187,000 rifles from Germany in 1897. The ultimatum expired at 5 p.m. on 11 October 1899 and, as soon as it did, Boer troops from the Transvaal and the Orange Free State invaded the Cape Colony and Natal. By the time the main British reinforcements reached South Africa, the Boers were already besieging Ladysmith, Kimberley – the headquarters of the diamond industry – and Mafeking.

The Commander-in-Chief of the British forces was Sir Redvers Buller, VC, who had been Haig's GOC at Aldershot and was already sixty-six years old. He was a veteran of many campaigns: the China War of 1860, the Red River expedition in Canada, the Ashanti wars in West Africa, the Zulu War (where he had won his Victoria Cross), the 1881 Boer War, the Egyptian campaign of 1882, and the expedition which had failed to relieve Khartoum in time to save Gordon's life. Although in appearance and manner a typical Victorian martinet, Buller was in fact an extremely compassionate officer who did his best to avoid casualties to the troops under his command.

The strength of the Boer forces was not known precisely but was now thought to be about fifty thousand. However, numerical strength was going to be less important in this war than other factors. The Boers were, of course, all fighting effectives: there was no wastage of able-bodied men doing administrative jobs. Every man had a horse, could ride superbly and shoot straight from the saddle. They had learnt their fieldcraft in fighting the Bantu. They had good artillery: Krupps and Creusot 75 mm field guns, and some 155 mm Creusots. All these outranged the British guns, which consisted of 15-pounders of the Royal Artillery, 12-pounders of the Royal Horse Artillery and 7-pounders of the Natal Field Force. This unequal balance of firepower was not appreciated in the United Kingdom, where it was assumed that after a few well-aimed shots the Boers would flee or raise a white flag. Still less appreciated was the enormous size of the terrain in which the war would take place, which was as large as France and Germany combined, while Britain's two main bases, Cape Town and Durban, were two thousand miles apart. There were no accurate or reliable maps, there were very few roads or bridges, and the fords (known as 'drifts') on the rivers had steep sides which made them dangerous to troops crossing: ambushes often took place at drifts. There were other hazards in South Africa which would become all too apparent later: heat and cold, water- and fly-borne diseases, insects and unknown infections. South Africa would also prove a graveyard for horses, which suffered enormously from privation and disease, and cavalry tactics which had met with everyone's approval on Salisbury Plain would there seem quaint anachronisms.

As there was no expeditionary force available for despatch overseas, one had had to be raised from troops who were normally fully employed on other duties. For the commanders, experience of warfare overseas was felt to be an advantage which outweighed the possible disadvantage of age. General Sir George White, at sixty-four, was only two years younger than Buller. In contrast, Lieutenant General Methuen was a young man, being only fifty-four, but unfortunately had no experience of command, having risen in rank entirely by staff appointments.

Haig was sent out with French as his staff officer AAG or Assistant Adjutant General on 23 September 1899 on the Union Castle liner *Norman*. On arrival at Cape Town on 10 October they heard of Kruger's ultimatum. They were then sent on to Durban – another five days at sea – and thence on to Ladysmith by train.

As they travelled, the war was beginning briskly. The Boers had invaded Natal and were at that moment driving towards Mafeking and Kimberley. The commander of the Natal forces, Sir George White, was pleased to see French and Haig arrive, and promptly put French in charge of a reconnaissance force of mixed cavalry and artillery. His brief was to assess the situation to the north of Ladysmith, on which strong Boer forces were said to be converging. In that area lay important coalfields and the towns of Glencoe and Dundee. It was obvious that the British forces in the region were too isolated and too few, but an encouraging note was struck when advancing Boer columns were checked by a British brigade at Talana Hill. The British brigade commander was killed while leading a charge and there were many other casualties, but the Boers withdrew. White therefore decided that the next move should be to occupy Elandslaagte, where the railway had been destroyed by the Boers, and where there were said to be British prisoners.

French's force, now consisting of a mixture of cavalry, infantry and artillery, set off at 4 a.m. in the direction of Elandslaagte. It meant a busy night for Haig, for his task was to draft the orders for the march. The British force met the Boers four miles south of Elandslaagte and drove them back to within a mile of the town. Good artillery fire then caused the Boers to withdraw and take up a position on a circle of small hills (*kopjes*) near the town. There they were attacked by the British infantry – a brigade commanded by Sir Ian Hamilton – in an orthodox action, with one battalion coming from the front and the other two on the right flank. At this stage some of the cavalry were dismounted to support the attack. The operation was successful, the Boers abandoned their position and the remainder of the cavalry pursued them on their retreat. British casualties numbered 263, Boer exactly 100 more, of which 188 were taken prisoner.

The aftermath of the battle gave Haig another busy night. He had to examine the prisoners, who included an extraordinary mixture of Boers, Germans, Dutch and American-Irish; all had fought well. They told Haig they would never have thought the British could have taken their position; they were also extremely indignant that fugitives had been speared by the lances of the pursuing British cavalry. This, they felt, was 'butchery, not war'. Haig noted in a letter to Henrietta that some 1815 brandy had been found in one of the Boer wagons, and that the Boer commander, General Kock, who was fatally wounded, had led his troops while wearing a top hat and a frock coat.

However, in spite of this encouraging success Elandslaagte was no place for the British to remain, for White had now learnt that Boer columns were converging on Ladysmith from the north, east and west. Unfortunately there was still a British brigade on Talana Hill and this needed to be brought back before it was cut off and annihilated. The task was allotted to French's cavalry and achieved successfully, though not without a skirmish with the Boers. Further reconnaissance established that the latter were too strong to be attacked until they came closer to the town, but once there must be checked before they could occupy the strategic point of Long Hill. An attack was therefore planned for 30 October.

In this operation the cavalry acquitted itself well, but the artillery met disaster. On the night march the mules in a mountain battery panicked and stampeded, thus disrupting the column and losing some of the reserve ammunition. By dawn this part of the column, which consisted of two battalions, found itself surrounded by vastly superior numbers of Boers and was forced to surrender; the total taken prisoner was 954. Haig considered that this would never have happened if they had been allotted cavalry to conduct a proper reconnaissance: presumably this would have enabled the unfortunate column to see the reception prepared for it and to take evasive action. Haig's opinion had not, of course, been sought. His task was to draft the orders for a decision which had already been taken. However, two days later, when White asked him for his opinion of the dispositions he was proposing to make, Haig gave a straight answer in a memorandum:

The line occupied is too extended for troops available – 9000 men. The perimeter is about ten miles long. The first requirement is a good defensive position suited to the numbers available for defence. Certain points should be strongly held as pivots of manoeuvre, and a large proportion of troops be kept in reserve for counter-attack. Cavalry and artillery to be set apart for this purpose, unless the bulk of the cavalry could be sent to Colenso to operate on the enemy's flanks and rear. Caesar's camp must be held at all costs because it commands the surroundings of Ladysmith.

The next morning, at 3 a.m., French set off with his cavalry to reconnoitre the situation twelve miles north-west of Ladysmith. Haig, of course, accompanied him, and it now seemed likely that they would spend the next few weeks around Ladysmith. However it was not to be: Buller had just arrived in South Africa, and one of his first actions was to send a telegram to White requesting that French and Haig should report to Cape Town immediately, if they could be spared. French was to take charge of the new cavalry division which was arriving from England shortly.

It was a fortuitous event for Haig. The Boers were closing round the town rapidly, and if they had remained both he and French would have been besieged. In the event, it was a close shave: their train was the last to leave Ladysmith for four months. Haig described the journey in a letter to Henrietta; if she was nervous about his safety, this letter can have done little to allay her fears.

A train was starting at 12.30 p.m. We got our kit and ten horses put in. The Railway Manager did not think we could get past the Boers as they had fired on the morning passenger train. However, we insisted on going. There was a guard's van with a first-class compartment at the rear end in which we travelled. There was an engine driver and a guard, the others on the train were ourselves and seven servants. All were enjoined to keep out of sight for the first two hours. Twenty minutes went by without any untoward event. We then got near a place called Pieter's station. Several bullets, in fact a regular volley, rattled along the side of the vehicles, and we heard several shells explode. We did not see anything for we had a wooden shutter up and we all four lay on the seats and floor of the carriage. The train went on and then suddenly stopped. The door opened and we expected to see some Boer inviting us to descend! We had got into one of our own posts left to protect the line and the individual who opened the door was a British officer. On we went again with the same precautions, for we were told we should be shot at again three miles down. Sure enough there was a very loud report and other shots. When we got to Colenso we examined our train and found a 2½ or 3 inch shell had got through the second truck. If this shell had hit a wheel, not to mention the engine boiler, we would certainly have been now on our way to Pretoria instead of in Durban.★ Or indeed if the Boers had torn up a rail, the engine driver would not have seen it because the moment the Boers began shooting he lay down amongst the coal.

Or, as Henrietta would no doubt have surmised, if the shell had hit the carriage in which they were travelling, they would no doubt be occupying graves by the side of the shattered train.

As soon as Haig arrived at Cape Town he set to work making

★ Pretoria jail, near the Boer HQ. Durban was in British hands.

the arrangements for the accommodation of the Cavalry Division, which arrived on 17 November. By this time Ladysmith, Mafeking and Kimberley were all under siege. But besieging small garrisons in relatively unimportant towns was not the best use of Boer resources. Rather than split up their army in this way, they should have concentrated into one or two powerful columns and headed straight for the Cape. If they had done so, they could have won the war outright. Their greatest error was to waste the criticial two weeks before the larger British reinforcements began to arrive. However, although it made poor sense strategically, the Boer investment of certain well-known towns embarrassed the British considerably. When the public learned that within a few weeks of Kruger's ultimatum he had locked up at least three British garrisons inside towns there was a demand that something should be done forthwith.

At the outbreak of war Buller had planned to concentrate his forces and advance to Bloemfontein and Pretoria. However, when Ladysmith and Kimberley were besieged he realised that these towns must not be allowed to fall into enemy hands. If they did, it would serve as a sign to the large numbers of Boers in the Cape who had so far not decided to join Kruger that they should now do so. Buller concluded that Ladysmith was the more important of the two towns, and therefore that he should take personal command of the operation to relieve it. This meant that the Commander-in-Chief would be separated from his subordinate commands by huge distances. However, he had not abandoned the idea of a central drive to the Boer capital and therefore assigned that objective to French's Cavalry Division. To Methuen's 1st Division he gave the task of relieving Kimberley, but decided that Mafeking would have to sit out its siege until the central group could make some headway towards Pretoria.

Neither General Gatacre, commanding another relief column, nor Methuen was equal to his task. Gatacre tried to push through a Boer position at Stormberg and was repulsed, suffering 696 casualties, while Methuen met a similar fate at Magersfontein with even greater casualties – a total of 948. But these disasters were overshadowed by a reverse to Buller himself: at Colenso, when he was trying to cross the Tugela River, his force sustained 1139 casualties and lost much of its artillery. These reverses all occurred between 10 and 15 December 1899. Not surprisingly, it was named 'Black Week' by the British public; ominously it implied that even now, against a stronger British force, the Boers could and would win the war.

The immediate effect of Black Week was, however, beneficial to Britain. The government was spurred into action and, as a first step, relieved Buller of his post as Commander-in-Chief. Young men in Britain and the colonies, Australia, New Zealand and Canada in particular, came forward in large numbers and volunteered their services. It seemed that, if the situation could now be stabilised, the Boers could still be defeated. Buller's replacement was even older than he was – the veteran Lord Roberts, 'Bobs', who was already sixty-eight. Nevertheless, Roberts was in an entirely different category from Buller, and so too was the Chief of Staff who accompanied him – Major General Kitchener of Khartoum, the victor of the Sudan campaign. Buller was not sent home but, with his main responsibility removed, was left in charge of the relief of Ladysmith. This was an unwise decision, for he was so anxious to avoid heavy casualties in his attempt to break through the Boer lines that he hesitated to make the all-out thrust which, in the long run, might have cost fewer lives. He was heavily defeated at Spion Kop on 24 January 1900, and further reverses occurred before the town was finally relieved on 27 February.

The campaign to relieve Ladysmith was no concern of Haig, except perhaps to confirm his view of Buller's ineptitude. Haig was now under a commander in whom he would come in time to have complete confidence, and this confidence would be mutual.

Roberts decided that his strategy should be to strike north-west to relieve Kimberley and then due east to capture Bloemfontein: French's cavalry division should lead. However, when Roberts made this appreciation he committed an initial disastrous mistake. Without consulting French, both Roberts and the War Office had decided that someone more senior than a captain holding the rank of brevet major should be acting as French's right-hand man. In fact, the War Office had already despatched Colonel the Earl of Erroll, who had commanded the Blues (the Royal Horse Guards) for four years. Unlike Haig, Erroll had not attended the Staff College and for that reason alone this was an unwise appointment.

French was furious when he learned what was happening, and sent a long and forceful telegram to Kitchener:

> May I point out that the appointment of Assistant Adjutant General to the Cavalry Division was promised by Sir Redvers Buller to Major Haig with the local rank of Lieutenant Colonel. I was officially asked to recommend an officer to fill his place as Deputy Assistant Adjutant General. I earnestly beg that the Field Marshal will be pleased to confirm this. Major Haig has performed the duty of Chief Staff Officer to a division since landing in Natal. He has acted in this capacity under my command in three general engagements and many smaller fights. I have several times mentioned him in despatches.

But his indignant protest was in vain. Roberts replied via one of his staff officers: 'Field Marshal Commander-in-Chief fully realises the very excellent services rendered by Major Haig and much regrets not being able to meet your views as regards his taking position of AAG of the Cavalry Division. That position however the Field Marshal thinks must be filled by the appointment of a senior officer and he feels sure you will find in Colonel the Earl of Erroll an efficient officer.'

The modern reader, who may not have had experience of the working and structure of the Army, may find some of these ponderous titles baffling. When armies were very small, it was sensible enough to describe the officer in charge of personnel as the Adjutant General and his counterpart in supplies as the Quartermaster General. Their deputies would have equally grandiloquent titles, even though they might be mere majors or captains. Sometimes the two deputy posts would be combined to give the sonorous title of Deputy Assistant Adjutant and Quartermaster-General, abbreviated to DAA and QMG; it was usually referred to as 'the DQ'. The term 'local rank' describes another means of saving official money. Local rank was temporary and, of course, unpaid: it could be removed at a moment's notice, and disappeared on a posting to another appointment.

Within a few days of his appointment, Erroll was found to be quite unqualified. French's ADC, Sir John Laycock, obtained an interview with Kitchener and explained the position. Erroll was soon removed and Haig resumed his former position. He had behaved very correctly and had seemed less concerned than his friends. Laycock was relieved when the position was restored, for he said of Haig: 'The thing that struck me most was Haig's extraordinary ability to express in concise form capable of being copied into a notebook on the field important orders for the movement and disposition of troops. In this he was an absolute master.'

Haig's signature appears again on the orders which were issued on the 13th. They are quoted here in full because they provide a good example of his style:

1. The enemy has retired from the Riet apparently in a north and north-westerly direction.

2. The General Officer Commanding intends to march to the Modder to-day and seize a passage over it, and establish the Division beyond it.

3. The Division will march at 9 a.m. to-day in the following order:

    (a) Porter's Brigade in the centre, Broadwood's Brigade on the right, Gordon's on the left.

    (b) The Mounted Infantry (under Colonel Alderson) will follow the cavalry as closely as possible, escorting the ammunition column and pontoons, and accompanied by the Bearer Companies and Field Hospital.

4. The baggage and supply columns with the ammunition wagons which are not horsed will follow with the detachment which marched into De Kiel's this morning under Colonel Porter, at an hour to be named by the latter.

5. The General Officer Commanding will march with the centre brigade.

    By order   D. Haig   Major DAAG

The British public was overjoyed to hear the first good news of the war – that on 15 February Kimberley had been relieved. This welcome victory was almost entirely due to French's initiative. The column had set off on 11 February at 3 a.m. That evening French's force was joined by 550 troops from Robert's Horse, 153 from Kitchener's, and 562 Mounted Infantry, as well as seven batteries of mounted gunners. This gave them a total of just under five thousand and was therefore about three thousand short of the number they had been promised. But it was no good waiting for more; they might never arrive. Instead, French decided to rely on surprise. In order not to be delayed, he left all the wagons behind except four ambulances and a cable cart. The weather was very hot and there were a number of heath fires on their way, but he pressed on with all possible speed. At one stage he was delayed by a force of some fifteen hundred Boers on a hilltop farm on the right flank, but dealt with this by detaching one brigade. His force reached the vital Klip Drift which the 12th Lancers crossed first, establishing a bridgehead. Here the Boers were so surprised to see them that in their flight they left all their supplies behind them: these included peaches and other fruit, and even hot bread.

However, the captured supplies were soon exhausted and the column had to wait until its own rations caught up. The following day they set off again. They had received a few reinforcements at Klip Drift but were still short of the number needed. 'However,' commented Haig,

we cavalry must not complain, for Kitchener has backed us up well, and is really the *working man* of the Obercommando.[*]

We had not gone three miles from Klip Drift northwards before our advanced squadrons were heavily fired on from some hills in their front – at the same time some Boer guns opened on us from a hill to our left (i.e. N.W.). The situation seemed to be that our friends of two days ago were holding the

---

[*] Haig had adopted, as military commanders often do, the terminology of the enemy. 'Commando' was a Dutch word used by the Boers to describe their independent fighting units.

hills in our front to stop us going to Bloemfontein, while Cronje from Magersfontein had extended his left to prevent us out-flanking him . . . There was an open plain towards Abous Dam between the two parties of the enemy. The ground rose from the river, so we could not see whether there were wire fences or not, but there seemed to be only a few Boers at the end of the rise. There seemed to be only one thing to be done if we were to get to Kimberley before the Boers barred our path, namely to charge the gap between the two positions. Half our guns were ordered to keep down the fire from the Kopjes in our front (which would be on the right flank of the charging cavalry) and half engaged the enemy's guns. The 9th and 12th Lancers were then ordered to charge followed by Broadwood's brigade in support. For a minute it looked in the dust as if some of our men were coming back, but they were only extending towards a flank. Porter's brigade followed with the Mounted Infantry and brought on the guns. Our lancers caught several Boers and rode down many others in the open plain and really suffered very little from the very hot rifle fire – about twenty casualties I fancy, and we passed within one thousand yards of the Boer position! We got to Kimberley at 6 p.m. The garrison made not the slightest attempt to assist us. Alone we cleared all the Boers investing positions in the south . . . The people of Kimberley looked fat and well. It was the relieving force which needed food, for in the gallop many nosebags were lost and 7 lb tins of bully beef is an unsuitable adjunct to one's saddle in a charge!

This had been an excellent and timely thrust by French, but the campaign was not yet over. The elusive Boer general, Cronje, was not in the trap they had set for him; even though the British now commanded the country up to the Vaal River, Cronje had managed to slip away eastwards and reach Paardeberg, twenty-five miles away. Orders were given to intercept him in the Modder Valley, though before he was eventually taken prisoner the British forces sustained heavy casualties: 140, of which 94 were officers.

Haig described his experiences in a letter to Henrietta. At Kimberley:

I have never seen horses so beat as ours on that day. They have been having only 8 lbs of oats a day and practically been starving since we left Modder River on Feb 11th. So many Colonial Skallywag Corps have been raised that the horses of the whole force could not have a full ration. The Colonial Corps raised in *Cape Colony* are quite useless, so are the recently raised Mounted Infantry. They can't ride and know nothing about their duties as mounted men. Roberts' Horse and Kitchener's Horse are good only for looting and the greater part of them disappear the moment a shot is fired on them in the prospect of a fight. You will see that the success of the Cavalry Division has been in spite of these ruffians, and notwithstanding short rations.

Despite these disadvantages, Roberts's army continued to press forward towards Bloemfontein, which was occupied on 13 March. Unfortunately for them and for the length of the war, they just missed capturing Kruger. After a short while spent in repairing the railway, they pressed on to Johannesburg and Pretoria. Kruger and his colleague Steyn had fled to an unknown destination. It looked as if the war was almost over; no one could have guessed it still had two more years to run. Mafeking was relieved. News came that Kruger was now in the neutral Portuguese colony of Mozambique, with as much gold as he could carry. Meanwhile it became obvious that a much more dangerous Boer general was at large, Christian de Wet. As a foretaste of his daring tactics, he pounced on and seized a station between Pretoria and Bloemfontein, effectively blocking all British communication for a week. Suddenly he abandoned the station and disappeared; three days later he swooped on another station twelve miles north and nearly captured Kitchener in the process. Meanwhile, Roberts pressed on to Mozambique, where he tried to persuade the Boer general Botha to surrender. Botha at first agreed to a meeting, then refused. Kruger departed for Holland and Roberts returned to England in November, after handing over his command to Kitchener. The British public, and particularly the British Cabinet, were rejoicing that the war was virtually over. In fact, as Kitchener realised only too well, the most difficult part was only just beginning, and was likely to continue as long as Botha, de Wet and the other great guerrilla leader, Smuts, were at large.

Haig, who shared the general view that the campaign was drawing to its end, took part in the march from Bloemfontein to Pretoria. His immediate problem was trying to see that the horses were properly fed and watered in such barren countryside. He was in constant touch with Henrietta, who sent him necessities and luxuries and also looked after his financial affairs at home. 'Many thanks for ordering me some shirts: please send me a sponge and some soap (nice soap) from Floris next time you are in London. The scent is capital – Some awful smells about here. Enteric very bad – many funerals every day. Fever will stop as soon as the frosty nights begin.'*

Haig arrived in Pretoria in June after a long trek, sometimes covering thirty miles a day. The horses suffered badly; no one had anticipated the harshness of the conditions and the inevitable wastage.

On 7 July French was ordered to set off immediately to assist General Hutton, who was protecting Pretoria against possible Boer guerrilla attacks. However, it turned out to be a false alarm and he was soon back. Haig wrote to Henrietta: 'I hope this movement [to complete the campaign] which really begins tomorrow will end the war in about three weeks. The policy of

---

* Army officers have a reputation for being addicted to scent, but there is a very good reason for it: it helps to disguise the odours of dirty clothing and unwashed flesh. It became popular with armies on the Crusades, and by the nineteenth century had become a feature of elegant Army officers even when there were adequate facilities for washing. In South Africa, to bury one's face in a scented handkerchief was a relief from one's surroundings and a reminder of more comfortable times. In the warfare of the Western Desert in the early 1940s, tank crews used scent liberally when available; water was often too scarce even to be used for shaving. Men went about smelling, as they crisply but crudely put it, 'like a whore's bedroom'.

treating the Boers with leniency has not paid so far: they surrender their arms and take an oath of allegiance, but on the first favourable chance they go out on commando again. I have not received any mail since I wrote to you last week.'

In August he mentioned in another letter that Sir Evelyn Wood had written to French saying that he, Haig, should be appointed to a cavalry regiment as he would be a much better commanding officer than most who held that position. French had objected, saying that Haig was much more useful as chief staff officer in a cavalry division. 'Personally I don't care what happens to me in the way of reward,' Haig said, 'for I despise those who only work when they hope to get something in return.' At that time his main anxiety seemed to be the non-arrival of some silk drawers he had sent for; in that climate, with long days in the saddle, the only suitable underwear seemed to be silk; everything else chafed.

In November of that year Haig himself narrowly escaped being captured by sixteen Boers; he was out riding with one other officer at the time. In December he wrote to Henrietta to tell her she could come out and see him in the following February – the visit was later cancelled. He referred to Sir Evelyn Wood's efforts to get him command of a cavalry regiment and added,

French is only too anxious to help me on but I think that in remaining on as his Chief Staff officer I did the best for the Cavalry Division, for him and for myself. One did not foresee this war lasting so long, otherwise I might have taken command of some scallywag corps or other. So don't make a fuss about my being now in the position I started in. Recollect many have gone lower down, and as to rewards, if you only knew what duffers will get and do get HM's decorations and are promoted you would realise how little I value them. Everything comes in time, and decorations come in abundance with declining years and imbecility. No one yet on the Staff, fortunately, has got a decoration of any kind, otherwise we might have achieved disaster like the other *decorés*!

By the end of the year the War Office had decided that the

guerrilla warfare tactics of the Boers necessitated a reorganisation of the British forces. Instead of large units there would be small mobile columns, and the movements of the Boers would be restricted by the adoption of Kitchener's 'blockhouse' system: the creation of a network of barbed wire enclosures, each incorporating a fortified blockhouse. Eventually the Boer families which had been supplying the commandos from their farms were moved into camps in the south of the country. During the early part of 1901 there was considerable apprehension that many of the Dutch farmers who had stayed on their farms might now decide to rise and join the guerrillas.

Haig was given command of mobile columns and enjoyed the work. In February he received a telegram from Kitchener congratulating him on his performance. In March he was engaged in hunting De Wet, who periodically made raids into the Cape Colony, but with lessening success. Both sides hoped that the other was becoming tired of the war: the Boers were apparently convinced that the British would soon go home and let them have the run of the country again. By now Haig was commanding three columns, comprising a total of 2700 men, and in April he was promoted to the command of all the mobile columns in the Midland District of Cape Colony. In spite of having to hurry from one point to another he seemed to be faring well. On 19 April he wrote to Henrietta: 'I also wired you today to tell you that the wine etc. had reached me and that "everything is excellent". The champagne, claret and port *could not be better* and all are much appreciated. Please see that it is all charged to me.'

Militarily the situation was slow to improve:

I like the change of work down here, which is different from what I had in the Orange River colony: there we merely cleared farms and made raids on them at night. But here the situation is different. Some people say it is the most difficult operation of the war and causes a certain amount of anxiety . . . Since then Kretzenger seems to have been allowed to run loose, while Molam has wrecked trains just as he liked. Now the local farmers have begun to join the Commandos and the situation is much more serious than when I was here before.

Don't think for a moment that I require a rest. On the contrary I enjoy myself immensely and have got quite used to getting about 300 telegrams a day.

Nevertheless in June he caught influenza, which put him to bed for three days. In August he was given command of the 17th Lancers who formed part of one of the mobile columns he was directing, but he continued to perform his former tasks as well as his new one. In his correspondence with Henrietta Haig makes light of his difficulties, although 'hunting the Boer leader is like trying to catch quicksilver with one's fingers'. His opinion of Kitchener seems to have improved little since the Sudan campaign: 'Lord Kitchener seems to meddle rather and does not give French a free hand. Personally when I was in command directly under K. I did not find this the case. Indeed I did just whatever I thought fit and never asked what he wanted but merely told him what I had done and the situation from day to day.'

Not the least of the British difficulties was the fact that the Boers often dressed in khaki uniforms and were thus able to approach very close without rousing suspicion. Wearing one's enemy's uniform was a risky procedure, for when they were apprehended – which they often were – they were promptly shot. There was little sympathy among the soldiers for the Boers, who disregarded the conventions of war, such as wearing distinctive uniforms, and even used explosive bullets.

In March 1902 Haig was in the Palehuis Pass, near Clan William. 'This is a bad part of the country for horses. I have lost two since I came. The old friend which I have ridden ever since Bloemfontein [March 1900]. Another horse (which one of my servants rode) ate some kind of poisonous bush when we were near Calvinia last month and died in about 4 hours.' Claret and champagne seem to have helped to alleviate the tedium, even for the relatively abstemious Haig. But he liked the country and several times suggested to Henrietta that she might like to buy a farm and settle there, remarking on the fertility of the soil and hoping that the British would settle there in greater numbers after the war.

Peace was signed on 31 May 1902 and Haig returned to England from South Africa in October, pleased to be back but convinced that this experience with all its hardships had been as useful as it had been enjoyable.

Haig's personal servant, Sergeant T. Secrett, who first joined him when Haig was commanding his independent column in 1900 and stayed with him until 1926, subsequently wrote a book, *Twenty-Five Years with Earl Haig*, which was published in 1929. Although Secrett was a great admirer of Haig he was not blind to the faults of the man whom he sometimes refers to as 'my master', though he produced anecdotes which indicate that the subsequent view of Haig as an insensitive martinet are far from true. Writing of the south African period, Secrett noted that Haig admired the Boers, possibly because they were first-class horsemen and excellent shots. After peace had been signed, he was quick to arrange a polo match between British and Boer teams. He also made friends with Smuts and Botha, and in the early days of the First World War he would appoint Botha's son to be one of his ADCs.

5
A Changing Scene

It HAS BEEN suggested by his critics that Haig's experience in the South African war confirmed him in his belief – some would say obsession – that cavalry was the most important arm on the battlefield because it cemented the final victory there. However, it is unlikely that Haig viewed the campaign in this way: undoubtedly the cavalry had played an important part in bringing hostilities to an end, but Haig knew as well as anyone that it was the methodical cordoning off by barbed wire and blockhouses that eventually brought the Boer leaders to the conference table. Without that long-term war of attrition, planned and executed by Kitchener, the cavalry could never have rounded up the Boer commandos.

Haig, as has been noted earlier, had an enormous respect for the abilities of his chosen arm. He was fully aware of the decisive effect that cavalry charges had had in the past, and he was unlikely to forget the value of the thrust French had made at Klip Drift. Cavalry was indispensable in mobile warfare because it enabled soldiers to cover long distances, effect surprise and police large areas. But it had to be used correctly: timing was all-important. Cavalry, he had observed, could be used stupidly and wastefully, as in the disastrous charge of the 21st Lancers at Omdurman. He would have been quite right, however, in assuming that at that stage in warfare there was in fact no alternative to cavalry, and there would not be one until fast tanks, tactical aircraft and helicopter gunships appeared on the battlefield. Although a few aircraft had already flown successfully, it would have needed a prophet of genius to see them playing a dominant rôle on the battlefield at the turn of the century. The horse was still the chief element of mobile warfare, and in some areas it would continue to be important long after armies had been mechanised.

Haig was, of course, well aware that cavalry could not win wars on its own, but needed gunners, engineers, signallers and, above all, infantrymen. Moreover, he was not unaware of the fact that since he had joined the Army there had been developments which boded ill for the future of cavalry. One was the machine gun, on whose effectiveness Haig had already commented, and another was the use of barbed wire on the battlefield. Fortunately for French, when he set out towards Klip Drift the Boers were either short of barbed wire or did not fully realise at that stage what a deadly obstacle it could be. Equally ominous was the rapid improvement in the accuracy of rifle fire; even in the days of muzzle-loaders, musketeers had been formidable opponents, and as personal weapons became more accurate and reliable, the threat to such large and inviting targets as horses must be taken seriously. Nevertheless it was not the first time that cavalry had been challenged on the battlefield, and Haig and his contemporaries reached the conclusion that, although cavalry would not be able to withstand the threat of modern weapons for ever, the end was not yet in sight. The Boer War, in spite of its heavy toll on horseflesh, had encouraged cavalrymen rather than depressed them. There might no longer be a future for glittering squadrons riding in close formation at the enemy, but there could be considerable scope in less conspicuous uniforms riding in open formation. It would probably mean a painful period of adjustment to changing conditions and the discarding of some time-honoured practices, but change could not be resisted – nor should it be. Although Haig had an impressive collection of books on past cavalry tactics, that fact did not necessarily mean his ideas were rooted in the past.

Nevertheless the cavalry needed to be diplomatic and to look for compromise at this time if it was to survive, for there was a strong movement in the War Office to abolish horses from the battlefield altogether.

Among adjustments which Haig had to make, the choice of suitable cavalry weapons came high on the list. Although he was now commanding a regiment which was formerly schooled in the idea of charging with the lance, he was aware that the days of the lance were over and that its replacements were the sword and the carbine. But not everyone felt the same. One of his officers in the 17th Lancers, Major the Hon. H. A. Lawrence, felt that he was too old a dog to learn new tricks and resigned his commission. He already had good connections in the City and proceeded to make a success of his career there. However, when war was declared in 1914 Lawrence did not hesitate to return to the Army, although by that time he was in his fifties. Ironically, he eventually became Haig's Chief of Staff and the pair worked together very well.

In the spring of 1903 a Royal Commission was appointed to look at the lessons of the South African War and identify the changes that might result from its findings. Haig's contribution was to suggest that cavalry should have light transport attached to them, as the cavalryman was now almost immobilised by the amount of kit he had to carry into action:

> Equipped as he was with an unnecessarily heavy saddle and wallets, a nosebag of horse food, rifle, sword, lance, great coat, blanket and other paraphernalia, the cavalryman looked more like a travelling showman than a death-dealing soldier. No one knows better than the cavalryman himself how all these goods and chattels retarded his progress in pursuit of the wily Boer and to what extent they were responsible for knocked-up horses.

But as commanding officer of the 17th Lancers, whom he had trained to a pitch of unprecedented efficiency, he felt he must put in a token plea for the lance to be retained in certain regiments. However, his arguments were weak, as he must have realised: 'Strategical reconnaissance must culminate in a tactical collision if the enemy possesses cavalry: we want a lance for this.' *Must* culminate? *If* the enemy possesses cavalry? However, even though this plea is unconvincing, he was adamant that an army must have cavalry if it was to possess mobility at all. The core of his argument was that the cavalry must be highly trained and skilled, and he was convinced that there was no value in mounted infantry, as it did not possess the necessary skills. There seems to be more personal antipathy than logic in this broad condemnation, and it was perhaps coloured by the fact that in South Africa the hastily raised local regiments had not shown up well. They were neither cavalrymen nor infantrymen: they had the faults of both without the virtues of either. The regular units from Britain were, of course, in a different category: they were first-class infantry who used horses, which most of them could ride very well, to give them extra mobility. Mounted infantry normally use their horses to approach the battle area, then dismount and fight on foot. Horses are merely a form of transport and the riders are armed as infantry, not as cavalry. Haig was no doubt incensed by the fact that the Mounted Infantry in South Africa tried to fight as cavalry, a function for which they had not the weapons, horsemanship, or experience to do.

In the event he did not have to fight this particular battle for long, for at the end of 1903, when he had been in command of the 17th Lancers for only a year, he was suddenly faced with the choice of two attractive posts. The first, offered by Sir John French, was to be commander of the 1st Cavalry Brigade at Aldershot; the other offer, that of Inspector General of Cavalry in India, came from Kitchener, who was now Commander-in-Chief there. Haig went for the latter. His career was leaping ahead: he was forty-two, and in his new post he was given the local rank of major general – the youngest in the British Army – with the substantive rank of full colonel.

Before he left to take up his new appointment, Haig was invited to stay at Balmoral by Edward VII. There he was made a Commander of the Victorian Order and the King instructed him to write regularly about the course of events; this order, of course, repeated the one that Haig had been given when leaving for the Sudan in 1898.

At the same time he received a letter from a very different level of society – one of his former troopers:

Sir,

Will you please pardon the liberty I am taking but I see you are shortly going out to India (will you please accept my sincere congratulations on all your well-deserved honours). I am taking the opportunity to say how much my wife and I would appreciate one of your photos if it is not too much to ask for. I for myself would like to thank you for all your great kindness to me. You perhaps do not know, sir, how much I have to thank you for, but there was a time in India when I (a young fool) was being rapidly led away by bad companions, when suddenly the thought struck me 'what would Capt Haig think of me if he saw me now' and I put down the glass and said 'I have done with drink'. That was 15 years ago, and I have touched none since. I am not a teetotaller, but I made up my mind and stuck to it. I have bitterly regretted those months I could not break from my so-called Friends. This will seem foolish to you, sir, no doubt but I wanted to tell you how much I have to thank you for, and to tell you that it is through my deep respect for you that I have been able to raise myself to my present position.

I shall soon have completed my service and shall have to sever myself from the dear old regiment.

Goodbye, sir and Good Luck.

Although Haig enjoyed his second term in India, it was not without its difficulties. The Commander-in-Chief, Lord Kitchener, had been persuaded to take up his eminent position without any realisation of its concealed hazards. The core of these was the system of 'Dual Control', which stipulated that, although the Commander-in-Chief was expected to train the army to the highest level of efficiency, all other military matters were the responsibility of the Viceroy, Lord Curzon, an ambitious and intellectual civilian. On the Viceregal Council he had a major general to whom he delivered his opinions about military responsibilities: these were then passed on to Lord Kitchener as directives. To put it mildly, Kitchener was not pleased to be given orders by an officer of lower rank than himself, and the fact that

Curzon was not really interested in military matters and held the military in contempt sharpened the experience. Haig soon became aware of the tense relations between the C-in-C and the Viceroy, but was not personally involved: in fact, the situation tended to benefit, rather than handicap, him, for it meant that Kitchener left him very much to work out his own destiny. He referred to the Dual Control in a letter to Henrietta:

> The C-in-C India really has very little power. All the Supply, Transport and Finance are under an individual called the 'Military Member of the Council'. That is to say that Lord K. may order men to Thibet but he does not know whether they will starve or not because he has nothing to do with the supply arrangements. Such a system is obviously ridiculous. It is like a pair of horses in double harness without a coachman. The latter ought to be the Viceroy but he has too many things to attend to already even if he were capable of discharging such duties, which the majority of viceroys are not.

With the advantage of not having the C-in-C breathing down his neck, Haig was able to arrange cavalry training in a manner he knew from his experience to be necessary. He helped to form a cavalry school at Sangor in the Central Provinces, and he visited each cavalry regiment in camp, taking a personal part in their training. This practice may have been somewhat irksome for the commanding officers of the regiments, but their feelings were not recorded for posterity. While the troopers had a busy time, the officers were not neglected. Staff Rides became a regular feature of cavalry training – much to the dismay of the more idle officers who had come to India with the intention of enjoying themselves rather than improving their professional skills. In his three years as Inspector of Cavalry Haig held five Staff Rides, each lasting a working week. Although the whole future of cavalry was under threat in the British Army Haig introduced large-scale operations in India, mostly based on his South African experience. His conclusions from these exercises were later published in his one and only book, *Cavalry Studies, Strategical and Tactical*, which did not appear until three years after he had left India. An old friend, Colonel Sir Lonsdale Hale, had encouraged him to write it. Like Kitchener, Hale was a Royal Engineer but he had been an instructor at Sandhurst, the Staff College, and the RE Depot at Chatham. Hale was an able officer, with a good reputation as a military historian, though he clung somewhat illogically to the view that the day of the cavalry was not over but only just beginning. Ignoring all the threats to the very existence of this arm, he prophesied that the future would be even more important than the past. Hale, with whom Haig was constantly in touch by letter, seems to have been responsible for encouraging him in some of his more reactionary ideas. Thus Haig wrote:

> It must be borne in mind that the days of small armies are past and it is a simple fact that *large armies entail large numbers of cavalry*. The Army, then, which assumes the strategical offensive, has, as a general rule, the best chance of employing the most effective manoeuvres but much depends on the quality and handling of the cavalry. Cavalry, then, sharing enormous power conferred by the low trajectory rifle and rapidity of fire, plays a rôle in grand tactics of which the importance can hardly be over-estimated.

His contemporaries, who read to their surprise that cavalry was also a defensive, as well as an offensive, weapon and that the low-trajectory rifle would favour it, rather than destroy it, assumed that Haig must have been in the Indian sun far too long. He supported his thesis by quoting two authorities, one from 1898 and the other from 1882.* He continued:

> The rôle of the cavalry on the battlefield will always go on increasing because:
>   1. The extended nature of the modern battlefield means that

---

* The first was General Maillard, Professor of Infantry Tactics at the Ecole de Guerre in France. Haig also mentioned Colonel von Pelet-Narbonne's lecture to the Military Society of Berlin in 1862. His second source, from 1882, was a German military historian, Skobeloff.

there will be a greater choice of cover to favour the concealed approach of cavalry.

2. The increased range and killing power of modern guns, and the greater length of time during which the battle will last, will augment the moral exhaustion, will affect men's nerves more and produce greater demoralisation amongst the troops. These factors contribute to provoke panic, and to render troops (short service soldiers nowadays) ripe for attacks by cavalry.

3. The longer range and killing power of modern arms, the more important will rapidity of movement become because it lessens the relative time of exposure to danger in favour of the cavalry.

4. The introduction of the small-bore rifle, the bullet from which has little stopping power against a horse.

5. The rôle of cavalry, far from having diminished, has increased in importance. It extends to both strategy and tactics, it alone is of use in the service of exploration and it is of capital importance in a general action.

For the year 1906, these views were not as absurd as they become later when read against the background of the First World War – in the context of Flanders, for example, the statement that on the modern battlefield there would be a greater choice of cover was ludicrous nonsense. But, of course, Haig was not talking about a war which neither he nor anyone else could see or visualise. He was speaking as the holder of an important post in an imperial territory, and his purpose was to raise morale, encourage efficiency and broaden aspects of leadership. Cavalry warfare had changed very little over the previous two thousand years and had been suited to the terrain on which it was fought. The Boer War had been an example of just how large a battlefield could become. If Haig cast his mind to the setting of a future war, he would no doubt have seen it spread over much of Europe and possibly Poland and Russia. The fact that he expressed such views at that period does not mean that in a changed situation he would continue to cling to the same beliefs. Haig was not a fool. As will become clear later, his aim was the impeccable one of trying to create mobility on the battlefield, and when, in 1918, he managed to escape from the confines of trench warfare, he was able to win victories by cavalry-style tactics. As late as 1925, long after the experience of the First World War, he still believed that cavalry had a rôle – but not, of course, on battlefields such as those of north-east France between 1914 and 1918.

In retrospect, it may be of interest to compare Haig's view on tactics ten years before the outbreak of the First World War with the opinions of the generals of the Second World War ten years before 1939. In 1929 many senior officers in the British and German Armies were dismissing plans for tank warfare as dangerous visionary nonsense. Prophecies of weapons such as amphibious tanks, dive bombers, sub-machine guns, midget submarines, wooden bombers and ballistic missiles would have been regarded as the fevered imaginings of a twisted brain or, at least, as toys with no relevance to the battlefield. Yet Montgomery, Eisenhower and Wavell were censured for not having foreseen the use of these weapons and other developments of the Second World War. Valid criticism of Haig, therefore, must be based on stronger grounds than not being able to see ten years into the future.

6

Domestic Interlude

IN 1905 HAIG married the Hon. Dorothy Vivian, sister of the 4th Lord Vivian, and many years younger than himself. This was not unusual in those days, when officers were expected to have reached an appropriate rank and financial position before embarking on matrimony. Haig was on leave from India at the time, and so his time was limited, but even so the speed at which this important even took place surprised everyone. The circumstances of his engagement and marriage were so romantic that they seemed totally out of character with the deliberate, careful, self-contained major general that Haig had now become. A friend who expressed his surprise was taken aback by what seemed a somewhat ungracious comment from Haig: 'Why not? I have often made up my mind on more important problems than my own marriage in much less time.' In fact the remark showed a sense of humour which Haig possessed but rarely disclosed: if the friend thought the comment was serious, he must have been remarkably naïve. Haig's marriage was enormously important to him and was always a very happy one.

Dorothy Vivian was a Maid of Honour to Queen Alexandra and was extremely beautiful. She had seen and admired Haig on several occasions before she met him that June, and thought him attractive and impressive, though she understood that he had little time for women. But when Haig was invited to stay at Windsor Castle for Ascot week that year she found herself in a foursome with him for a game of golf. One of the other members was the

Duke of Devonshire, who was such an incompetent performer that the others had to wait for considerable periods while he hacked his way out of bunkers. Haig and Miss Vivian chatted politely as he did so. At the time she thought that Haig seemed rather impatient, for he kept pulling out a gold watch and looking at it. Later she learned that the watch had been given to Haig by his mother so that in due course he could present it to his future wife.

Dorothy Vivian asked him various questions about his life in India which he, though not an expert on small talk with attractive young women, was able to answer easily. Nevertheless she formed the opinion that he had not enjoyed the occasion and was therefore surprised when, on the walk back, he asked her to play a game with him the next day. Afterwards they spent the day together at Ascot races and talked again at dinner. They arranged to play golf again the following morning before breakfast. However, on arrival at the course Haig told her he did not wish to play, and paid off the caddies. They then looked for a quiet seat where they could sit and just talk, but could not find one. To her astonishment he suddenly said, 'I must propose to you standing.' Although Dorothy thought that a proposal might be in prospect in the not-too-distant future, it was totally unexpected at that moment. Nevertheless, she accepted.

There were considerable problems of protocol. As Dorothy was one of her Maids of Honour, it was imperative that Queen Alexandra should be told immediately. However, the Queen was not at the castle at that time and diplomacy had to be exercised to see that she was informed promptly. Another problem was Dorothy's mother, whose permission should also have been requested. Haig therefore set off to ask formal permission from Lady Vivian to propose to her daughter. On arrival at her house he was confronted with a flat refusal to see him, as Lady Vivian did not like strangers, whether major generals or anyone else. Haig sent in a message to say he would not go until she agreed to see him and, when at last he was admitted, opened the conversation with a formal request for her daughter's hand in marriage.

All this came as a great surprise to those who thought they

knew Haig well. He had met someone he had never seen in his life before and, less than thirty-six hours later, had not only proposed to her but been accepted. This impulsive action had been taken in full awareness that it was in defiance of all the normal conventions, a situation which was enhanced by the fact that it was taking place on the fringes of the royal circle. However, there were no serious problems and, in view of the fact that Haig's leave would soon be over and he would have to return to India, an early wedding was desirable. It took place on 11 July, scarcely more than a month after their first meeting, in the Private Chapel at Buckingham Palace.

The honeymoon was spent at William Jameson's Warwickshire house, Radway Grange. They drove there by car and on the way stopped in Oxford where Haig showed his new bride his rooms in Brasenose. As Oxford was on vacation, Dorothy thought everything looked very gloomy and desolate – as Oxford used to look in the vacation before the colleges were profitably taken over for conferences and conventions – but Haig was so enthusiastic about the happy times he had spent there that she concealed her feelings.

There was only a fortnight of Haig's leave left, but much of it was spent in the company of Henrietta, who stayed for a week at Radway and then travelled as far as Paris with them on their way to India – they embarked on a French ship at Marseilles. Dorothy was well aware that Henrietta, who was childless, might resent her brother's marriage. However, Dorothy herself seems to have borne the presence of a devoted sister with fortitude, even feeling sorry for her, though neither Haig nor Dorothy was sorry when eventually they were by themselves on the journey.

Not surprisingly, Haig was slightly concerned to know how Kitchener would react at finding his bachelor major general had returned to Delhi with a bride. Kitchener was said to be a woman hater, but this was untrue. His first love had died very young and he was thought subsequently to have become a misogynist, though informed gossip later said there was some other lady in his life, and in 1989 it was rumoured that certain very informative letters between Kitchener and 'another woman' had come to light and would shortly be published. Nevertheless Kitchener was shy in the presence of women, and when Haig presented his new bride he became totally inarticulate. Dorothy observed them closely and noted that when they played billiards in the evening Kitchener liked to win.

Haig did not let marriage interfere with his military life. Dorothy recalled many years later that she heard one of his fellow officers say that he spent more time than ever on exercises, and a number of his staff found themselves scarcely able to sit down after long spells on horseback. Haig rarely addressed his wife as Dorothy but preferred 'Doris'. Doris was a name first used in an early-nineteenth-century play and which became popular a hundred years later. It is, of course, a particularly British characteristic not to use the given baptismal name: Haig himself, when young, had been called 'Dougal', which means 'black stranger', rather than Douglas.

Apart from his long periods in the field, which his puritan conscience probably told him were necessary to show that marriage had not made him idle and unprofessional, Haig was a model husband. Much though he disliked them, he went out to dinners and balls night after night. However, after several enjoyable weeks Dorothy noticed him in the early hours of one morning 'hiding so well his boredom'. She decided, with remarkable unselfishness, to pretend she was bored too, having been warned, quite seriously, by Edward VII that she must not let marriage interfere with the military work of his best and most capable general.

Secrett recounts various stories about his experience with the Haigs in India at this time. Haig had a white polo pony which he rode successfully in many tournaments. To his embarrassment, this pony was soon assumed to have miraculous healing powers and attracted a stream of diseased and crippled Indians, who firmly believed that to touch the sacred animal would produce the desired cure. Haig tried to explain that this was simply an ordinary pony, but when his words had no effect he established a clinic near the stables where the afflicted could receive free treatment from qualified doctors. It was to no avail. The supplicants continued to arrive, even from long distances, and many who believed themselves to have been cured by touching the pony tried to leave rewards.

However, contact with the Indians was not always so benign. On one occasion, Haig agreed to watch the famous Indian rope trick. With others, he sat in a circle around the fakir and his boy. Secrett, who was sceptical, decided to watch from the verandah, where he was out of earshot. To his surprise, he saw Haig and the others in the group look upwards as the fakir began his incantation, even though the boy remained motionless next to the rope during the whole proceedings. Somewhat unwisely, Secrett darted out and explained what he had seen. To his surprise, Haig and the others were reluctant to believe that they had been mesmerised when they thought they had seen the boy climbing the rope, while the fakir was, not unnaturally, extremely angry.

The same night, Secrett awoke, thinking he had heard a foot-step outside his bungalow room. He switched on a torch and saw a viper crawling along the floor towards his bed. He grabbed his revolver and blew its head off. The snake, when examined, was discovered to be of a type not found in that part of India.

In general, Haig's relationship with holy men and mendicants was good. He provided food, clothing and medical necessities, but had a firm rule against giving money. According to Secrett, Haig never minded paying over money by cheque, but had a strong dislike of taking it out of his pocket.

When Haig left for a tour of the military posts early in October, Dorothy found herself back temporarily in the formal social whirl at Viceregal House in Delhi. She mentions that during that winter Haig had a number of very debilitating attacks of malaria. However, his next posting was as Director of Training, based at the War Office in London, so it was hoped that the attacks might become less frequent in a cooler climate. In view of the fact that Haig was plagued by a malignant form of malaria which can lead to serious complications, it was astonishing that he managed to continue working; the stresses and strains of the burden of work he took on might have crushed a less dedicated man. It seems from his letters to Henrietta that at this stage he began to see himself as a man with a mission – a mission first to reform the Army, then to command it at the highest level.

On arrival in England, Haig wasted no time before taking up his duties at the War Office. In 1904, as a result of the findings of the Esher Committee on the South African war, an Army Council had been set up. It consisted of four military and three civilian members. The former comprised the Chief of the General Staff, the Adjutant General, the Quartermaster General and the Master General of the Ordnance; the civilian members were the Secretary of State for War, the Parliamentary Under Secretary and the Financial Secretary. The Army Council, which had numerous sub-departments, began slowly and ineffectively, mainly because the Prime Minister, Arthur Balfour, showed little interest in encouraging it. However, when Balfour's Conservative government was succeeded by Campbell-Bannerman's Liberals in 1905, a new Secretary of State for War, Richard Burton Haldane, was appointed.

Haldane was a Scottish lawyer who had made a name for himself at the English bar and was not without a sense of humour. On arrival at the War Office, he had immediately been asked by the Chief of the General Staff, General the Hon. Sir Neville Lyttelton, what reforms he was proposing to introduce: his answer was, 'As a young and blushing virgin just united to a bronzed warrior, it is not expected by the public that any result of the union will appear until at least nine months have passed.' Later he commented that he spent half his time apologising to the government for the existence of the Army and the other half apologising to the Army for the existence of the Liberal government! However, the Army liked Haldane and felt that good would come of him. His fellow Liberal politician Lord Esher had suggested to him that Haig should be a member of the Council, on the staff of the Chief of the General Staff, replacing the Director of Staff Duties, Major General H. D. Hutchinson. The two men got on well from the start. They made a good team because Haig knew how to put to the Army the reforms that Haldane wished to make.

The problems of reorganisation were considerable. In view of the European situation, the first need was to establish a potential expeditionary force. The South African war had shown how sadly deficient Britain was when it was necessary to despatch a force large enough to engage in a major campaign. The agreed number was six infantry divisions and one of cavalry, properly armed and equipped. For home defence, and also as a source of reserves for the expeditionary force, the existing conglomeration of Volunteers, Yeomanry and Militia would need to be combined into a unified territorial army. These proposals did not suit everyone. Field Marshal Lord Roberts felt the idea of a territorial force was unworkable, and that the only solution to the Army's manpower problems was to have compulsory military service in peacetime. There was also opposition to the quality and quantity of the equipment to be allotted to the territorial army, a principal argument being that the voluntary soldiers would not have the time to acquire the necessary skills and experience in using heavier weapons.

The opposition to Haldane's reform did not come solely from diehards in the War Office. The Militia had been regarded as the backbone of home defence since what was regarded as 'time immemorial' – that is to say it could trace its history back to pre-Norman times. Most of those holding key positions in the Militia were men of wealth and influence in their districts, where they tended to own most of the land on which their recruits worked. Haldane's attempt to win these men over proved ineffective, so he abolished the Militia completely and in its place established a Special Reserve which would be available for the Expeditionary Force. The Yeomanry and Volunteer Forces were then incorporated into the Territorial Force. In theory the Territorial Force could not be called on to serve overseas, but at that time no one could foresee the emergency created by the German invasion of France in 1914.

These changes, which were spread over several years from 1907 onwards, meant a huge amount of work for Haig. In his post as Director of Training he had to arrange for the publication of the training manuals, for the provision of training areas, for exercises, for call-up, and for the organisation and establishment of the newly created armies. The Territorial Force had an establishment of twenty-eight divisions – fourteen infantry and fourteen cavalry – and he was also responsible for the training of the Expeditionary Force of another seven divisions. Haig refused to accept the idea that the Territorial Force should have an inferior scale of equipment, and insisted that all should be standardised throughout.

As always, there were frequent suggestions in Parliament that the Army was costing too much, and was being made unnecessarily large in order to combat a threat which did not exist. Happily, Haldane received invaluable support from the Foreign Secretary, Sir Edward Grey, who felt that the danger of a German invasion of France was very real. Eventually Haldane turned the tables on his opponents by announcing that not only was the Army bigger and better, but it would also cost less in 1908.

The Haigs' first child, Alexandra, arrived on 9 March 1907. The birth took place in London at 21 Prince's Gate, Henrietta's house, although the Haigs had rented a house, Coombe Farm, at Farnborough, near Aldershot. There Haig used to ride every morning before catching an early train to London, returning late in the evening. However, his bouts of malaria had given him an enlarged liver, and very reluctantly he had to take ten days off from work and 'take the waters' at Tarasp in Switzerland. Dorothy enjoyed the visit but had some difficulty in shaking off the attentions of the local doctor, who was very anxious to extract all her teeth – drinking spa waters, bathing, walking and having one's teeth extracted were popular remedies for a wide variety of ills at that time, and soon the extraction of appendices would be added to the list. Dorothy was somewhat concerned on arriving back at Farnborough to discover that all her three servants had given notice, though for what reason she never discovered.

Although Haig was kind and considerate in his domestic life, he regarded that and his military sphere as quite incompatible. Dorothy mentions in her book that on a memorable occasion she was allowed to attend some manoeuvres near Leighton Buzzard. With other wives, she was staying with the Rothschilds: 'He had purposely taken a horse for me to ride, but when I met him out with the troops and dared to go and speak to him, he just looked at me as if he had never seen me before. His blue eyes, which were usually so kind, took on a steady hard look which quite alarmed me. He was altogether too military. The other highly placed officers, however, were most kind when I went and talked to them.'

Haig was probably too inarticulate to explain that his reactions were much the same as hers would have been if, in a period when rigid domestic hierarchies existed, he had entered the nursery or kitchen at their home, taken an intelligent interest in the cooking and child-rearing, and chatted socially to the servants. At times Dorothy found her husband's behaviour so restrained that she was baffled and annoyed. On a visit to Ascot she was asked to make herself agreeable to a party of German officers who were also staying with the Rothschilds, because it was the intention to restrict their activities during the manoeuvres.

Mr Leopold Rothschild asked me to make myself particularly agreeable at dinner, because one of these officers was to take me in. I thought him extremely common, but tried to carry out what had been asked of me, apparently so successfully that during dinner he became very drunk and proceeded to make love openly, daring to call me '*Süsse Doris*', much to the amusement of the whole party. After dinner I hoped that the creature would not come near me again, but to my extreme discomfort he lurched across to where I was sitting, and openly asked me to go into another room. We all laughed and there were many jokes, perhaps more so because Douglas took it all so calmly and politely answered the man when he spoke to him.

The following morning we got up very early to see the finish of the night operation, and we were all having breakfast when the wretched man began addressing me in the same familiar way – evidently still drunk. In the evening the creature discovered where my bedroom was and sat in the garden under the window looking up. I complained to the German attaché, who himself was a gentleman and much liked in London. He was ashamed of his brother officer's behaviour and let him know at once what he thought of him. I had no more trouble but the story was too good not to be talked about and I had to put up with a lot of chaff. The German officer was in no way ashamed of himself, and Douglas continued to show him polite courtesy and did not join in the general amusement, which really saved the situation. The officer afterwards showed his appreciaton of this by sending Douglas his photograph.

How does one interpret this? Was Haig using the occasion to discourage Dorothy from ever again taking any active interest in his military life, or was he seething with rage but bound by protocol to allow the German to pester his wife? By this time Britain and Germany were openly suspicious of each other's intentions and the Germans would probably have welcomed any opportunity to restrict the access of the British to any of their own manoeuvres. A quarrel in England would have been a useful excuse and served as a mask to other motives.

The incident must have rankled with Dorothy, for she talks about it at length in her book *The Man I Knew*, which was meant to counter the views expressed in Duff Cooper's biography of Haig, published in the same year, 1936. Clearly Haig never offered any explanation to her of why he behaved as he did. He may have had reason to suppose that the German wanted to challenge him to a duel: duels of honour were recognised by the military code in Germany up until 1914. Haig did not lack moral or physical courage, but he was scarcely a match for an accomplished duellist. Perhaps the Germans had decided that Haig, the renowned military organiser, might cause them trouble and wanted him out of the way. Or the 'drunken' German officer might have been an agent provocateur, who could have killed Haig in a duel in which, having been challenged, he would have the choice of weapons. On the other hand, perhaps in fact he merely decided that this was the correct way to behave, and that to provoke any kind of scene at a formal dinner with ladies present would be disastrous and less than courteous to his host. And possibly it was just a sign of his inarticulacy that he never offered any explanation to his puzzled and resentful young wife. It seems, not surprisingly, that she was not present at the time of any subsequent manoeuvres.

In November 1907 Haig was transferred from the post of Director of Military Training to that of Director of Staff Duties. Staff Duties, usually abbreviated to SD, is concerned with the organisation and co-ordination of the General Staff: it extends to the exact phraseology in which orders are given. This was a period of Haig's life which did not subsequently attract criticism. Although staff officers are not popular with regimental soldiers, their existence is recognised as being necessary: the normal complaint against them is that they are often out of touch, physically and mentally, with the experience of the fighting soldier. Haig organised and co-ordinated a General Staff which could make the arrangements to mobilise, despatch, supply and maintain an Expeditionary Force overseas and a Territorial Force at home. Although occasionally the complicated arrangements broke down, the general organisation and administration of the BEF in France in 1914–18 was something of a miracle. Haig also had the responsibility of organising the Imperial General Staff – that is, the co-ordinated organisation for the armies of Britain and the Empire. At that time the Empire forces were under British command, and when Britain declared war on Germany in 1914 Canada, South Africa, Australia, New Zealand and all the countries of the Empire – which had not at that stage attained the degree of formal independence that would later be known as 'Dominion Status' – were automatically at war too. It was a different story in 1939, when the Dominions, as they were then known, each declared war separately after making a decision in their own Parliament.

Haig never slackened in his efforts, even though at times he had to take sick leave. Fortunately he worked in complete harmony with Haldane, who obtained parliamentary approval for the plans that Haig made. In 1909 Haig was created a Knight Commander of the Royal Victorian Order. By that time his family had increased, for another daughter, Victoria, had been born on 7 November 1908. In the same year that he received his knighthood Haig was offered the post of Chief of the General Staff in India under the new Commander-in-Chief, the genial General Sir O'Moore Creagh, VC, who was to replace Kitchener. Although the offer came in April, Haig delayed taking up the post until he had finished his work at the War Office. The Haigs set off for India in October 1909, leaving the children behind in the care of Henrietta at Stowlandtoft in Suffolk.

Although Haig had looked forward to another tour in India, the situation he found there on this occasion was more serious than the one which had existed before, and concerned him much more closely. Before he left on the earlier occasion, one of his Army contemporaries had said: 'I would rather have Haig's luck than a licence to steal horses.' Haig had certainly been lucky in his rapid promotion and the jobs which had gone with it, but the time was coming when he would feel that he might have been a happier man if he had been a little less fortunate in his ambitions.

Although the Curzon–Kitchener dispute over Dual Control had been partially resolved, the implementation of any decision still required much bureaucratic manoeuvring. It was often unclear whether certain procedures were in the province of the Commander-in-Chief or that of the Viceroy. The newly appointed C-in-C, Sir O'Moore Creagh, had served for forty years with the Indian Army and felt that his predecessor's changes had all been unnecessary. He did not agree with Kitchener that the Indian Army should be organised to fight overseas, but believed it should never leave India. This was also the policy of Lord Morley, who was the Secretary of State for India back in London. Curzon had left India some years before and been succeeded as Viceroy by Lord Minto; within a year of Haig's arrival Minto would be succeeded by Lord Hardinge, who agreed entirely with Morley and instructed Haig that all plans for Indian troops to serve overseas must be dropped forthwith. Haig disobeyed the accompanying order to destroy the mobilisation plan, and secretly filed it: it was brought out again in 1914, when it proved invaluable.

Totally frustrated in his plans to train the Indian Army for European warfare, Haig had to concentrate on raising its general level of efficiency; in doing so he travelled throughout the subcontinent. The Haigs were given quarters in the Fort in Calcutta and Dorothy enjoyed herself acquiring furniture in the bazaar, giving their rooms an old-fashioned look which, she said, 'will make the present generation scream'. She liked Calcutta: 'One got away from the eternal military circle and came across many very interesting people.'

In her book Dorothy Haig recounted several stories about their time in India which suggest that she enjoyed the social life rather more than her husband did. On one occasion, when he was away visiting, she gave a dance for a couple who had recently become engaged. Not knowing much about wine and how much would be needed, she left the ordering to the C-in-C's ADC. The bill did not come in until Haig returned from his travels. When he saw it he said, with reason, that they must have drunk enough for an army. Dorothy thought he would be very angry, but he laughed it off, although he knew it was absurdly high: a naïve young ACD had ordered from a local supplier without realising that he was giving the latter an opportunity to make a small fortune. The dance had been extremely rowdy: late in the evening the guests had played 'pigsticking', with the women riding on the men's backs and using billiard cues as spears. Stories of this and other incidents were reported to Haig, but he was merely amused: army dances and mess games can often be childish and dangerous – as this one turned out to be – but are sanctified by long custom. However, he could well have been annoyed by the fact that the younger generation had taken the principle 'When the cat's away . . . ' rather far, and exploited Dorothy's innocent kindness.

Innocent though she undoubtedly was, she also had an inner core of toughness. She belonged to a first aid class, and arranged with the Viceroy's doctor that it should get some practice at a hospital in Simla. Bed-making and bandaging of sound limbs passed off uneventfully, but Dorothy felt they should have more realistic experience. She therefore arranged that they should go to the out patients' department of the local hospital. She recorded:

We were rather unfortunate on our first day. A man, who had been bitten by a snake, was brought in and his finger was an appalling sight from having had a tourniquet on it. Arrange-

ments were made to have it amputated. I noted down everything that happened but my class gradually faded away because
they could not bear to look on. Afterwards they told me how
horrified they had been to see me as they left, still standing
taking notes while the finger was being taken off.

Haig encouraged Dorothy's medical studies, 'because he felt
that the existing medical and nursing arrangements for war were
most unsatisfactory'. She recounted that she 'learnt the hard work
and sadness entailed in nursing patients, and came across cases of
kalazar, plague, cholera and many types of malaria and leprosy'. In
spite of her comfortable and sheltered early life, Dorothy seems to
have been undeterred by the horrors of Indian hospitals: her
eventual reward was that her first-aid classes led to the formation
of Voluntary Aid Detachments (VADs) in India.*

In Calcutta in 1911 they again had problems with truculent
Germans. The Crown Prince arrived on an official visit, accompanied by a large party. He was accorded every honour by the
Viceroy, but everyone knew that he was probably out to make
trouble and, in any case, had brought with him Count zu Dohna,
a leading figure in German espionage. Lady Hardinge, the wife of
the Viceroy, asked Dorothy to help her in keeping the Prince at
Barrackpur and away from Calcutta. This meant that Dorothy
had to play golf with him every day – and he was a very poor
player. However, after a time the Prince became so insistent that
he must now leave and visit Calcutta that the two women
concocted a plan to persuade him he was ill and had a temperature.
Reluctantly, but accepting the fact that they knew more about the
local fevers than he did, he agreed to stay in bed until the day
before he was due to leave. However, even the one night he
eventually spent in Calcutta caused embarrassment, for he had
secretly arranged to visit an opium den, but was not allowed to do
so by the British. On an earlier occasion on this tour he had
slipped away to meet a Burmese princess. His German escorts had

---

* One of several organisations developed to handle the casualties of the
First and Second World Wars.

been horrified when they realised he had given them the slip, but eventually found him and brought him back. Dorothy also recalled that when the Prince had been shown the King's throne, which was used by the Viceroy, he had remarked that the Kaiser would soon be sitting on it. She paid little attention at the time, although the remark sent a little flutter of irritation through the rest of the party: three years later she realised the Prince had been serious.

Aware that the friction between the military and viceregal circles gave scope for mischief-making and intrigue, Dorothy tried to defuse some of it. The Haigs knew that, though personally respected, they were considered to be on the losing side, and it was therefore with some relief, in 1911, that Haig accepted the job of GOC Aldershot, offered in a personal telegram from Haldane. The particular attraction of this job to him was that it gave automatic command of 1 Corps of the British Expeditionary Force, in whose creation he had played such an important part. It also meant that, if war broke out in Europe, he would already be on the scene instead of being marooned in a backwater.

In the event he could not take up the new post immediately, for King George V, who had acceded to the throne on the death of Edward VII in May 1910, would be coming to India the following year. This visit was one of the most important functions that the new King could perform, as he was, of course, also Emperor of India. At the resplendent Delhi Durbar he received all the Indian princes and reviewed the Imperial troops. Haig was required to stay until the Durbar was completed on 12 December 1911, and at the concluson of the ceremony he was made KCIE (Knight Commander of the Indian Empire). He sailed from India on 23 December.

Like her husband, Dorothy did not leave India unscathed by local disease. Her particular ailment was dysentery, which Haig believed she had contracted at the Durbar, where they all had to sleep in damp tents.* When they arrived, the two tents allotted to

---

* Dysentery is not, of course, caused by dampness but by a bacillus or a protosoon.

them, which were very close to the royal tent but on slightly lower ground, were waterlogged: the boxes holding her Durbar dresses were floating in water. She was first on the scene, saw the appalling mess, and insisted that the tents should be drained and refurbished. Haig arrived a day later, by which time all was well, though damp. Although Dorothy enjoyed the Durbar, during which she had the satisfaction of seeing a very conceited young officer bucked off his horse in a most undignified way in full view of everyone, the dysentery she had incurred nearly killed her on the way home.

7

The Clouds Gather

HAIG TOOK OVER Aldershot Command on 1 March 1912. His predecessor had been Sir Horace Smith-Dorrien, an infantryman of three years' seniority to him who had already commanded two divisions and was therefore much more experienced. Although normally urbane and charming, Smith-Dorrien was liable to outbursts of violent temper when anything upset him, and bearers of bad news felt like those messengers of classical times who did not know until their messages had been deciphered whether they were going to be rewarded lavishly or executed. On this occasion, however, all was well, for Smith-Dorrien was leaving to take up the post of GOC Southern Command.

Observers soon noted that Haig thought very highly of a young Royal Engineers captain, John Charteris. He had first encountered Charteris when making one of his tours of inspection in India, and considered that he had the qualities of articulacy and fluency which he himself lacked, as well as technical achievements – though he disliked his often scruffy, dirty appearance. Charteris was undoubtedly a fluent talker and was well aware of it, though he in turn seems to have gone out of his way to exaggerate Haig's own deficiencies in that respect. At Aldershot Charteris was Haig's Assistant Military Secretary; he went on to become his Chief of Intelligence and eventually Brigadier General Sir John Charteris. He did not die until after the Second World War, in 1946, but long before that he had been criticised for supplying Haig with absurdly optimistic intelligence, and thus contributing to some unwise decisions. Nevertheless, he wrote a lucid and comprehensive biography of Haig which contains many perceptive comments and stories.

There were significant moves and promotions in the political arena at this time. Haldane was made a peer and became Lord Chancellor; he was succeeded as Secretary of State for War by a soldier and big-game hunter turned politician, Colonel J. E. B. Seely.

Unfortunately for Haig, his first manoeuvres, which were held in East Anglia, were a disaster and a humiliation. The scenario was that Haig, commanding 'Red Force', had landed on the Norfolk coast and was advancing on London. 'Red Force' – the Army is addicted to such titles – consisted of two infantry divisions and an additional cavalry division commanded by his old colleague and rival, Major General E. H. Allenby. 'Blue Force', blocking the route to London, was deployed around Cambridge and was commanded by Lieutenant General Sir James Grierson, KCB, CVO, CMS.* Grierson's force was slightly inferior in strength to Haig's: although it contained two infantry divisions, its cavalry component consisted of only two brigades, one being regular, the other Yeomanry. An interesting aspect of this battle was that each army had an air component of one airship and one squadron of service aircraft. Sir John French, the Chief Umpire, was comfortably established in Cambridge, and on his advice Seely had invited the French General Ferdinand Foch and a Russian delegation under the Grand Duke Nicholas. The Ministers of Defence from South Africa and Canada were present, and King George V, anxious to see his Army in action, also arrived on the scene, having arranged to ride round the battlefield with Seely.

For Seely, as for Haig, the manoeuvres turned into a nightmare. It began with his horse going lame. A replacement was immediately ordered from the Remount Depot, but did not arrive as promptly as had been expected and so the King was kept waiting

---

* Grierson, a Scot, formerly Royal Artillery, had served in India, Egypt (the 1882 campaign), China (the Boxer rebellion of 1900) and the Boer War; he had also been Director of Military Operations in the War Office, and Commander of 1st Division at Aldershot in 1910.

for a short while. Seely's profuse apologies were accepted. The two set off to meet the representatives of the Dominions, but when the King halted for a minute to enquire exactly who he was going to meet, Seely was appalled to hear him suddenly cry out, 'I wish you would stop your horse eating my foot.' Horrified, Seely saw that his mount had bent its head round and caught the King firmly by the foot. Seely jabbed the offending animal, which then let go. He apologised once more, but the foot had been badly bruised and the King was not pleased.

Seely then galloped ahead to tell the Dominions ministers that the King was about to arrive, but as he came close he was dismayed to see them engaged in a fist fight! He rode between them, hoping George V had not seen, although of course he had. The South African had asserted that one South African was better than twenty Britons in a fight, and the Canadian had retorted that one Canadian was better than twenty South Africans. At that point they had decided to settle their differences with their bare hands. Seely apologised yet again to the King.

In the subsequent mock battle, Haig was completely out-generalled by Grierson, in spite of the efforts of the umpires and judges to make the contest appear more even. The crux of the matter was that Haig had not appreciated the importance of spotter aircraft. Grierson had so carefully concealed his men from aerial observation that Haig never knew where they were, while every move by Haig's troops had been observed by Grierson's aircraft. The 'battle' was therefore over quickly and Haig was defeated in front of his staff, foreign observers and King George V. It was clear to all who was the better general, and not only in his use of aircraft. If Grierson had lived, it is highly unlikely that Haig would have risen to become Commander-in-Chief of the British Expeditionary Force. However, within a few days of the outbreak of war in 1914 Grierson, very much overweight and inclined to be self-indulgent, died of an aneurism of the heart.

The disgrace of being defeated in the manoeuvres threw Haig completely off his balance. At the final conference, over which George V presided, the two commanders, Haig and Grierson, were called upon to explain their tactics and moves. Grierson explained his confidently, lucidly and vigorously, but when it was Haig's turn to speak his normal common sense appeared to desert him completely. Instead of reading out his written statement, which gave a 'clear and convincing account of his views, he did not even refer to it when he spoke but to the dismay of his staff attempted to extemporise. In the effort he became totally unintelligible and unbearably dull. The university dignitaries soon fell asleep, Haig's friends became more and more uncomfortable, only he seemed totally unconscious of his failure.' This account comes from Charteris, who never under-rated Haig's verbal deficiencies. Charteris should have realised his superior's dilemma and made some allowance, however, for it seems likely that Haig had little alternative to speaking off the cuff. The notes he had made for his speech would have assumed that the battle would be evenly balanced: after the result was declared, they would have sounded absurd if read out.

Nor was Haig's period as GOC Aldershot Command without other problems. When he and Dorothy had first met their children again after three years of separation they did not recognise each other, and once the children had taken the measure of their parents they became uncontrollable. Reluctantly Dorothy decided she must start spanking, and did, but without results, for on one occasion the children completely destroyed the drawing room. Haig, with memories of the stories told about his own childhood, was inclined to believe they would soon settle down, but was seldom at home to observe whether that was happening or not.

When the Haigs first arrived at Aldershot they had stayed at the Queen's Hotel in Farnborough, as so many military dignitaries have done, before and since. Here Haig became aware that German spies might be more active than he had suspected. There were German waiters in the hotel, as there were in most hotels and restaurants at that time, and one day when he returned to his room suddenly he was surprised to find a waiter just leaving it. Haig kept an unimportant map on his writing table, and when he looked at it he observed that it had been marked with drawing pins: someone appeared to have been tracing from it.

Among the Haigs' other domestic troubles was a fire in their house. This was extinguished by the servants, who were ably directed by their master. When the alarm was given Haig refused to allow the Army to come in: from his previous experience, he said, they did more damage to the furniture than the fire would do. He took the opportunity to pour a bucket of water over Charteris, who arrived rather late on the scene; on this occasion Charteris failed to appreciate a joke as much as Haig did.

Haig had learnt his lesson about the importance of observer aircraft and gave much encouragement to their development. There was a balloon school at Aldershot which had been in existence since 1892 as a Royal Engineers function, and in 1911 it became the Air Battalion Royal Engineers. Its former buildings later became the Royal Aircraft Factory, Farnborough. In 1912, the Air Battalion was renamed the Royal Flying Corps (Naval and Military Wing): from this developed the RAF and Fleet Air Arm.

In 1913, when there was another, larger, exercise in the Midlands, between 'Brown Force' and 'White Force', many more aircraft were used than in the previous one, and their potential as air spotters was appreciated. But there were still doubters. Foch was dismissive: '*Comme sport, magnifique; comme intérêt militaire, zéro.*' He would be converted later.

On the second exercise it was French's turn to make a fool of himself. He was commanding 'Brown Force', which consisted of two corps and a cavalry division. Very wisely he had chosen Grierson to be his Chief of Staff, and his corps commanders were Haig and General Sir Arthur Paget, while Allenby commanded the cavalry. The opposition 'White Force' was not designed to be a serious obstacle as it consisted largely of Territorials and Yeomanry.

Haig recorded the subsequent events in his diary: 'Sir John French's instructions for moving along the front of his enemy (then halted on a fortified position) and subsequently attacking the latter's distant flank, were of such an unpractical nature that his Chief of the General Staff [Grierson] demurred. Some slight modifications in the orders were permitted, but Grierson ceased to be his CGS on mobilization, and was very soon transferred to another appointment in the BEF.' French's deficiencies as the commander of a large force were now becoming clear to all, but they would not prevent him becoming commander of the BEF when war broke out.

In spring 1914 the Army was plunged into a crisis over what was known as the Curragh Incident. At the time H. H. Asquith was Prime Minister of the Liberal government which, though it had been in power since 1908, did not have an overall majority over the Unionists. Fortunately for the Liberals there were eighty-four Irish Nationalist members in the House, who voted with them in the expectation that eventually they would be rewarded by the granting of Home Rule. A bill to this effect had already been passed in January 1913, but would not become law until June 1914. Home Rule for Ireland meant that the Catholic-dominated Parliament in Dublin would also control the north, Ulster, where the majority of the population was Protestant. The Northern Ireland Protestants had no intention of passing meekly into the control of the Dublin Catholics, and in consequence had raised a well-armed militia of one hundred thousand, who were known as the Ulster Volunteers. They were a disciplined and trained force, well aware that they had sympathisers in the higher ranks of the British Army. Field Marshal 'Bobs' Roberts, Sir John French, now CIGS, and Major General Sir Henry Wilson, Director of Military Operations, were all of Protestant Anglo-Irish stock; Wilson was quite frank about where his sympathies lay. However, the real danger was among the lower-ranking officers, many of whom were also Anglo-Irish, who might soon be placed in the intolerable position of being asked to disarm their compatriots in the north and to fire on them if they resisted.

In May General Sir Arthur Paget, Commander of the British Army in Ireland, was summoned to a conference of the Army Council to discuss what action should be taken if any of the Anglo-Irish officers flatly refused to obey orders to march against the Ulster Volunteers. Paget does not appear to have obtained a very clear idea of what the Army Council wanted him to do – perhaps the Council was not very sure itself – and when he returned to Dublin he briefed his subordinate commanders to the effect that if any Ulster-born officer who still had a home there was ordered north, it would be acceptable if he simply disappeared until the crisis was over: his period of absence would be treated as official leave. However, there were a number of officers who, though not Anglo-Irish, had considerable sympathy with the Ulster viewpoint; these were informed brusquely that if they refused to fight against the Ulstermen they would be dismissed from the Army. One of them was Hubert Gough, who would later command 5th Army in the murderous battles of 1917 and 1918. Although Gough was originally Anglo-Irish, he no longer lived in Northern Ireland and could not 'officially' disappear, even if he had wished to take advantage of that loophole. At this time he was commanding 3rd Cavalry Brigade, who were at the Curragh Military Training Centre in Co. Kildare. Gough decided that he would resign if he was ordered north and when he explained the situation to his seventy officers he was informed that fifty-eight of them would join him.

Gough's younger brother, Brigadier General John Gough, holder of a Victoria Cross, was Haig's Chief of Staff in Aldershot. Haig was drawn into the dispute because John Gough decided that, if his elder brother was forced to resign his commission or be dismissed from the service, he too would resign. Haig told him to keep calm, which was not the sort of advice likely to appeal to the Goughs, and took him to London to talk with Haldane who, though now Lord Chancellor rather than Secretary of State for War, still had decisive influence.

Meanwhile, Hubert Gough's statement to his officers at the Curragh had brought him a peremptory summons to explain himself to the Secretary of State, Seely, the CIGS, French, and the Adjutant General, Sir Spencer Ewart. Seely informed Gough that he was making a mountain out of a molehill and that the Army would only be sent to Ulster if it became necessary to protect the arms depots which lay in that area. He then told him that he should return and take command as before, which Gough refused to do unless he was given a written undertaking that neither he nor his command would be asked to take any military action to enforce the Home Rule Bill. A document was prepared which stated that the original instruction, which was that the Army might be required to protect the arms depots in Ulster, had been misunderstood, but that it was nevertheless the duty of soldiers to obey all orders emanating from the Army Council. Gough protested that this satisfied neither him nor the men under him. In consequence, Seely added a few words saying that the Government had 'no intention whatever of taking advantage of this right [the duty of the Army to obey] to crush the political opposition to the policy or principles of the Home Rule Bill'. This additional statement was initialled by French and Ewart.

Although the amended document pleased Gough, the repercussions were traumatic. Asquith informed Seely that he had no business to have added the words, and forced his resignation. French and Ewart also felt obliged to resign, and their posts were given to two virtual unknowns. On Seely's resignation, Asquith added the role of Secretary of State for War to his own post – few less suitable holders could have been found. This version of the timing and sequence of events is only one of several about a confused situation, but it seems the most probable and the most straightforward.

The Curragh Incident left bad feeling all round at a time when harmony was extremely important. The Army felt that its deep suspicion of the intentions of politicians was fully justified, and the Liberals, of whom Lloyd George was one, suspected the incident showed that the Army was trying to demonstrate that it was not the obedient servant of the government which its constitutional position said it should be. George V was particularly annoyed that he had not been informed first-hand and that his information had come from newspaper headlines. Haig was not directly involved, although for a time it looked as if he might lose his promising Chief of Staff over the affair; he realised it had been a bad moment for the Army, which should not have been put into a position in which sectarian loyalties and military obligations might come into conflict.

Meanwhile in Europe the instability of what was then known as the Balkans – Turkey, Greece, Serbia, Albania, Romania, Bulgaria, Bosnia, Herzegovina and Montenegro – which made that area a matter of interest and concern to the Great Powers – Great Britain, France, Germany, Austria-Hungary and Russia – had meant that sooner or later it might provide the detonator for a wider conflict. The danger to world peace in 1914 did not, of course, come from the strength of the Balkan countries but from their weakness, their nationalism and their geographical position.

Germany was interested in the Balkans because they occupied the area through which it awaited a favourable opportunity to expand into the Mediterranean. Russia was interested for precisely the same reason and considered it had made a useful move in befriending Serbia, which today, with Bosnia, Herzegovina and Montenegro, forms Yugoslavia. Serbia had aspired to add Bosnia and Herzegovina, at this time part of the Austro-Hungarian Empire, to its own domain because they already contained a large number of Serbs, but had been frustrated in this aim when Austria annexed them both in 1908. Italy had ambitions to wrest some colonial territory from Turkey and in 1912 had acquired Tripoli, changing its name to the former Roman one of Libya. The Turks had then turned to Germany for assistance, and immediately before the 1914–18 war had been receiving advice and assistance from German officers. Soon after the outbreak, Turkey decided to come in on the German side, a decision which subsequently involved Britain in the Gallipoli landings, the exhausting Mesopotamian campaign and the eventual conquest of Palestine.

On 28 June 1914 the Archduke Franz Ferdinand, the heir to the Austrian throne, made a state visit to Sarajevo, the capital of Bosnia. While there, he was shot dead by a Bosnian who leapt on to the running board of his car. Although the assassin was an Austrian subject, he was also a member of the Black Hand, a nationalist Serbian society which had supplied him with his pistol. He could not have chosen a more unsuitable target, because the Archduke was a liberal and, if he had lived to succeed his uncle, the elderly Emperor Franz Josef, would probably have helped, rather than hindered, the Serbs in their ambitions. However, there were others in power in Austria who were anything but liberal and they decided that the assassination, and the Serbian government's suspected complicity in it, meant that the time had arrived to crush Serbia. The Austrians assumed that if they could gain German backing this would effectively warn off Russia and prevent her intervening. When the Kaiser gave this assurance on 5 July Austria began preparations for an attack on Serbia, which was launched on 28 July.

Needless to say, Russia was not prepared to stand by and see its Serbian protégé crushed and her own ambitions of an outlet into the Mediterranean disappear. It therefore ordered a general mobilisation. Germany, not willing to see its Austrian ally defeated by the Russian colossus, decided to declare war on Russia before the latter could complete the call-up of forces from its far-flung territories. But at the same time Germany had other plans up its sleeve. Since 1871, when Germany had defeated France in a short but devastating war, it had suspected that the French might one day want to take their revenge. The most likely time for that was when Germany was involved in a conflict with France's ally, Russia, a possibility that seemed likely in view of Germany's expansionist policy. The German general staff had nightmares about being involved in a major war on two fronts, east and west, and much thought had gone into the diplomatic and military plans necessary to prevent this happening. The eventual solution, if the worst came to the worst, was that France must be knocked out with an overwhelming blow, delivered without warning. When this had been successfully accomplished, Russia could be dealt with at leisure and Napoleon's dream of ruling from Moscow might become a German reality.

The plan for disposing of France, irrespective of what was happening elsewhere, was conceived by the general staff as early as 1895 and named after its then chief, Graf von Schlieffen. It was quite simple. The bulk of the German army, with its left flank pivoting on Metz, would swing round in a great arc, likened to a door on its hinges, and by violating the neutrality of Belgium and Holland would outflank all the French fortifications – which did not, of course, cover the Belgian frontier. The Germans would then enter France, encircling Paris with the right wing and finally clinching victory by trapping the French armies to the east of Paris. The closing of the trap would see Paris in German hands and the French army, or what was left of it, being attacked in the front and from the rear. In devising this strategy the German General Staff had given no thought to Britain which, it was assumed, was a maritime colonial power with no interests on the Continent.

This carefully conceived, ruthless plan soon broke down in execution, but the early stages went remarkably well for the Germans. Their artillery proved much more effective than even the optimists had forecast and demolished the Belgian fortifications without difficulty. However, to German surprise and mortification, the British were not content to sit back and watch all this happen. Britain recalled that in 1839 it had signed a treaty guaranteeing the neutrality of the then newly created state of Belgium: it was therefore legally and morally bound to come to the aid of Belgium if that country was attacked.

If Britain had not entered the war, Germany and Austria would almost certainly have defeated France and Russia, and they would probably have been assisted by Italy in doing so. In the event, Italy threw in its lot with the Allies rather than Germany and Austria, although it was already linked with the two latter powers in what was known as the Triple Alliance. The factor which influenced the Italians to join the Allies was undoubtedly the realisation that Germany and Austria would now eventually be defeated, but Italy was influenced, too, by Britain's support of Belgium, for by that Britain had taken a stand on moral principles and loyalty. Ironically, the other signatories to the famous 1839 treaty (which the Kaiser is reported to have described as 'a scrap of paper') were France, Austria and Prussia: the two latter, far from defending Belgium's neutrality, were now violating it.

So Britain entered the war on moral grounds, though in theory it had no reason for taking up arms against Germany at that stage. It is true that Britain was linked to France and Russia by what was known as the Triple Entente, but the Entente was an understanding, not an alliance, and had come into being to serve as a general warning to Germany and Austria, rather than as a military pact. Britain had ample reason to be wary of Germany's long-term intentions, which had been indicated by the great naval building programme of the pre-war years, by various sabre-rattling gestures and by the Kaiser's encouragement of the Boers. None of these was likely to lead to a declaration of war, though realists might suggest that if Germany successfully crushed first France, then Russia, Britain's turn would have come next. Britain had long been aware of the Schlieffen Plan without necessarily believing it would ever be implemented – all countries prepare contingency plans against possible emergencies, and there was no reason to suppose that the Germans' grandiose plan was anything more.

The fact that Britain began the war in a strong moral position had three significant effects. It gave Britain a voice in the early stages of the battle of France which was considerably in excess of what might otherwise have been accepted by the French. Later, when France had been exhausted by Verdun and the Nivelle offensive, it fell to Britain to save its ally; faced with the dire situation of 1917 Britain could perhaps have made its own terms with Germany and extricated itself without loss of anything except respect from the French. The fact, however, that Britain never contemplated such an action, nor would be likely to, had a considerable influence in drawing America into the war. And the knowledge that America would soon be bringing the weight of its arms into the war, and more than replacing the Russians who were withdrawing from it, certainly encouraged Britain to struggle on at whatever cost

It has sometimes been claimed that, after Germany's unprovoked attack on Belgium, its subsequent behaviour in that country has been exaggerated for propaganda purposes. Furthermore, it has been suggested that within a few months of the outbreak the Allies had forgotten why they had gone to war and were merely concentrating on beating Germany. This is not so. German behaviour in Belgium, well documented, was not forgotten. Canada, Australia, New Zealand and South Africa were well aware that the British Empire was engaged in a conflict in which the *casus belli* had been a moral one. That knowledge, if nothing else, enabled them to accept the enormous losses they suffered on such battlefields as Gallipoli, Vimy, the Somme, Arras and Passchendaele, to quote but a few: they were losses incurred in a form of crusade. The awareness that Haig, who was Commander-in-Chief of the BEF for the last two years of the war, was a man of integrity and high moral virtue made him an entirely suitable leader in their eyes.

All the complex events leading up to the outbreak of war would eventually affect its course and outcome. It has therefore been appropriate to look at them now, before the great battles of 1914–18 began. Haig would later have good reason to ponder them, for they would provide him with some tactical dilemmas. The conflict turned out not to be a mobile one, as he and many others had anticipated, but a war of attrition, a war in which the defence had the advantage over the attackers, and a war in which the most important factor was the quantity of artillery land shells available to either side.

8

The World at War

FROM THE OUTBREAK, it was clear that the war which began in August 1914 involved such a diversity of peoples and interests that it was certain to be extremely complicated. Even though Haig would only be concerned with one sector of that war and was never Commander-in-Chief of the combined Allied forces, his decisions would often be influenced by events happening thousands of miles away from his own area of command. In view of the complexities of the First World War, a brief summary of the main events will help to show the framework within which Haig would have to work.

The immediate effect of Germany's invasion of Belgium was that Britain declared war and despatched an expeditionary force to France. This, of course, was the force which had been organised by Haig and Haldane eight years earlier. As soon as it had disembarked, it marched up to meet the Germans at Mons. Although driven back, the British at Mons and the French at Charleroi held up the Germans long enough to disrupt the grandiose Schlieffen Plan to encircle Paris. At the same time the outer right flank of the German 'door' was running out of supplies, impetus and morale. Instead of making the sensible move of occupying the Channel ports, which would not have been difficult at that stage, the Germans decided to concentrate everything on capturing Paris. By 5 September 1914 they were only fourteen miles from their prize, but by then the shrewd French General Joffre had weighed up the situation and calculated that the rapid advance had left the German forward troops in disarray. Mustering every man he could, some of whom were brought to the front by Parisian taxi-cabs, he counter-attacked along the River Marne. So unexpected was this action that the Germans began to retreat and fell back on the River Aisne.

Now that it was too late, the Germans decided to take the Channel ports. The attempt to do so meant that the full weight of the attack fell on the British, who at this stage were on the extreme left of the Allied line. The name given to this phase of the war, which took place during October and November 1914, was the First Battle of Ypres. Ypres was an ancient Belgian market town close to the French frontier and, as will be seen, was held by the British, with the addition of a narrow strip of land to the east of the town itself. Seven miles north-east of Ypres lay the village of Passchendaele, on a low ridge – nevertheless a 'high point' in this flat landscape – which the Germans had no difficulty in occupying. Ypres was not an important town to hold from a military point of view, but had enormous diplomatic importance because it represented a prestigious toehold on Belgian soil. For the British, who had guaranteed Belgian neutrality but had been unable to prevent the Germans over-running most of the country, it was important to retain a piece of territory which would serve as a symbol of their determination to make Germany disgorge its other gains.

After the battle of the Marne both sides tried to make outflanking movements. These, of course, were always met by counter-movements and soon resulted in the hasty construction of a line of earthwork defences stretching from Flanders to Switzerland. Although this trench line was the result of hurried improvisation, it remained astonishingly static: and for the next four years it stayed in much the same position, in spite of continuous bombardment and attempted breakthroughs. In some sections the trench line was very poorly sited from a tactical point of view and there were various attempts to improve this situation without yielding ground. As the years passed the original defences, little more than deep ditches, were gradually transformed into highly complex fortifications with barbed wire, concrete dug-outs, gun sites and

1 Haig's statue outside School House, Clifton College, Bristol

2 Haig at Darmstadt, Germany, in an awkwardly posed photograph

3 Henrietta, Haig's elder sister and close confidante. She married
  William Jameson

4   Haig with staff at
     Aldershot, 1912. Left to
     right: Captain Baird,
     General Robb, Haig,
     General Davies,
     Captain Charteris

5   Dorothy Haig, 1905, the
     year of their marriage

6 Facing left to right: Field Marshal von Hindenburg, Kaiser Wilhelm II, General Ludendorff

7 German dugout on the Somme 1916. This is a good example of the careful defensive preparations the Germans had made in the area

8 General Robert Nivelle, a former artillery officer, replaced Joffre as Commander-in-Chief on 12 December 1916. His subsequent offensive was disastrous

9 A Mark IV tank 12 October 1917 at St Julien. The track has been blown off by gunfire

10 Left to right facing: At XIV Corps HQ, Meaux, 12 September 1916,
    Albert Thomas, French Minister of Munitions, Haig, Joffre, Lloyd
    George; the latter seems unimpressed by Haig and Joffre's arguments

11 Left to right, facing: General Sir Herbert Plumer, Lt General the Hon. Herbert Lawrence, Field Marshal Sir Douglas Haig. Taken at GHQ, BEF 1918

12   Haig riding at the head of the Peace Procession, 1919

13 Haig at the poppy factory at Richmond, with Major Howson, on 27 January 1928. He died suddenly the next day

long communication trenches. The Germans seem to have been more efficient than the British or French at making trench fortifications, and in consequence many Allied lives were lost by underestimates of the strength of opposing positions. Certain sectors of the line remained relatively quiet throughout the war; others were almost continually in action, often because they were inherently vulnerable, a temptation to the enemy and a spur to the holders to try to improve their hazardous position. The classic example was at Ypres where the British were occupying land for diplomatic, rather than military, reasons: it proved a costly piece of diplomacy, for the total Allied casualties incurred in fighting to gain the seven miles of territory leading up to the strategically important low ridge on which the village of Passchendaele stood eventually mounted to a quarter of a million. The German defenders paid a similar price.

The trench warfare which began in 1914 quickly developed predictable tactics. Each side would make a heavy artillery bombardment and then launch an infantry attack. The bombardment, which was meant to demolish the opposing defences, rarely did so, and the infantry who followed it were usually mown down by the machine gun or small arms fire of the defenders. In April 1915, for example, the French launched a massive attack in the Artois sector and made a breakthrough three miles deep. The Germans then closed the gap and drove the French back to their original line. The French had gained nothing and lost four hundred thousand men. They had already lost fifty thousand in other rash offensives elsewhere on the front.

The Germans were by no means passive recipients of these attacks, and in spring 1915 launched an offensive known as 'the second battle of Ypres'. They achieved surprise by using gas, but failed to consolidate their sudden gains. The British tried to break through at Neuve Chapelle in March, but the result was nothing but heavy losses. In September that year they went over the top again at Loos, but failed through shortage of shells, inability to cut the German barbed wire and misuse of reserves. The French offensive in Champagne, which was meant to complement this action, also proved abortive.

While this was happening in France, there was considerable activity elsewhere. In spite of their wish to avoid doing so, the Germans found themselves fighting on two fronts simultaneously. The Russians had invaded East Prussia in August 1914, and the Germans were extremely alarmed when the Russian colossus began rolling towards them; they summoned Field Marshal von Hindenburg from retirement,* and with the help of the Chief of Staff, Ludendorff, he defeated two large Russian armies in turn at Tannenberg. The Russians lost many of their guns and incurred huge casualties.

However, Germany soon found that the Austrians were less reliable as allies than they had hoped. The Russians quickly drove back the Austrian Army through Galicia (which would later be incorporated into Poland) and seemed certain to enter Hungary, but by that stage the Russian stocks of ammunition were almost exhausted and could not be replenished from outside. The Germans therefore took the opportunity that this presented of launching a heavy counter-attack – although it involved them in the risky manoeuvre of temporarily transferring troops from the Western Front to the East. In a series of brisk attacks they drove the Russians out of Galicia, the campaign being completed in May 1915. Hypothetically, the fact that Germany had thinned out its Western Front by deploying troops in the East should have given the Allies scope for considerable success in their own attacks. Instead, they suffered the setbacks of Artois and Neuve Chapelle. The explanation appeared to be the time-honoured thesis that one man in defence is the equal of three in attack.

Flushed with their success against the Russians in the south, the Germans decided that the summer of 1915 was an appropriate time to complete the Eastern campaign by attacking the Russian Army in the north. German armies therefore drove through Poland and even reached Lithuania. There, on an easily held line, they rested and pondered whether to continue and, in a further sustained offensive, try to drive Russia completely out of the war.

* Hindenburg had a distinguished record, including service in the Austro-Prussian War of 1866 and the Franco-Prussian War of 1870–1.

During early 1915 the Allies had decided that the more pressure they could put on the Germans on the Western Front, the more likely were Russian successes in the East. But as we have explained, this would prove an illusory hope. In February 1915, however, the Allies had also decided that, if a successful landing could be made in the Dardanelles, Turkey could be neutralised, a route to Russia could be opened up, and the Russian steamroller could be assisted to further conquests by copious Allied supplies.

It soon became clear what had happened to the Russian offensive of spring 1915, and before long a similar setback was to follow in the Dardanelles. The Turkish forts had been bombarded in February that year and this had given the Turks and their German advisers ample warning of Allied intentions. When the invasion force landed in April they gained such a small, vulnerable piece of territory that they became bogged down in trench warfare and no further advance was possible. A year later, after horrific casualties and prolonged suffering, the last of the Allied troops were evacuated. Germany was delighted, the Turks had gained confidence and prestige, and the Anzacs (Australian and New Zealand troops), who would have been invaluable on the Western Front, had been slaughtered for no gain at all. Furthermore, the ammunition wasted at Gallipoli could have been used very profitably in France, as Haig did not fail to point out.

Meanwhile other events in the Balkans began to imply that if the Allies did not win the war in the West, and win it quickly, they might soon find they had already lost it in the East. So far Bulgaria had remained uncommitted. However, that country had a long frontier with Serbia, which the Austrians had attacked but not subdued, and if Bulgaria could be induced to attack Serbia with German help it would be rewarded by large pieces of Serbian territory. A contented Bulgaria would then allow Germany to cross its territory and supply its Turkish ally on Bulgaria's other frontier.

The German/Bulgarian offensive took the Allies by surprise; when they realised the danger posed if Serbia was defeated and removed from the war, they hastily despatched divisions to Salonika (now Thessaloniki) in Greece, with orders to proceed to Serbia by train. In the event this preventive measure was too late, for the Bulgarians were already in Serbia. It would have been sensible for the Allies to evacuate Salonika forthwith, but they did not do so for two reasons: first, by having a presence there they felt they could forestall German moves against Greece, and secondly, there was always a chance that the port could be used as a base for a possible Allied offensive through Romania. The belief that Germany could be invaded through the back door, or, as Churchill later put it, 'the soft underbelly of Europe', appealed more strongly to politicians than to the military and naval personnel who would be required to provide the necessary troops and naval forces. But clearly there was an urgent need to forestall any German move to link itself more closely with Turkey. So far there were German liaison officers and instructors with the Turkish Army: the thought of this co-operation ever being expanded to the point at which German and Turkish regiments would be fighting side by side was a daunting one.

With the hope that Romania might eventually throw in its lot with the Allies, it was decided that the force at Salonika should be built up for future action. This was achieved by reinforcing it with divisions from Britain and France, and with smaller contingents from Russia and Italy. The Serbian Army was also rebuilt there. This gave a total of half a million men, but, not without reason, the Germans mockingly described it as 'the largest internment camp in Europe'. The Salonika force suffered badly from disease of various types and did not make an effective entry into the war until the autumn of 1918, when Germany was almost at the point of total collapse.

For those in France who believed that the quickest way to end the war was to drive a path to Berlin, the effect of hearing of this sequence of dismal failures may be imagined. But Gallipoli and Salonika were not the only disasters draining Allied manpower resources. There was also a Turkish threat to Egypt which had to be countered, though the small number of troops required to do this could be justified. And there were misgivings about the Mesopotamian campaign. Britain had acquired Basra, on the Persian Gulf, to safeguard the supplies from the Persian oilfields, but an extension of the British positions, which involved pushing nearly two hundred miles into the centre of Mesopotamia (now Iraq) seemed unnecessarily venturesome. The ultimate aim was the capture of Baghdad from the Turks, but the invading column was neither large enough nor well enough equipped for the task. The end of this phase of the Mesopotamian campaign came when the invasion force was besieged in Kut and starved into surrender by a Turkish army. The loss was only a small one in relation to the vast numbers engaged elsewhere in the war, but the loss of even two divisions seemed a prodigal waste of critically scarce resources.

The opinion of all the Allied commanders in France was that the sooner Britain stopped dissipating her resources on wildcat schemes the better it would be for all concerned. In their view, for as long as the war continued there would always be frivolous plans to create diversions in order to break the deadlock on the Western Front, even though the quickest and least complicated way to win the war was to smash a way through the German defences there. It would no doubt be costly in terms of lives, but in the event it would prove far less expensive than the ridiculous efforts around the Balkans. If possible, Russia must be kept in the war because Russian manpower would always present a threat to eastern Germany, but from the point of view of the Allied High Command, Russia could never win the war: that must be done by action on the Western Front.

In August 1914 the German Army vastly outnumbered the Allied forces and had achieved dramatic successes by treachery and surprise. It had acquired valuable strategic territory in Belgium and France and would not yield it up lightly. But as the trench line extended across France, the Allied generals quickly realised that the war would be unlike any of its predecessors. Cavalry tactics, as they knew them, could have no place on this front. Cavalry would still have a vital role, but it would only be after the breakthrough. Then, as had always happened, defeat would be turned into rout by pursuing the enemy with cavalry. There would be no time for the beaten army to improvise defences and rearguard actions on the retreat: the cavalry would move too quickly for that to happen. Haig himself never lost sight of this idea that the cavalry continued to have a part to play, and in the final stages – but only in the final stages – he was proved right. Long before that happened, however, he had made up his mind that the way the war could be won was by orthodox methods – artillery bombardment followed by massed infantry attacks. The cost in lives was appalling, and he was well aware of it. In the long history of warfare there have never been so many bitterly contested fights for ground as in north-eastern France during 1914–18. Usually those pieces of terrain would have been pounded by shells before the infantrymen occupied them and moved on to the next blood-soaked few yards of soil.

In every battle fought on the Western Front it was important, often essential, to know the fighting qualities of the men defending the desired objective. It was important not to allot too many men and resources to capturing each objective, for there were many demands on manpower; but it was also vital not to underrate the difficulties, use too few men and thus suffer dismal failure. Everything therefore depended on accurate knowledge of the number and quality of the enemy troops holding each objective. In France they might be the élite of the enemy's forces or they might be unwilling conscripts, tired, cold, and with no interest in the task they were expected to perform. They might be soldiers provided by unwilling allies, often men who hated their allies more than they hated the enemy. Such men might surrender easily or even change sides: any action they took when unwillingly fighting for someone else's cause was no measure of the courage they might display when fighting for their own.

These factors made the provision of high-quality intelligence vital. Information about such troops is gained from deserters, captured prisoners, papers on dead bodies and listening devices. Patrols would be sent out each night to find out what the enemy was doing, and if possible to capture a prisoner who might provide more information, intentionally or unintentionally. This activity was organised by companies – units 120 strong in the front line. Before an intended attack, staff officers would inform battalions that they needed information about the quality of troops holding the opposite position. The battalion would distribute the order to companies, and company commanders would increase the number of their routine patrols in order to capture prisoners or obtain information by any other means that chance presented in their sector.

This was all standard procedure – although over-earnest patrolling often caused unnecessary casualties – and the information gained was probably considered to be of not much more than local interest. Clearly a corps commander, still less a Commanderin-Chief, would not be concerned with local reports and would rely on summaries made by staff officers. That was where the system began to develop faults. Staff officers would read company reports and interpret them as they thought fit, emphasising some points and doubting others. Selections from the reports would then be made to build up a daily summary. From these daily summaries a broad view of enemy intentions, morale and composition would be formed. From such filtered documents the Commander and his operational staff would decide when and where the next attack should be launched.

Neither Haig, nor anyone else, had any conception of the task ahead when Britain settled down into trench warfare in the autumn of 1914. There were the usual optimistic forecasts. The Royal Navy would quickly starve the Germans into surrender. The might of the British Empire, with its sturdy Australians, New Zealanders, Canadians and South Africans, would soon frighten the Germans out of the positions they were illegally occupying. Britain had learnt all the necessary lessons in the Boer War of 1899–1902, whereas the Germans had not seen real action since 1871. In fact the war would probably be over by Christmas and the troops could go home.

Haig, though not unduly optimistic, took a positive view of Allied prospects. Nevertheless he could see reason in the view of Kitchener, now Secretary of State for War, that if Britain was to win it would have to raise an army of at least a million, and that victory would take three years. Haig had considerable misgivings about the ability of Sir John French to manage the exacting task of

Commander-in-Chief of the BEF, to which he had been appointed in August 1914. He blamed French for the fact that the British
Army was to be deployed as far forward as Maubeuge. In fact this
was not French's decision. It was due to a misunderstanding over
an agreement reached three years earlier when Sir Henry Wilson,
the British Director of Military Operations (DMO), had met
General Dubail, the French Chief of the General Staff, in the
presence of the French Minister for War. The agreement had
specified that in the event of war the British would be deployed
thirty miles west of Maubeuge, though they would have preferred
Amiens; it was an ominous indication that serious misunderstandings between the British and French general staffs could occur all
too easily. The French had initially decided that, whatever the
German tactics, they themselves would fight the war according to
their own agreed plans. Although they knew of the existence of
the Schlieffen Plan, they doubted if it would work. In their view
any advancing German troops would quickly be turned by French
cavalry. By the third week in August they had revised these ideas
and were fighting for their lives.

As GOC Aldershot, Haig became Commander of 1 Corps. It
was an efficient, well-trained unit which contained two divisions
only – there is no upper or lower limit to the number of divisions
in a corps. First Division was commanded by Major General
Lomax, in whom Haig had complete confidence, and 2nd Division by Major General Monro, of whom Haig had doubts because
he was somewhat overweight – in the opening stages of this
gruelling war, physical fitness was going to be of great importance. Grierson, who had defeated Haig in pre-war manoeuvres,
had collapsed and died, and the weather in that critical August was
very hot.

First Corps had its initial encounter with the Germans on 23
August, east of Mons. The French plan to drive forward through
the Ardennes had quickly turned into a hasty retreat, and the
British, who had been deployed too far forward, found themselves facing the full weight of the German attack launched from
the north-east towards Paris. The British 2 Corps came under
heavy German attack at this time, and as it withdrew asked Haig if

he could spare reinforcements. He sent three battalions, but by now the French armies were in full retreat and it was necessary to fall back to prevent a gap appearing between the British and French forces. The British had to try to disengage, regroup and link up with the French force which should have been on their right (which was Haig's right flank). The ensuing lengthy retreat was a formidable test of the courage, resilience and fitness of the British Army. Most of the weight of the German attack had so far fallen on 2 Corps, commanded by the volatile but reliable Smith-Dorrien. Their casualties had been horrific. At Mons they had lost four thousand, and when they made another stand at Le Cateau this figure went up by another eight thousand. As they withdrew, they were described as being too tired to march further but not too tired to lie down and fire their rifles. Smith-Dorrien managed to repel all the German attacks on his weary corps at Le Cateau and then, on the orders of GHQ, marched them back towards St Quentin. It was impossible to co-ordinate the withdrawal with the French – the best that could be hoped for was not to lose touch with them altogether. But at least the British had avoided being outflanked by the right wing of the German Army.

Meanwhile 1 Corps, also acting under GHQ orders, fell back through Guise and crossed the Oise. The aim of the retreat was to keep the British and French armies in line, but to allow the Germans to over-extend themselves and lose their co-ordination; it was going to be a long, exhausting process. Although not having suffered the mauling which 2 Corps had experienced, 1 Corps was also thoroughly weary. Haig therefore acquired a train to carry some of the kit and the more exhausted of the soldiers. It was a revealing but depressing start to the campaign.

Apart from one day when, suffering a severe attack of diar-rhoea, he had travelled by car, Haig spent all the time in the saddle. Every evening he wrote the orders for the following day in his own entirely legible handwriting. Charteris reported of this time: 'His Headquarters moved at the rear of the main columns in close touch with the rearguards but each day he himself rode along the whole length of the line. His uniform was neat as in peace time; his

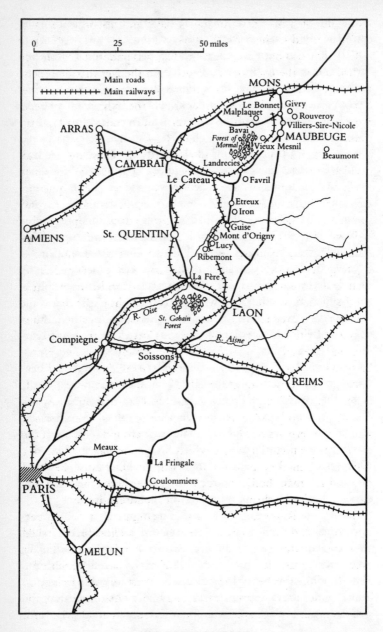

THE GREAT RETREAT

face immobile; his horse fully groomed; and his presence gave confidence and strength to all who saw him.'

Charteris was not exaggerating. Haig was undoubtedly as well turned out as the conditions allowed, and the fact that he supervised the retreat as if it was an orderly manoeuvre which he himself had planned gave confidence to the exhausted soldiers. Rearguard actions are notoriously difficult to control, and retreat can all too easily turn into a disorderly rout.

At one point Haig was almost caught by the Germans. He had decided to spend the night with the Guards Brigade in the small town of Landrecies. As evening fell he was given the disquieting news that the advance German units had caught up and were now surrounding the place. A brisk infantry attack, supported by artillery, began on the outskirts, but the Guards have a long tradition of not being pushed aside and after a few hours the fighting died down. By that time Haig had given orders to destroy all important papers and prepare the local barracks for a last ditch stand, where he and his staff would fight to the end. Haig was quite prepared to die in battle. There would be plenty of other competent officers to take his place as Corps Commander if he died and the campaign continued; undoubtedly he would rather be dead than live to see a German victory. At midnight, however, since the fighting had slackened, Haig, General John Gough, Haig's Chief of Staff and Charteris slipped out of Landrecies in a car showing no lights. It evaded the thin screen of troops which was all the Germans had been able to throw around the back of the town. At one point Haig's party was ordered to halt, but was not fired on when they paid no attention; an hour later they had rejoined the main body. The next day, after heroic fighting, the Guards also broke through the cordon round Landrecies.

The Great Retreat, lasting from 24 August to 5 September, came to an end forty miles from Paris. The soldiers had marched an average of fifteen miles a day for two hundred miles, falling asleep almost as they halted. None of them had experienced a marathon like this before, and even the fittest found marching in heavy boots on cobbled roads a nightmare. Astonishingly, the soldiers never lost confidence that one day they would stop, turn, fight and beat the Germans. The fact that every day they saw their Corps Commander, not merely staying with them but also keeping close to the rearguard in the position of most danger, undoubtedly helped to maintain their confidence.

It was subsequently said that in the First World War the soldiers never saw their commanders. Field Marshal Lord Montgomery used to say that in the First World War he never saw a senior officer. (Since, after being wounded and evacuated in 1915 he returned to France the following year and served for the remainder of the war in various senior staff appointments, one can only conclude that if he did not see any senior commanders he must have had very selective eyesight.) The troops whom he commanded certainly saw Haig, not only on the Great Retreat in 1914 but many times afterwards.

9

The Road to
Ypres

ALTHOUGH THE ORDER to halt at the end of the Great Retreat suggested to some that the war had come to an end, they were not allowed to persist in their delusion for long. Haig set out his troops like chessmen on a board and moved from point to point, exuding confidence in the outcome of the next phase. Following their reverse on the Marne, the Germans had drawn back to regroup in preparation for their next attack. The British soldiers in the forward positions were able to see the wanton destruction the Germans had inflicted on the French villages they had temporarily occupied; they were therefore now anxious to give the Germans a taste of their own medicine. Haig found some of the officers rather less enthusiastic than their troops: their morale had been badly shaken and they would have preferred to take a few days' rest before going into action again. To these he gave special attention, with talks to rebuild morale.

On 7 September 1 Corps began to move forward again – at first, surprisingly, meeting no opposition. On the 8th they caught up with the German rear troops. A brisk action followed, after which the Germans retreated again in disorder. Haig came well forward to observe the progress of this action, and put himself within range of the enemy machine gunners. They soon spotted him and his staff and gave them a lively welcome with bullets. Haig's party had to take hasty refuge behind the tombstones in the local churchyard until the Germans fell back again. Progressing carefully, by 12 September 1 Corps had advanced seventy miles.

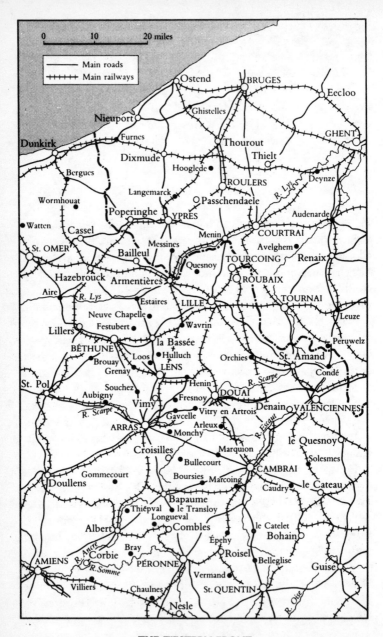

THE WESTERN FRONT

On the 13th they crossed the River Aisne and renewed the attack at the base of the Chemin-des-Dames Ridge, which would later be the scene of much bloodshed. But by this time the Germans had decided that they had retreated far enough and that the line should be stabilised. First Corps dug in, little realising that this part of the line would remain static for years. In view of the fact that he was accused by later writers of neglecting his air component, it should be recorded that Haig used aircraft to 'spot' for his own artillery. The lessons of 'Red Force' *v* 'Blue Force' had not been forgotten.

Then the Germans counter-attacked. At this point the brunt of the fighting fell on 1 Corps; 2 Corps had not recovered from the battering it had sustained on the Great Retreat, and the French on Haig's right flank were unable to make headway. However, morale was high, the Aisne had been crossed (giving this particular phase of the war the name of the Battle of the Aisne), and reinforcements were arriving regularly from Britain.

At home, the British public was elated by the news that the German thrust had been checked and put into reverse. Wild rumours began to circulate about the precise means by which this had been achieved, and the story of the reinforcements delivered by Paris taxi-cabs was inflated to the point of incredibility. A more interesting theory was that British troops in France had been reinforced by Russians hastily brought over for the purpose. They had landed in Scotland in conditions of great secrecy, it was said, and come south by night before crossing the Channel at Dover. Their timely presence might not have been known had it not been for the sharp eyes and ears of a porter at King's Cross. He had seen the actual snow on their boots and heard them talking in Russian. The distinction between the Gaelic and Slavonic languages is probably not easily recognisable by someone who speaks neither.

For Haig, the opening months of the war had been an educational experience. The Germans had proved much better than he expected and the French much worse – the latter would, of course, recover, and fight with the utmost courage and tenacity in later battles, but Haig would never fully regain his former confidence in them. Although he admired Joffre, both as a person and as a general, he had misgivings about the ability of the French to do battle with the Germans. He would change his mind to some extent later when he observed them locked in a struggle to the death with the Germans at Verdun, and, judging by their victory on the Marne, the French might always produce a surprise, but he found their administration so slovenly that it was likely to affect the morale of their fighting troops. In the Great Retreat he had learnt that the French commissariat had failed badly, while his own, run by the ultra-efficient Sir William Robertson, had met all the demands made on it and had had rations to spare for the neighbouring French corps.

In the opening stages of the war Haig had been more than satisfied with the troops under his command, whose morale had remained steady under the most depressing circumstances. He had also discovered a lot about himself. He had been faced with the possibility of sudden and unexpected defeat, but had managed to maintain a calm outward appearance. Although he had been under fire before, this was the first occasion when he had had more than an even chance of being killed. The wars in the Sudan and South Africa, although testing, bore no comparison to the one in which he was now engaged. Up until now he had been involved in theory rather than practice: now there would be no manoeuvres, Staff Rides and Tactical Exercises Without Troops (TEWTS). Every move would cost lives, and any mistakes would mean the needless slaughter of hundreds, if not thousands. He had been quick to realise that this would be a long, hard struggle and if in earlier days he had been something of an aloof dandy, from now on the impression he would give would be one of dogged pugnacity.

The retreat from Mons and the subsequent recovery had taken the BEF well away from the sector of the line which had originally been allotted to it. Sir John French therefore proposed to Joffre that it should now move away from its position on the Aisne and be deployed on the left, south from the area immediately to the east of Ypres. Joffre agreed readily. This meant that 1 Corps would be protecting Ypres, while 2 and 3 would be holding the sector in the Armentières area as far south as La Bassée. In the meantime, an attempt was made to relieve Antwerp, which was being besieged by German forces. For this, a British naval division had been organised and disembarked at Dunkirk. However, it was unable to break through the German besiegers' lines, and when Antwerp surrendered it had to retire hastily to the Ypres area. Further reinforcements which had arrived too late to save Antwerp were now absorbed into 4 Corps, which was put under the command of Major General Sir Henry Rawlinson. This new corps took up a position with the BEF, on the right of 1 Corps. However, between the British and the coast was a contingent of inexperienced French under General d'Urbal, and Belgian troops who had also fallen back from Antwerp now held the extreme left flank.

Sir John French was already demonstrating the limitations which made him unsuitable as Commander-in-Chief, BEF. He failed to realise that the German line had now been strengthened in depth, assuming that it was still thin enough to make a British breakthrough possible. On 19 October he instructed Haig to advance from the Ypres sector and capture Bruges and Ghent. The fact that 1 Corps had only recently taken part in a gruelling retreat, followed by some brisk fighting, did not seem to enter French's calculations. Haig tried to carry out the absurd order but was checked at the beginning, sustaining heavy casualties in the process. First Corps had run headlong into the German 4th Army, whose commander had decided that this was an appropriate moment to curl around to the right of the Allied line (in the northern sector as it faced them) and thus, having outflanked the main position, be once more on the road to Paris.

Another victim of self-delusion was Foch, who was overall Allied commander in the northern sector. He now decided that d'Urbal's inexperienced force should mount an attack and reach the vital railway junction of Roulers. Roulers lay beyond Passchendaele and would in fact evade capture until the closing stages of the war. To assist d'Urbal, Foch sent up the French 9 Corps, but this offensive failed to make much headway.

Sir John French's dream of the BEF making a dramatic breakthrough east of Ypres was now looking absurdly optimistic to

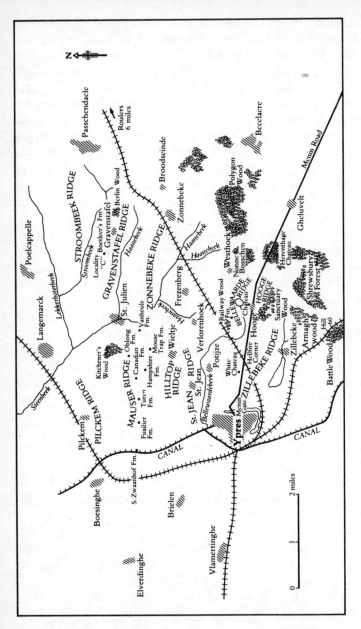

YPRES, 1914–15

everyone except the veteran of Klip Drift himself; here there was not just a single obstacle to be brushed aside but rank upon rank of well-sited German positions. To make matters worse, the British were just beginning to encounter a limiting factor which would affect them for the next two years: shortage of shells. The Germans did not seem to have the same problem, and whenever there was a British attack the response was a German counter-attack well supported by an artillery barrage. Although Haig shared French's view about the need to break through the German line and create havoc with the British cavalry, he could see this ambition rapidly disappearing as the German resistance stiffened. His headquarters at this time were in the château at Hooge, though later in the war the château would completely disappear above ground level and the surrounding territory would become a morass of mud and corpses.

But while French and Foch had been making their optimistic plans for a successful breakthrough, the Germans had been nurturing a similar idea. The sector which Haig was holding with I Corps, which had now been strengthened with another division, was to be breached by eight German divisions – three of which were cavalry to exploit the gap – and a suitably large artillery component. Haig's sector contained Gheluvelt, which was a ridge slightly above the surrounding countryside – since the area on which the fighting was taking place was a plain of low-lying ground, the few ridges acquired a special importance. At the start of the fighting the mixture of pasture and arable land had been drained by an ingenious system of ditches. In rainy weather these were scarcely able to remove the surface water, for the whole area was at, or below, sea level. For this reason it was impossible to dig adequate trenches: a few feet below the surface, and sometimes even closer to it, they would fill up with water. When the shelling started in earnest, the irrigation channels were destroyed and blocked and the whole area became a nightmare of water-filled shell-holes, liquid mud and the detritus of battle. That process was only just beginning: it would reach its nadir in 1917, when the rains were unseasonably heavy and prolonged. For both sides, physical conditions influenced this battlefield as in no other war in history. Whereas in other battles it would have been considered the utmost folly to deploy troops on forward slopes, where they would be in full view of the enemy artillery, in the Ypres salient they often had to take up such a vulnerable situation because there was no alternative.

The German attack began on 29 October and was continued in greater strength on the following day. Haig quickly realised that, far from being in a position to attack the enemy himself, he would be hard put to it to hold their own attack. The German attacks on 29 and 30 October began at 5.30 a.m. and 6.30 a.m. respectively, but later both sides would realise that onslaughts which began precisely on the hour or half-hour were less successful than those which began at a less predictable time, such as 06.21 or 11.19.

Although 1 Corps held up the Germans they sustained heavy casualties in doing so, and also lost over two miles of ground. It was obvious that the Germans were preparing for a major assault. They desperately needed a quick victory and a speedy culmination of the campaign in France, for the news from the Eastern Front was ominous: the Russians were advancing in armies of unknown but clearly enormous strength. The Kaiser, who made a habit of showing himself near the line when important offensives were to be made, now visited the headquarters of the German commander, Crown Prince Rupprecht, who was destined to stay in France for most of the war.

On 31 October the attack began at 6 a.m. The three spearhead divisions came head on to 1 Corps and were stopped, with heavy losses. Frustrated, the Germans decided to soften up 1 Corps with intensive artillery fire. The rain of shells destroyed the temporary trenches which 1 Corps had made and, when these were evacuated, the Germans pressed forward with two divisions. At a heavy cost in casualties, they occupied Gheluvelt and were now a mere four miles from Ypres.

At this point a disaster struck the British. Somewhat unwisely, 1st and 2nd Divisions in 1 Corps had chosen Hooge Château for their joint headquarters. In the early afternoon of the 31st it came under heavy German shellfire. General Lomax, who had been commanding 1 Division with great expertise, was killed, as were six staff officers. General Monro was lucky to escape without serious injury, and Haig was fortunate not to be there himself for, as mentioned earlier, he had used Hooge as his battle HQ before the Germans penetrated the British line. His present HQ was one mile outside Ypres, on the spot which later became known as 'Hellfire Corner'; it took its name from the fact that in the later stages of the war the Germans shelled it day and night with merciless accuracy.

As yet unaware of the disaster at Hooge, Haig and a small escort rode slowly up the Menin road, which runs through Hooge, until he reached the heart of the battle. Although he rode in silence, the fact that he was moving up towards the line rather than away from it gave great encouragement to his troops, whose morale had now become very fragile. If a general is going up to the front it gives fresh heart to those who think the battle is already lost. When he comes back, preferably looking cheerful, the reinforcements moving up will think, 'It can't be too bad up there if the general is returning unwounded.'

On his return, Haig was met with the news of the deaths of Lomax and his staff. He at once ordered up a replacement, Brigadier General Landon from 3rd Brigade. But meanwhile the unbelievable had happened. Shortly before he was killed, Lomax had asked Monro for any reserves he could spare; his own had already been committed. Monro was hard pressed, but produced the 2nd Battalion of the Worcestershire Regiment. They had been held in reserve in the oddly named Polygon Wood, halfway between Zonnebeke and Gheluvelt. Put under the command of Brigadier General Fitzclarence, VC, an Irish Guards officer who relished a fight, they surged into Gheluvelt and took it at the point of the bayonet. This feat was so extraordinary that unless it had happened nobody would have believed it possible. Fitzclarence, sadly, was killed three days later.

The Germans, astonished that they could have been attacked and lost ground so unexpectedly, cautiously withdrew from their forward positions and consolidated their new line. It was not the last attempt they made at capturing Gheluvelt, but the later one was no more successful. By now, 11 November 1914, the Belgian winter appeared to have settled in, and they decided to leave the recapture of Gheluvelt till the following spring. When that came, they planned to surprise the Allies and complete the task they had set themselves. Meanwhile the two armies began the long, continuous artillery duel which would go on throughout the war and make this the most notorious battlefield in history.

This opening battle became known to military historians as First Ypres. There were fifty thousand British casualties, twenty thousand French and Belgian, and one hundred and fifty thousand German. The ratio had been the expected one of twice as many casualties among the attackers, but in fact the British losses had been the more serious. 1 and 2 Corps, on which much of the German attack had fallen, contained the 'Old Contemptibles', that hard core of well-trained, pre-war regular soldiers. They were the men whose steady rifle fire, 'fifteen rounds a minute', had been so fast and accurate that the Germans had believed it must be coming from machine guns. Their qualities could not be replaced easily or quickly; there were volunteers coming forward by the thousand but, until they could be thoroughly trained, all the courage and morale they undoubtedly possessed could not compensate for lack of experience. Many of them were killed while still acquiring the necessary skills to survive.

Meanwhile the Germans shelled Ypres steadily. From the positions they had gained in the opening stages of the battle they could observe most of what went on in the town. Their greatest asset was the low ridge of hills which ran like the rim of a bowl around the seven miles by twenty which constituted the Ypres salient. On the right lay the Messines Ridge, north-east of Ypres was the village of Passchendaele* and due north was Pilckem, which would later become a sea of mud.

Although the Germans held most of the valuable higher ground, the position at the end of First Ypres was considered reasonably satisfactory by the British. The Germans had been held in that sector, and the immediate danger to Ypres and the Channel ports had been averted.

---

* The Belgians have now changed the spelling of the name to Passendale.

Haig had been lucky to emerge from the battle with a whole skin, for he had visited the front line every day and had several times been caught in shell fire. He was, however, quite relentless. Although sympathising with the hardships and losses that the corps had sustained, he was not prepared to accept the fact that men's minds could be as vulnerable as their bodies. He did not see why every battalion should not fight to the last man: the Germans were doing it, and so should the Allies. He was particularly unsympathetic to subordinate commanders who reported during the battle that their men could not possibly mount another attack without some form of rest. When it was reported that some men had fallen back without orders, they were promptly court-martialled: their eventual fate is unknown. Ruthlessness was necessary, Haig thought, or such a malaise would spread. He did not believe in shell shock or battle fatigue, and if he had he would have thought the best cure for these was victory or the attempt to achieve it. Nevertheless, when there was a lull in the battle he spared no effort to see that proper arrangements were made for leave.

At the end of November he took a week's leave himself. Dorothy found him less tired than she had expecterd: the modest success of First Ypres, the fact that the Germans had been held and that his corps had behaved so creditably served as a tonic. Instead of relaxing in the country, however, he spent much of his leave in the War Office, making sure that everyone gained the benefit of his experience. An urgent priority was to obtain a faster supply of shells, and he made clear his views on how the newly raised troops should be trained. Nobody could doubt that Haig had thought carefully about the preparations, equipment and organisation required to win the war.

When he returned to France at the end of November, 1 Corps was in reserve but training hard for the next phase of the battle. This would not be until the following spring. There was, however, a small, unsuccessful attack on the Messines–Wytschaete Ridge on 14 December mounted by 2 Corps which achieved nothing but casualties. This area contained Spanbroekmolen,* and

* The famous mine crater, over 400 feet wide.

also the trenches in which Hitler served later. There was no proper artillery barrage, the German wire had to be cut by anyone who survived to reach it, and the approaches were deep in mud.

The official history records: 'In the close fighting the superiority of the German hand-grenades was very marked.' This was hardly surprising. The official history gives the 'recipe' for making a British 'jam pot' hand grenade. 'Take a tin jam pot, fill it with shredded guncotton and tenpenny nails, mixed according to taste. Insert a No. 8 detonator and a short length of Bickford's fuse. Clay up the lid. Light with a match, pipe, cigar or cigarette and throw for all you are worth.' A variant of this was the 'hairbrush' grenade. A slab of guncotton was made fast by wire to a flat piece of wood of hairbrush shape, which afforded a convenient handle for throwing. It was ignited in the same way as the 'jam pot' grenade. Fortunately the first Mills bombs began to arrive in spring 1915, but not in sufficient quantities.

The situation with trench mortars was even worse. These simple weapons were basically pipes which projected a grenade at an angle of about 45° into the air in the direction of the enemy trenches. They were almost as dangerous to the user as to the opponent. Forty mortars were obtained from the French to make up the deficit – though even these were seventy-five years old. Some were used in the battles of 1915. Fortunately the much improved Stokes mortar would soon be in production; it was named after its inventor, the managing director of a factory making lawn-mowers.

The Official History also makes the following extremely relevant point about this early period in the war:

It must be borne in mind that many of the words used in 1915 had a value quite different from what they acquired later in the war. A 'trench' was a slight narrow excavation with steep sides and six to nine feet wide traverses, lacking duck-boards and drainage and revetment worth the name. A dug-out was merely a hole in the ground with splinter-proof covering. An aeroplane photograph was a blurred picture on which little else but trenches could be picked out. Mining had scarcely begun.

The signal service at the front, with its wireless, buried lines, earth circuits, pigeons, etc, was in the making. Air warfare and anti-aircraft defences were still in their infancy. The possibilities of strategy, as the Dardanelles proved, was limited by want of means to carry out what were the best and most effective strokes. The tactical conduct of battles was hampered not only by difficulties of communication, but by the incomplete training of the reinforcements and the new units, and the inexperience of the staff. Commanders had to handle, under novel conditions, far larger bodies of troops than they had ever been allowed to contemplate, and to do so with the aid of officers who had little or no staff training.

It might have added: 'All activities had to be conducted in the face of attack by an enemy who had for long been preparing for the moment and whose equipment was altogether better.' However, adequate criticisms of the performance of First World War generals rarely seem to take into account the almost insuperable problems they had to face. Probably the greatest handicap was the inability to act promptly on information about enemy moves because of inadequate communications.

At the end of 1914 the British Expeditionary Force, which had grown considerably in size in spite of casualties, was organised into armies. Haig was given command of 1st Army, which contained his former command, 1 Corps, as well as 2 Corps and 3 Corps. Second Army was commanded by Smith-Dorrien. Commanding 5 Corps under him was Lieutenant General Sir H. C. O. Plumer, who had been one of Haig's instructors at the Staff College. Despite his unimpressive appearance and a tendency to take an unacceptably independent line, there were many people who thought that Plumer should already have been an Army Commander, and when he became one later he showed outstanding ability.

Another important change which took place at this time was the replacement of Sir Archibald Murray as Chief of the General Staff at GHQ, BEF. Although the name of Henry Wilson, French's deputy Chief of Staff, was put forward for the appointment, both Haig and Kitchener demurred on the grounds that Wilson was too prone to accede to French requests, however inconvenient and hazardous those might be. Instead, Sir William Robertson, who had been a great success as Quartermaster General, was given the position, and Robertson and Haig would work closely together for the remainder of the war. But Wilson was by no means out of the picture, for he was appointed Chief Liaison Officer between Sir John French and Marshal Joffre.

The problem which now confronted French was how to break the stalemate which had developed after the first few months of fighting. There were many better minds which were also concentrating on the task. Chief among them was Kitchener, who had returned to England from Egypt in August 1914 in order to take up his present post of Secretary of State for War. He regarded Britain's existing arrangements with scorn. The original expeditionary force numbered 125,000 men. There were also 60,000 regular troops overseas, but these could not be sent to France unless other troops were despatched to replace them in their former stations. There were 250,000 Territorials, but they were quite untrained for modern warfare and had enlisted on the basis that they would only be used for home defence and would not be required to serve abroad. It did not require a very discerning mind to see that this mixture was unlikely to be adequate against a trained German Army of one and a half million men – though part of the German Army would, of course, be deployed to confront Russia and to bolster up the Austrian Army. Kitchener had predicted that the war would last at least three years and would require a British Army of at least a million. If he had asked the government to bring in conscription at that point it would undoubtedly have agreed, and the whole country would have accepted it as a sensible course. However, he thought that at this stage conscription might produce more problems than solutions, so he appealed instead for 100,000 volunteers.

The decision to create Kitchener's armies, of which 'The First Hundred Thousand' were quickly enrolled, did not please everyone. They had rallied to the call of 'Your Country Needs You' on Kitchener's famous recruiting poster. In consequence thousands of well-qualified men, who would later have been invaluable as doctors, engineers, scientists and staff officers, were being enlisted into infantry regiments. Most of them would be slaughtered at Loos and on the Somme. In the event, the Territorials also volunteered for overseas service and provided useful stiffening to the BEF, but there was a marked coolness between them and the 'Kitcheners'. Kitchener did not really trust the Territorials: like Haig, he had acquired this prejudice in the Boer War when certain locally raised units had been virtually useless.

Incredible though it may seem today, there was distinct resentment at the presence of some of the reinforcements in the regular battalions. It was not a matter of social class, for many of the newcomers had been school or university contemporaries of the regulars. But they were regarded as intruders, who had chosen not to be in the peacetime Army which saw itself as a form of élite, direct heirs to the medieval knights with all the panoply of ancient military traditions. The astonishment and bitterness of the new arrivals when they were treated as outcasts and sent off to learn riding and do saluting drill under junior NCOs when temporarily out of the line, may be imagined.

Although Kitchener was now serving in a civilian post, he was a field marshal and saw no objection to over-ruling Sir John French when it suited him, even though the latter was Commander-in-Chief of the British Expeditionary Force. Kitchener despised French; French responded by hating Kitchener – though none of this was shown in public, of course. Meanwhile, Churchill's special project had begun; but within a few months it would become obvious that the Dardanelles would be the scene not of a major breakthrough but of appalling losses. It was not only on the Western Front that men could be mown down by machine gun fire.

There were ominous portents that 1915 was going to be a year of disasters, and all too soon they were realised. Apart from the failure of the Dardanelles expedition, there were expensive but frustrating battles at Neuve Chapelle, Aubers Ridge, Festubert and Loos. In addition there was the endless trickle of daily casualties through artillery fire, small attacks and disease. On all occasions, large and small, the shortage of guns and ammunition was a limiting factor. Many of the casualties occurred in the Ypres salient. The BEF would have been happy to see a withdrawal from it, enabling them to concentrate behind the Yser Canal, further back and more easily defensible. However, Foch had grandiose ideas about the value of the Ypres salient as a pivot for launching vast, sweeping attacks into the German lines. In fact, the salient was never used for that purpose and never looked remotely like being so. However, three years later the fact that the British were in the salient and able to bring pressure to bear on the Germans saved the French Army from total collapse after their 1917 mutiny. Foch's strategic ideas may have been over-optimistic, but his instincts were sure enough.

The winter of 1914–15 was enough to reduce the stoutest heart to despair. January saw continuous rain, snow and flood: the River Lys rose seven feet and in places extended from two or three yards to a width of one hundred yards. Some trenches became ditches full of water which could not be pumped out. Those which could be manned contained so much water that men were standing knee-deep in it. The Army became acutely aware of what was called 'trench foot', a painful disease of the feet which could become gangrenous and lead to death. It was caused by cold and wet, combined with static positions. Twenty thousand men were invalided out because of trench foot in 1914–15.

The British guns were not merely inferior in numbers to the Germans but at that time were limited to four rounds of ammunition a *day*. The soldiers, standing in freezing water, could not understand why their own artillery did not try to make a more effective response. Nevertheless, in spite of all their disadvantages they managed to repel German attacks at Cuinchy, Givenchy and St Eloi.

In March, when the weather seemed to have brightened up, Haig launched an attack on the village of Neuve Chapelle. The ultimate aim was the capture of Aubers Ridge, which rose sixty feet from the sodden plain and was therefore a very important objective. Haig's plans had an inauspicious beginning, for late in February he lost John Gough, who was his Chief of Staff. Gough, who had just been given command of a division, was killed by a sniper when he went up to the front to say goodbye to his old regiment, the 2nd Rifle Brigade.

The Neuve Chapelle battle was only a modest success, but it was an occasion from which many lessons were learnt. It was not Haig's choice of a point for attack, but Joffre's. The Germans knew well enough that an Allied attack was coming in that area, for they could observe many of the British preparations from the high ground which they themselves held. It was decided that, in an area with strong defence in depth and with a slope to climb, the chances of a breakthrough and cavalry pursuit were negligible. Furthermore, instead of infantry platoons covering each other in alternate advances, the procedure now was that all would advance together under the cover of an artillery barrage. In theory this barrage would 'creep' along just ahead of the advancing troops, but in practice it was soon discovered that the barrage could either fall short, preventing an advance, or 'creep' too quickly and leave the attackers behind. Once the barrage had passed, the surviving defenders would emerge from their trenches and mow down the advancing infantry.

The early stages of Neuve Chapelle went very well for the British. On 10 March twelve battalions, four from the Indian Corps and eight from 4 Corps, captured the German front trench which the artillery had already saturated with shells. The Indian Corps displayed superb courage and dash, but suffered heavy casualties. Neuve Chapelle itself was captured and, as this made a considerable breach in the enemy line, it seemed for a moment as though a cavalry breakthrough might still be feasible. Haig, who had advanced his HQ to Merville, brought forward a cavalry brigade in case this could be realised. However the Germans still held the flanks, which meant that the breach could not easily be widened and might even be closed by attack from the flanks. There was an urgent need to exploit the initial success, but the British reinforcements had been delayed through misunderstandings and the Germans had already organised a further defensive line; they were also rushing up reinforcements which, as they were travelling by night, were not spotted by British aerial observers.

Most of the telephone cables had been destroyed in the barrages, and the most reliable method of keeping in touch was by runner or horseman: this meant that artillery fire was haphazard and speculative.

On 12 March, the Germans counter-attacked after a heavy artillery barrage. Although a thick mist enabled their infantry to come closer to the British trenches before being spotted, they were then checked and sustained heavy losses. An attempt was made to mount further British attacks but, as there were no fresh troops for the purpose and ammunition was now very short, the battle drifted to an end. Neuve Chapelle had been captured, and two thousand prisoners had been taken, but the British force had sustained eleven thousand casualties. The German losses were probably as high.* The British had won a victory, but it was far from decisive – if they could only have gone a little further and faster they could probably have secured the coveted ridge and then made a deep hole in the German line.

Neuve Chapelle was typical of the tactical approach which would now become the standard pattern for the rest of the war. There would be no more open warfare of the type which had characterised the famous battlefields of recent centuries, but a reversion to the old pattern of siege warfare which had developed from the investment of castles in medieval times to the tactics for defending and attacking towns in the seventeenth and eighteenth centuries. By the time Haig had reached the Staff College, these tactics of siege warfare had seemed obsolete and slightly ridiculous; it was assumed that a fast-moving column could always outflank the defenders and cut their supply routes. But this was a simplistic view: castles and fortified towns had survived because they took time to capture, yet invading forces dared not leave such hazards unscathed on their lines of communication. The techniques of siege warfare were now to be used all over the Western Front: mining, howitzer bombardment, approach by saps and siege lines, and deep communication trenches. Both sides would

* It was always difficult to ascertain German casualties because accurate records were seldom kept. The reason was said to be that there were insufficient clerks available for the purpose.

look eagerly for a point where a breakthrough could be made, or hope for a new weapon which would breach the defences, but in lines which had stabilised on a relatively narrow battlefield there was no easily discernible alternative to a war of attrition. The Germans thought they had such a weapon in gas, and the British later assumed the tank was the answer, but both were to be disappointed.

The principal limiting factor on British tactics in 1915 was the shortage of shells. Although the worst effect was on the soldiers in the trenches, who had to endure bombardments of apparently unlimited German high explosive to which no effective reply ever seemed forthcoming, the 'shells scandal' had political repercussions at home. British production was a mere 22,000 a day, compared with the French 100,000, and 250,000 a day from Germany and Austria. Once a barrage began, the expenditure of shells was enormous; and several attacks, like Neuve Chapelle, had to be discontinued because the guns had quite simply run out of ammunition. The reason for the low British production was lack of industrial modernisation: some of the equipment in use was as much as seventy years old. Production with existing plant was not helped by a workforce which seemed deaf to pleas for larger output to ease the problems of their fellow countrymen in the trenches. Scapegoats were sought – it seemed easier to find them than to produce more shells.

After the battle of Neuve Chapelle, Haig visited GHQ to learn what future policy would be. He was horrified to find that the prospects of successful action in France were bleak; many of the available supplies were now being diverted from the French front to the Dardanelles. He commented bitterly in his diary: 'The lack of ammunition is more than serious: it is completely preventing us from profiting from our success by driving back the enemy before he can reorganize and strengthen his position.' As there was no prospect of any immediate action he took a few days' leave, most of which he spent playing golf at Folkestone, firmly refusing to give interviews to any politicians and politely asking to be excused from visiting King George V. His disillusionment with 'higher authority' was completed when he returned to France and learned that, although the battle of Neuve Chapelle had been pronounced a success, the entire credit for it had been attributed to the planners in GHQ. He forebore to ask whether they had also planned that the attackers should run out of ammunition at the critical moment.

A further cause of frustration at the time was the assumption, mainly fostered by the French but with British supporters, that the French were far superior tactically to the British. Where and how this myth had originated was not obvious, in view of the fact that the French had been constantly outfought in the Napoleonic Wars, had not shown up well in the Crimea, and had been trounced by the Germans in 1870. However, the myth survived the French disasters of 1917 and was sufficiently strong in 1939 for the BEF to listen reverently to French forecasts of German tactics and weaknesses. In both wars, of course, the French Army was much larger than the British at the outset, which gave them greater authority in conferences; and in both wars the French had assumed that the British would be capable of little more than defensive, holding operations. However, by spring 1915 both the German and French were taking a revised view of the attacking capabilities of the British: the former were now beginning to put more Germans in the line opposite British units than against French. It was an interesting, though not necessarily welcome, form of flattery, and derived much from the performance of 1 Corps under Haig.

It was becoming clear to many people in England that, of the military leaders thrown up by the war, Haig looked the most competent and promising. Almost as soon as he had arrived back in France there was a steady stream of visitors to his 1st Army Headquarters: it was impossible to avoid them. They included Asquith, Haldane, Curzon (whom he recalled without affection from his India days), and Kitchener, who was now being unfairly blamed in England for the shell shortage. Haig was tactfully polite to all his visitors, appearing to speak frankly and in confidence but in practice saying no more than was necessary.

In April 1915 Ypres became the focus of attention once more. The Germans had discovered that the line north of the town was now held by a newly arrived French Algerian division and French Territorials and decided that these would be suitable recipients for the new weapon of chlorine gas. This should not have come as a surprise to the Allies, for deserters and captured prisoners had for some weeks previously spoken of the presence of metal cylinders in the trenches, and one man had even brought a gas mask with him. The British left flank, which adjoined the French on this section of the line, was held by the Canadian division who were also newcomers to the battlefield. When the greenish yellow cloud drifted over the Algerian lines on 22 April the occupants promptly fled, closely followed by the French Territorials. This was the worst action that they could have taken: had they stayed in position, choking and blinded as they were, some of the effects might have been avoided as the gas drifted over and past them. By running back, they were ensuring that they were still exposed to the drifting clouds. The Canadians did just the opposite. Although they had no idea what this lethal new weapon and its fell effects might be, they stood firm and met with steady rifle fire the oncoming German infantry that followed in its wake. There was now a gap in the Allied line a mile wide, but the German efforts to press forward were half-hearted as they were afraid of the residual effects of their own gas. When the French artillery had ceased firing, it was obvious to 1st Army that urgent action was necessary and reinforcements were sent up.

The new German secret weapon, which had been designed to bring the war to a rapid conclusion, failed at Ypres, but had added another dimension to a battlefield that was already filled with horrors. The Canadians emerged from the battle with the highest credit. One of their number, whose name is unknown, had recognised the smell of chlorine and suggested that pieces of rag soaked in urine would give adequate protection if held against the mouth and nose – chlorine is water-soluble; urine contains ammonia, an alkali. The news travelled like wildfire. Four days later every man in the British Army was equipped with a cloth pad impregnated with a less homely substance than urine. These makeshift devices did duty until a more efficient type of mask was produced: later in the war, when both sides were using gas, usually mustard or phosgene, everyone was well provided with masks. A method then employed was to mix with the gas a substance designed to penetrate the mask and make the recipient sneeze; he would then pull off the mask and receive the lethal effects.

Although the Germans had not made proper use of the opportunity that gas had presented, there now began the long, gruelling campaign which became known as the second battle of Ypres, or just Second Ypres. The British sector here was now held by 2nd Army under the command of General Sir Horace Smith-Dorrien. He had already incurred the displeasure of Sir John French by electing to stand and fight at Le Cateau in the Great Retreat when French would have preferred him to continue the withdrawal. Now he decided that he would exercise his initiative once more, in spite of what French might think, and decided to withdraw slightly from the tip of the salient which was anyway virtually untenable. Having done so, he informed French that he wished to withdraw even further, to a more suitable defensive line. French's reaction was to replace him.

Smith-Dorrien's easily inflamed temper was well known, and the task of conveying French's decision to him was not an enviable one. It was therefore given to Robertson. Robertson, who rose from private to field marshal, spoke several foreign languages impeccably but never lost his original pronunciation of English. The exact words used to Smith-Dorrien are not known, but it is said that they were simply, "Orace, you're thrown!' An alternative version is "Orace, yer for 'ome.' The former would probably have appealed more to Smith-Dorrien as a cavalryman, but whichever it was, the expected outburst failed to materialise.

The dismissal of Smith-Dorrien* was a lucky event for Haig, for it removed one of his principal rivals from possible later competition for the highest post – that of Commander-in-Chief.

---

* Smith-Dorrien was appointed to command the East African Forces who, up to this point, had been unsuccessful against the German forces in the area. He was a popular and successful commander. In 1918 he was appointed Governor of Gibraltar and held the post till 1923. He died in 1930. His wife was an indefatigable war worker who concentrated on helping the wounded.

Haig had already overtaken Plumer, his former instructor at the Staff College, who now took Smith-Dorrien's post and in that capacity proved himself one of the most capable commanders of the war. Although it is difficult to see Smith-Dorrien as a successful C-in-C, there seems no doubt that Plumer would have been well-qualified for that post, as his subsequent career showed.

10

Attrition

IN MAY 1915, a co-ordinated Anglo-French offensive was launched along the whole front. Joffre had planned two principal French attacks – one through Champagne, the other through Artois – and proposed that the British should simultaneously capture Aubers Ridge, on the east side of Neuve Chapelle, in a two-pronged attack. After these successes, the combined front would push on for another five miles.

For this purpose Haig's 1st Army was allotted a further three divisions of Territorials. His own former corps was now in the charge of his friend Lieutenant General C. C. Monro, and included Major General R. C. B. Haking, the expert on Staff Rides, commanding 1st Division. One Corps also included 1st Canadian Division, led by Lieutenant General E. A. H. Alderson, and 47th London Division, who were Territorials. The Indian Corps, which had performed so gallantly in the battle of Neuve Chapelle was reinforced by another of the British Territorial divisions, the 51st (Highland). Four Corps, which was commanded by Lieutenant General Sir H. S. Rawlinson, contained 7th Division under Major General H. de la P. Gough, as well as the 49th (West Riding), another Territorial formation.

The arrival of the reinforcements helped to give 1st Army a huge superiority in numbers in this sector, for it could now muster ten divisions in all: the lines opposite were held by a mere three German divisions. It was assumed to be a situation which could not go wrong. The official history records:

Sir John French had written to the War Office on the 3rd of January 'in view of numbers and German commitments in Russia it seems of the utmost importance that we should strike at the earliest possible moment with all our available strength.' Breaking through, he urged, was chiefly a question of having larger supplies of ammunition, especially of high explosive for destroying the defences, and until the impossibility of breaking through on the Western Front was proved, there could, he said, be no question of making an attempt elsewhere.

However, the official history also records that French 'considered that although a victory of the Franco-British armies in the West might force the Germans back to the Rhine, the ultimate decision of the war would have to be gained on the Eastern front'. The total unsuitability of French as a commander-in-chief must have been obvious to all throughout the whole of 1915, but not until the end of that year was he to be replaced by Haig. The difference between the thinking of the two men was that French was an optimist who believed that victory could be bought immediately by superior numbers who would smash a hole through the enemy defences, whereas Haig had now come to believe that a limited advance, in small stages – which would also be costly in casualties but would at least achieve results – was the only possible formula.

The attack which 1st Army launched on 9 May was a total disaster. It began with a 5 a.m. artillery bombardment by 637 guns which was limited to forty minutes: this was totally inadequate, for it failed to make the necessary gaps in the wire and the six-foot-high German breastwork defences. When the infantry went in at 5.40 a.m. they came up against uncut banks of wire, and devastating fire from machine guns and rifles which had been carefully sited to meet this eventuality. The bodies of the unfortunate infantrymen piled up in heaps. Those who broke through the outer line were confronted with defence in depth. Haig did not at first realise how high the casualties had been and was still organising a fresh attack when he visited the Indian Corps HQ. Here he learned that, fighting with incredible gallantry, the Indians had suffered devastating losses. He postponed the next attack, originally scheduled for midday, until 4 p.m.; once again it failed. At the end of that day the casualties were as high as they had been for the whole of the fighting for Neuve Chapelle in March. Haig thereupon decided there would be no point in trying to renew the attack until suitable artillery cover could be arranged. In the near future that seemed to be impossible.

But that was not the full extent of the disaster for the British. The French had done much better. There had been one essential difference between the French and British attacks: whereas the British had bombarded for only forty minutes, the French had begun with four hours of intensive shellfire. They had then penetrated nearly two miles and captured two thousand prisoners and twelve guns. This had frightened the Germans so much that they had removed the two divisions waiting behind the three divisions on 1st Army's front, and sent them to help hold the French. The effect of this on Anglo-French relations may be imagined.

Sir John French found the comparison between the French and British attacks embarrassing, for the French made no secret of the fact that they thought their allies had let them down badly. Sir John ordered Haig to try again, encouraging him with the information that the Germans had used up all their reserves in combatting the French attack and that, once Haig made a breakthrough, victory was assured. Haig hoped he was correct.

The next attack, around Festubert, was scheduled for 15 May and this time was preceded by a two-day artillery bombardment on which Haig had insisted: it used up 100,000 shells. The assault began at 11.30 p.m. and it was hoped that this night attack – the first to be made by the British in the war – would surprise the enemy. It did. However, the successes achieved were uneven. Although the German line was penetrated in some places, in others it had held firm. The first phase of the battle of Festubert ended at 9 a.m. on 16 May.

On the 17th, after a preliminary bombardment, the attack was resumed. The weather, which at this time of year might have been expected to be improving, instead consisted of continuous, sheeting rain. The battlefield was a chaos of water and mud in which small advances were made with the utmost difficulty. Ten days after the offensive had begun the artillery ammunition had run out, the troops were totally exhausted, and the Germans had had sufficient time and warning to construct efficient defences in depth. British losses were given as 16,648, as against 5000 by the Germans.

As the French were now bogged down in their sector, which lay to the west of Vimy Ridge, Joffre was continually pressing Sir John French to maintain his efforts and make the Germans draw off as many troops as possible from the Vimy region. Sir John passed this on to Haig with the proviso that further attacks should not require more than the minimum of ammunition and troops. Haig allotted this operation to Rawlinson's 4 Corps.

It became the battle of Givenchy and lasted three days, from 15 to 18 June, at a cost of 3811 casualties. It gained nothing. The Western Front then settled down to passive trench warfare until the next large offensive could be mounted with the appropriate artillery barrage and adequate numbers of troops. Meanwhile, because the shell shortage was still continuing, the average number of rounds allotted to each gun was fifteen a day. It was better than four, but a pathetic figure in relation to the apparently unlimited resources of the enemy.

In hindsight, many of the major and minor tactics of the 1914–18 war have come in for severe criticism, much of it directed at Haig. However, by the time Haig became Commander-in-Chief most of the pattern of trench warfare had already been evolved from directives laid down by Sir John French, who, as already described, was mentally incapable of grasping the size of his problems. A directive on how soldiers should conduct themselves in the trenches had been laid down by French in February 1915, and was conveyed in a memorandum signed by Robertson:

1. The Field Marshal Commanding in Chief desires me again to draw attention to the importance of constant activity and of offensive methods in general in dealing with the enemy immediately opposed to us.

2. For reasons known to you, we are for the moment acting on

the defensive so far as operations are concerned, but this should not preclude the planning and making of local attacks on a comparatively small scale, with a view to gaining ground and of taking advantage of any tactical or numerical inferiority on the part of the enemy. Such enterprises are highly valuable and should receive every encouragement, since they relieve monotony and improve the moral* of our own troops, while they have a corresponding detrimental effect on the moral of the enemy's troops and lead in a variety of ways to their exhaustion and general disquiet.

3. Further, as you are well aware, enterprises of this nature constitute the most effective form of defence, since by throwing upon the enemy anxiety for his own security they help to relieve our own troops from the wearying and demoralising effects produced by unexpected attacks on the part of the enemy.

He continued by explaining that such raids should not be aimless 'but methodically initiated' and must 'invariably be well thought out beforehand, and careful preliminary arrangements made for their execution'.

The efforts of muddled thinkers like French and Foch to stimulate morale meant in practice that initiative was strongly discouraged. Although many of the recruits of 1914 and 1915 were highly intelligent men, it was assumed they should be treated in much the same way as their soldier predecessors of fifty years earlier who had to be taught which was their right and which their left foot before drill could begin.

At this time Robertson was Chief of the General Staff in the BEF, and French's memorandum was circulated to staff officers. They would probably have been unwise to leave their comfortable billets and explain it to men in waterlogged trenches, in which they were constantly trying to shore up collapsing parapets, for it was the sort of directive which produced vitriolic hatred of all senior commanders and their representatives, the staff officers.

* That generation used 'moral', where later the word 'morale' would be appropriate.

Sir John French appears to have imagined that the British troops were sitting in warm shellproof dugouts, idling away the time by playing cards, and totally lacking all initiative. He had no conception of the fact that the weather often seemed a worse enemy than the Germans, and that to men in the front line the Germans were regarded more favourably than their own staff. The enthusiasm for aggressive patrols was strongly favoured by battalion commanders who never took part themselves, but even they had second thoughts when they realised that such activity led to a steady drain on their best and most experienced officers and NCOs.

The incessant demands by higher authority for an aggressive raiding and patrolling policy became perhaps the most detested feature of British trench life. The chance of raids of half a dozen men achieving a favourable alteration in the line were clearly nil. The French took a more realistic view and saved their men for the big attacks when men could gain ground or be killed. The French held a much longer sector of the line than the British, who held only seventy miles out of three hundred, and the French could, therefore, not afford the inevitable losses brought about by perpetual minor trench warfare. Later in the war, trench raiding fell into abeyance in some sectors, particularly when the French and Germans confronted each other in areas of no special tactical importance. The situation was summed up by Colonel Howard Green, drawing on his experience of the fighting at this period:

> The French, unless an offensive was actually in progress, had a sensible 'live and let live' policy. Not so the British . . . they would go all out to gain the upper hand. Regular shellings and machine-gunning of the German line, mining, fighting patrols to dominate No Man's Land, and trench raids all started. While showing the right offensive spirit, this policy was not entirely wise. The Germans generally held the advantage of ground, they had heavier guns, and were no mean trench fighters themselves. On balance the British policy probably cost more lives than it gained advantage.

However, as so frequently happens, once a routine has been adopted it continues whether it is doing good or harm. Sometimes a bad custom continues because it has become an attitude of mind.

But if there were routines which were of doubtful value in the trenches, there were even more damaging ones at the highest levels of government at home. The shortage of shells was a well-known topic in Whitehall, but finding a solution to the problem of quicker and greater production seemed to produce little but arguments about alternative methods. At the same time there was much criticism of Kitchener for his performance as Secretary of State. Sir John French's private life was so scandalous that there were many who felt that a man with his record was unfitted for the post of Commander-in-Chief.* But he was by no means alone in having scandals in the background of his so-called private life, for even the Prime Minister, Asquith, was vulnerable to this charge.† None of this would, however, have been of importance if all the ministers had seemed able to forget their personal animosities and work whole-heartedly to increase production.

Although sporadic fighting continued during the summer of 1915, it was widely recognized that Allied progress could only be made by a large, combined offensive in the autumn. The French felt that this should be in the area around La Bassée and Loos. Haig had doubts about the suitability of this sector, but was aware that Joffre had persuaded Sir John French that this was the most appropriate area. Haig reluctantly began making plans for 1st Army's offensive. He knew better than anyone how quickly 'the fog of war' can descend on to a battlefield. At Neuve Chapelle he had been so frustrated by the slowness of communications from the front line that he had visited divisional and brigade headquarters and tried to assess battlefield intelligence there. And these had been limited-area attacks: he could imagine only too well the confusion that would develop in what was to be the biggest battle of the Western Front so far.

* It included an affair with the wife of an ambassador.
† Asquith had an affair with a woman half his age, and used to write love letters to her during Cabinet Meetings.

Charteris records that the ever-industrious Haig now decided to improve his knowledge of the French language. Haig suspected that some of the translations made by interpreters were by no means faultless, and it would be as well if he had a reasonably sound idea of what was being said by the French. 'He therefore enlisted the services of his French liaison officer and for two hours a day sat down studying French – working out exercises and compositions, much in the same way as any public schoolboy works at the language at home. He made rapid progress and at the end of the summer was able to converse fluently.' Charteris was surprised to find that Haig now became able to 'express himself far more coherently and articulately than in English'. When speaking in his native tongue Haig would sometimes leave a sentence unfinished, expecting his listeners to supply the remainder for themselves: another of his mannerisms was to omit the verb. 'In consequence,' said Charteris, 'only staff officers who thoroughly understood their Commander's mind could grasp his meaning from the spoken word.' Even Charteris, though, conceded that Haig's written expression was impeccable.

An alliance which few would have thought likely was forged at this time. Lord Northcliffe, founder of the *Daily Mail* and *Daily Mirror*, owner of the *Evening News* and *Times*, among many other successful enterprises, visited Haig at 1st Army Headquarters. Northcliffe took an immediate liking to his host and later said, 'That is the one indispensable man in Britain today.' Having made up his mind, he swung the weight of his considerable influence behind Haig, which proved a useful asset when his protégé was later caught up in political conflict.

The lull in the fighting during the summer after the failure of the Festubert and Givenchy attacks gave Haig the opportunity to introduce a reform which he knew would bring great benefits in the future. Independently of the service operating from Sir John French's GHQ, he established his own close links with the French intelligence service, and set up a special intelligence unit of his own for studying the organisation and resources of the German Army.

He read all the papers which came before him, paying particular attention to those relating to court martials in which the death sentence had been recommended. Not all sentences of death were carried out, but many were 'for the sake of example'. The phrase 'shell shock' had not been invented in 1915, and if a dazed man picked himself up and walked towards the rear rather than forward he might be unlucky enough to be accused of cowardice in the face of the enemy. Haig could not be aware of the background to each offence of desertion or cowardice; all he could do was to study the papers relating to the court martial and assure himself that the correct procedure had been meticulously followed. Secrett said that Haig was more likely to mitigate sentences for other ranks than for officers.

Every day he took two hours physical exercise to keep his body in trim. According to Charteris he was 'obsessed with dislike – almost amounting to horror – of the approach of old age and infirmity. Special diets appealed strongly to him and he would devote himself assiduously to every one which attracted his notice. "Sour milk", "whole meal bread" and "Sanatogen", each in turn had its trial.' Writing in 1928, Charteris found Haig's obsession with diet somewhat bizarre. No doubt he would have been incredulous if someone had told him that by the end of the century most of the more advanced Western countries would share Haig's food obsessions. Haig's 'sour milk', for example, was doubtless yoghourt, and the fact that Haig's health stood up to the strain of active service commands at the highest level for four years suggests that his dietary fads cannot have been very misguided.

Haig's visitors in the summer of 1915, who included Asquith and Kitchener, seem to have assumed that if he was an authority on military strategy in France he must be equally knowledgeable about such matters elsewhere. Most of them had some special axe to grind, and hoped that by seeking Haig's advice they would also be able to enlist his support. He was therefore asked whether he thought it advisable that the Dardanelles should be more strongly reinforced and whether alternative landings should be investigated. Invariably he showed polite interest, but always emphasised that the campaign on the Western Front was the top priority and that no ventures should be attempted which might weaken the British Army in that area.

One of the most productive discussions seems to have been with Kitchener, who was not finding his Cabinet responsibilities an easy burden to bear. In the past he had become accustomed to being the man whose word was law; in 1915 he found he was but one of many highly competitive equals. Admiral 'Jackie' Fisher believed that a successful attack on Germany could be made via the Baltic, whereas Lloyd George thought that Syria would be a more suitable area. Sir John French had been subordinate to Kitchener in the Boer War and had not impressed. French resented the fact that Kitchener still seemed to regard him as a junior officer, and in newspaper interviews had covertly encouraged the press to criticise Kitchener; Kitchener had been aware of this but had disdained to use similar tactics. Haig agreed that Kitchener had been right in his attitude to French, but hoped that the two might somehow be reconciled. In his diary he recorded that Kitchener had told him he was 'ready to do anything – even to blacken French's boots to obtain such an agreement'.

Haig took Kitchener on a conducted tour of the front-line trenches and explained the opinions he had formed of the tactics necessary to win this war, which was so different from anything either of them had previously experienced. There was no scope for manoeuvre or finesse: the only possible tactic was that of a sledge-hammer directed at a limited objective. To effect an adequate breach in the German lines, Haig thought now, at least half a million men and one thousand guns would be necessary. Kitchener accepted Haig's calculations without demur. Neither man could guess at this stage that the war of attrition would involve hurling in ever vaster quantities of men and shells to gain merely local advantages. On this 1915 tour it looked as if half a million men might produce a decisive breakthrough which could be turned into victory: eighteen months later, half a million men had become casualties to gain seven miles, and the end of the war was as elusive as ever.

Haig disagreed with Kitchener over manpower. He believed that conscription should be introduced immediately, while

Kitchener felt that voluntary recruiting was working well, producing all the men who could be equipped and trained at that time. Unfortunately, as Haig pointed out, voluntary recruitment was taking the best of the available manpower and wasting leadership and other potential. Moreover, the supply of volunteers could not continue much longer, and then conscripts would be brought in without a suitable proportion of highly motivated potential leaders. At the conclusion of their series of talks Kitchener was giving Haig full backing, even over conscription. However, he was not sure that he could influence his Cabinet colleagues to do the same.

Although the science (or art) of public relations was as yet unnamed, Haig was well aware of what was required in that field if the Army was to gain the whole-hearted support it required. Although he must have found the stream of visitors a time-consuming distraction, he made every effort to see that they were properly received. Among them, according to Charteris, was Ben Tillet, the leader of the successful dock strikes of 1889 and 1911, and founder of the Dockers' Union which later developed into the Transport and General Workers' Union. He was accompanied by Monsieur Bruhl, a French socialist of similar standing. Haig received the pair, both of whom made no secret of the fact that they detested militarism and the upper classes, and gave them facilities to move around freely and meet whomsoever they pleased. He gave specific instructions that when they were talking to men they must do so without officers being present. This reception so impressed them that they both revised their attitudes towards the war effort: Tillet, who became Labour MP for Salford in 1917, became an unswerving supporter of the Army and, in consequence, of Haig.

Haig knew that the Army needed all the backing it could get, and could be defeated by apathy and even hostility in Britain. Within his abilities he did his best to obtain that backing, on and off the battlefield. He was no Montgomery, who could gather a few hundred men around him and explain his war aims, but he could speak from experience. He knew what it was like to be under fire and face defeat. He knew that bullets do not discriminate and that death is no respecter of rank or class; he never used the prevalent, traditional expression, 'officers and men' in his orders, always preferring the term 'all ranks'.

At all levels and on all occasions Haig needed to call on the iron self-discipline he had developed for himself. Often he had to suffer fools gladly, and to listen patiently to obvious nonsense. Lloyd George had insisted on the formation of a Munitions Committee, and one of its first tasks was to visit the Army in the field – that is, Haig's headquarters – and examine the situation from there. One of its members found the shell shortage difficult to understand because he believed the enemy was still using solid cannonballs, which he thought should be easy enough to manufacture. There were other examples of naïveté which were nearly as bad. But they were the Munitions Committee and, as such, had the power to resolve the problem of the German gunners having many more shells at their disposal than the British.

Although the French and British higher command did not see eye to eye on everything, both were agreed that there must be a major battle before the winter of 1915 set in. The most appropriate month would be September, which should ensure reasonable weather and allow time for any large-scale breakthrough to be properly exploited. At whatever cost, this battle must produce a decisive victory. The losses and gains of the earlier months of the year, which had been costly in casualties, seemed to have ended in a stalemate which suited the Germans but not the Allies. A victory was urgently needed to boost morale, not merely in France but on the other fronts too. The hope that Russia would draw off large numbers of German troops and kill them in the East had proved an illusion. It was the Russians who were suffering on the Eastern Front and the Germans, far from being weakened, were having a succession of victories. Italy had come in on the Allied side, but there was nothing to show for it except two defeats. The Middle East presented a gloomy story: the Turks seemed to be fully capable of holding their own, and the British landings in the Dardanelles, from which so much had been hoped, were clearly a costly failure. The situation in the Balkans was depressing: there were rumours that Bulgaria would soon throw in its lot with

Germany and Austria and enable them to crush Serbia, while any hope of the Allies making a successful intervention in that area seemed to have been killed off by the Dardanelles setbacks.

Joffre, full of confidence in his own judgement, decided that the attack in France should be on a broad front. The major blow would be struck by the French near Reims, with thirty-four infantry and eight cavalry divisions from their 2nd and 4th Armies. At the same time, the French 10th Army, using seventeen infantry and two cavalry divisions, would attack further north in co-ordination with Haig's 1st Army, which would deploy six infantry divisions, with 114 heavy guns – 1st Army's artillery strength was approximately one-tenth of that available to the French in each of their sectors. Haig and d'Urbal, commanding the French 10th Army, would both be under the overall command of Foch. In reserve were three infantry and two cavalry divisions; these were to exploit the expected breakthrough. The feature of the battle most likely to produce the expected break-through was the use of gas, which on this occasion would come as a surprise to the Germans.

With over sixty French divisions being used in the broad assault, in conjunction with a mere six British, it is not surprising that the French thought they should have the first and last word about tactics. Nevertheless there was no overall Commander-in-Chief – a post which Joffre tended to assume – and therefore there was considerable discussion over the organisation of the attack. In order for the French blow in the Reims area to be as weighty as possible, Britain had taken over the sector of the French line which had previously been held by the French 2nd Army. It was now being manned by the British 3rd Army, commanded by Monro.

Joffre wanted Haig's 1st Army to attack in the area south of Givenchy along a thirty-kilometre front; their objective was a line south of the La Bassée canal down through Loos to whatever point the French 10th Army had reached after starting from the Grenay area. Tenth Army were planning to occupy the Vimy plateau eventually.

Haig found much that was unsatisfactory in the arrangements made for 1st Army. He felt that Sir John French had been

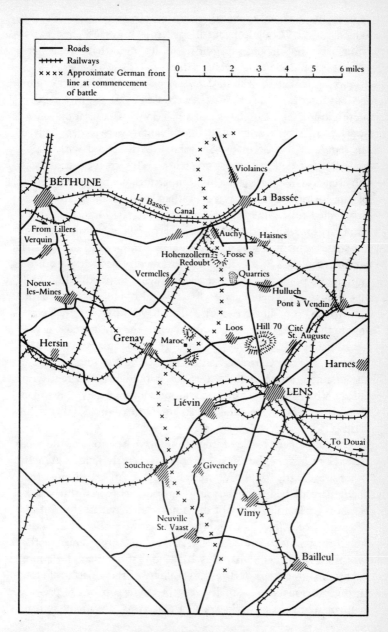

Roads
Railways
× × × × **Approximate German front line at commencement of battle**

0 1 2 3 4 5 6 miles

Violaines

BÉTHUNE

La Bassée Canal

La Bassée

From Lillers
Verquin

Auchy   Haisnes

Hohenzollern   Fosse 8
Redoubt

Vermelles   Quarries

Noeux-les-Mines   Hulluch

Pont à Vendin

Loos   Hill 70   Cité
St. Auguste

Grenay   Maroc

Hersin   Harnes

LENS

Liévin

To Douai

Souchez   Givenchy

Vimy

Neuville
St. Vaast

Bailleul

THE BATTLE OF LOOS

extremely weak in agreeing to an infantry assault in this area which was, as Rawlinson put it, 'as flat as my hand', and extraordinarily foolish and misguided in his idea that the general reserve should be held well to the rear. Haig's experience of reserves was that they should always be close at hand to exploit any advantage, or the opportunity would be lost again while they were closing up. But his main objection was to mounting an attack at all in an area in which the advantages lay so decisively in the hands of the Germans. Sir John French agreed with Haig's view but felt that it was not possible to refuse co-operation with the French while Joffre, like his compatriots, considered that most of the British troubles were of their own making: they had despatched four vitally needed divisions to the Dardanelles on a futile venture and had wasted much artillery and ammunition in supporting them. Kitchener shared Haig's misgivings but felt that a military success at this time was so urgently necessary from the diplomatic point of view that all risks were justified. Meanwhile five thousand gas cylinders, each weighing 140 lb, were taken into the British front-line trenches. All that was now required was a favourable wind on 25 September, when the great attack was to be launched. In the event Joffre's grandiose plans were to be doomed, for the Germans had no intention of giving ground in the Champagne sector and 10th Army would be no more successful at Vimy than it had been in previous attacks. The main strength of the German defence, therefore, would fall on the British.

The subsequent battle of Loos could have been one of the most decisive in history, but in the event was a costly failure. As with other great battles on the Western Front, the Allies had more than their share of bad luck; but any battle which costs nearly sixty thousand casualties, many of them in the first twenty-four hours, for a gain of a few thousand yards, must be reckoned a disaster unless the territory gained is of vital strategic importance. Here it was not. However, what this battle did show was the almost superhuman courage and resourcefulness of the British infantry. In the previous year a small hard core made up of the pre-war regular Army had checked a German army advancing with a massive superiority of men and artillery. In 1915, its successors were being asked to fight back and eject the Germans from well-prepared positions, and to do so without matching artillery support. The Allies had to accept the fact either that the Germans would not leave until they had imposed a crushing peace treaty or that they would have to be driven out at the point of the bayonet. As the idea of admitting defeat was unthinkable, Britain, short of artillery as it was, had no alternative to winning the war with flesh and blood alone. Even so, until September 1915 nobody realised how great the cost of that would be. The battles of the Somme, Vimy Ridge, Arras and Passchendaele lay in the future: Loos was the first indication of the huge price which would have to be paid.

If one accepts the fact that the German Army had to be beaten whatever the cost, an intriguing question arises: could anyone but Haig have provided the necessary leadership? Critics of his part in the battle of Loos suggest that he was an incompetent who chose to fight a battle over unsuitable territory and was indifferent to the pain and loss it caused. That view is totally mistaken. In reality, as Haig's correspondence with Robertson reveals, he was only too well aware of the problems the Army faced at Loos. He knew that the ground over which the attack was to be launched was dangerously unsuitable. In addition to long, open slopes on which advancing infantry would be mown down by German machine guns, there were slag heaps, cottages and mine workings. The soil was chalk, which made digging in extremely difficult, while rain made the surface so slippery that at times it was almost impossible for a man to keep his balance.

At 5.50 a.m. on the morning of 25 September the gas cylinders of Haig's 1st Army were turned on, releasing the first wave of 150 tons of chlorine gas. For this to be fully effective there should have been a suitable breeze and double the quantity. On the right the gas drifted over the German lines, where it killed men and rusted rifles and artillery breech blocks, making them unusable; on the left it drifted back over the British lines. The British troops had gas masks, but did not expect to have to use them until they reached the German lines; the Germans were unprepared for the gas, but the survivors knew that an infantry attack would follow and so they had their machine guns ready.

At 6.30 a.m. the British artillery barrage lifted and the infantry went forward. No Man's Land varied in width from one hundred to four hundred yards; in addition to the hazards of advancing over open ground, some of the wire had remained uncut by the artillery barrage. To the disgust of the British troops who found themselves confronted by this problem, their wire-cutters were unequal to the task; those who survived the deadly German machine gun fire were either pinned down or left hoping that someone would find a gap nearby.

Nevertheless Loos and a fortified hillock known as the Hohenzollern Redoubt were quickly captured, and Hulluch was reached. The cost in lives had been enormous, many of them in the new Kitchener divisions – from which little had been expected but which, in the event, had proved outstanding. But the 7th King's Own Scottish Borderers in 15th (Scottish) Division had been virtually wiped out. The 6th KOSB, in 9th Division, lost all twenty of their officers, all but one of their NCOs and six hundred men. Many other regiments had similar devastating casualties and great stories of heroism, not least the Highland Light Infantry, the Devons, the South Staffords, the Warwickshires and the Royal Welch Fusiliers.

The figures given by the official history for 1st Army's casualties at the end of the first day were 470 officers and fifteen thousand soldiers. These were, in fact, ten thousand below the overall real figure. The bitter tragedy of it all was that much of the sacrifice had been in vain because the reserves who could have pressed home and consolidated the advantages gained were nowhere to be seen. By the time they arrived the Germans had recovered and reorganised their defence.

There can be no doubt that Sir John French was to blame for this disaster. Haig was so confident that the general reserve would be arriving quickly on the scene that he had thrown all his own reserves into the attack. French's view was that he needed time to assess the battle before bringing forward the inexperienced 11 Corps, which had scarcely been in France for a fortnight. This may well have been a wise and prudent course in relation to 11 Corps, but it should not have prevented him deploying troops from other parts of the front and using them to continue the momentum in the areas where there had been a breakthrough. Eleventh Corps could have been used to take their former places.

Eleventh Corps was commanded by Lieutenant General R. C. B. Haking, who had at his immediate disposal the Guards Division, and 21st and 24th Divisions. Later he would be able to use 12th (Eastern) Division and 46th (North Midland) Division, but by then 21st and 24th would have been destroyed. On the battlefield, Haking was considerably less effective than he had been when organising Staff Rides. In the battle for Aubers Ridge the previous May he had commanded a division, but had lost most of it by recklessness. This had given him a reputation for fearlessness and forcefulness, but had also convinced Sir John French that Haking had not yet fully appreciated the killing power of modern defence weapons. With the best possible motives French had wished to hold back 11 Corps until they could be used to good effect with minimum casualties; in the event, this delay meant that they were plunged into the battle when the Germans had recovered. They were therefore given the impossible task of advancing through uncut wire and without an artillery barrage.

The experiences of 21st and 24th Divisions were both horrific and bizarre. When they were at first ordered forward they were expected to advance through narrow roads congested with traffic. One brigade was stopped by a military policeman on the outskirts of Béthune because its commander had no pass to enter the area. Other units were also delayed by over-officious MPs. Rain made the tracks slippery and reduced visibility. When they arrived on the battlefield on the morning of the 26th, after marching by night with inadequate rest and limited food, they were deployed without benefit of staff officers who knew the area or large-scale maps; some features, such as Hill 70, were not even marked on any map. Even if they had had the advantage of aerial photographs, however, they could have had no idea that the previous night the Germans had worked feverishly to construct a trench system protected by wire four feet high and twenty feet deep.

The Germans were very active that night, though not always successfully. A party of three hundred, hoping to recover three guns abandoned the day before, advanced towards the British lines and called out, 'Don't shoot, we are the Welsh coming back.' Unknown to them, the trench was held by the 1st Battalion the South Wales Borderers, who listened to the German version of their native tongue and held their fire until every German was in their sights. Very few of them survived.

The battle of Loos may have been a disaster, but ironically it also came very close to being a devastating Allied victory. Major General Richard Hilton, who fought in it as a Forward Observation Officer, subsequently wrote:

A great deal of nonsense has been written about Loos. The real tragedy of that battle was its nearness to complete success. Most of us who reached the crest of Hill 70 and survived were firmly convinced that we had broken through on that Sunday, 25th September 1915. There seemed to be nothing ahead of us but an unoccupied and incomplete trench system. The only two things that prevented our advancing into the suburbs of Loos were, firstly the exhaustion of the 'Jocks' themselves (for they had undergone a bellyful of marching and fighting that day) and secondly the flanking fire of numerous German machine-guns, which swept that bare hill from some factory buildings in Cité St Auguste [a suburb of the town of Lens] to the south of us.

All we needed was more artillery ammunition to blast those clearly located machine-guns, and some fresh infantry to take over from the weary and depleted 'Jocks'. But, alas, neither ammunition nor reinforcements were immediately available, and the great opportunity passed.

Sir John French lacked the steeliness of Haig, who would have put 21st and 24th Divisions into the fight earlier, even though he knew their casualty rates would have been enormous – but in so doing he would have probably achieved victory at far less than its ultimate cost. On 26 September, when French should have been actively considering what options he had left, he was visiting a dressing station at Noeux-les-Mines and talking to the wounded and dying. Haig would not have done that – not because he lacked compassion, but because he realised that unless a commander-in-chief was in a position to take instant decisions about the battle which was raging, the dressing stations were likely to become even fuller than they were already.

In contrast to Sir John, Joffre was so closely in touch with events in the French 10th Army that on the morning of the 26th he had called off the French offensive because their artillery had failed to neutralise the German guns on Vimy Ridge. Joffre, in what must have been one of the most treacherous acts ever perpetrated by an ally, gave strict instructions that no word of the cancellation must reach the ears of the British. Nevertheless, bad news travels fast, and by the evening of the same day the British knew. They now had to endure the full strength of the German resistance to their offensive.

The battle of Loos dragged on through October and into November, with Sir John French urging that preparations should be made for a final assault before the winter. However, by 4 November Haig told him that a further assault at this stage had been made impossible by the combination of heavy rain and constant enemy shelling. And so, as the bad weather was now beginning to set in, the Commander-in-Chief cancelled plans for a further offensive.

Sir John French's handling of the battle of Loos finished his active military career and caused him to be branded as a failure. It is, however, worth noting that if 1st Army had been a bit luckier with the weather, and the gas attack had been 100 per cent successful, as it might have been, he would have been considered one of the most brilliant British generals of all time. The official history considered that Haig enhanced his reputation at Loos but that Sir John French had made a series of incorrect decisions. The British casualties between 25 September and 16 October (three weeks before the end of the battle) amounted to 2013 officers and 48,367 other ranks. Eight hundred officers and fifteen thousand men were killed or missing. 'Such was the tremendous sacrifice made by all ranks to support fully and loyally our French Ally,

and the price paid in flesh and blood for unpreparedness for war,'
wrote the official historian. The German losses for that period
were less than half those of the British – 441 officers and 19,395
other ranks. An accurate figure for German losses was always
difficult to ascertain, but the total German casualties on the
Western Front between August 1914 and December 1915 were
given as 2,597,052.

The high casualty figures for the British were partly the result
of the French failure to draw off German divisions from the Loos
area. Had the French made the expected headway in the Champagne region, or threatened to take Vimy Ridge, there is no doubt
that the Germans would have rushed up reinforcements to both of
those areas, and some of those troops would have come from
around Loos. The German reinforcements *might* have checked the
French attack, but their departure from the area opposite 1st
Army would have made the British task infinitely easier. Thus, if
one is looking for a scapegoat for the failure to make the breakthrough at Loos, attention should not necessarily be focused
entirely on Sir John French: Joffre too must be in the dock. This is
not only because he withheld vital information on the second day
of the battle, but also because his whole concept was based on false
hopes. Before launching the French armies into the attack in the
Champagne area, he should have made sure that they could make
genuine progress.

When the battle was four days old, Haig wrote to Kitchener.
Once again this seems to be another example of Haig going
behind the back of his immediate superior with a view to
enhancing his own prospects of promotion, but one may say here
that the fault – if it was one – was not on his side only. Like Sir
Evelyn Wood, to whom Haig sent unofficial reports in the Boer
War, Kitchener wished to see the battle from a slightly different
viewpoint than that of the Commander-in-Chief's reports. He
had therefore instructed Haig to let him know if he had any
problems or doubts. He may have done the same with Plumer, in
charge of 2nd Army, and Haking, commanding 1st Division, but,
if so, they left no record.

My dear Lord Kitchener,

You will doubtless recall how earnestly I pressed you to ensure an adequate Reserve being close in rear of my attacking division, and under my orders. It may interest you to know what happened. No Reserve was placed under me. My attack, as has been reported, was a complete success. The enemy had no troops in his second line, which some of my plucky fellows reached and entered without opposition. Prisoners state the enemy was so hard put to it for troops to stem our advance that the officers' servants, fatigue men, etc. in Lens were pushed forward to hold their 2nd line to the east of Loos and Hill 70.

The two Reserve Divisions (under C-in-C's orders) were directed to join me as soon as the success of First Army was known at GHQ. They came in as quick as they could, poor fellows, but only crossed our old trench line with their heads at 6 p.m. We had captured Loos 12 hours previously, and reserves should have been at hand *then*. This, you will remember, I had requested should be arranged by GHQ, and Robertson quite concurred in my views and wished to put the Reserve Divisions under me, but was not allowed.

The final result is that the enemy has been allowed time in which to bring up troops and strengthen his second line, and *probably* to construct a third line in the direction in which we are heading, viz, Pont-à-Vendin.

I have now been given some fresh divisions, and am busy planning an attack to break the enemy's second line. But the element of surprise has gone, and our task will be a difficult one.

I think it right that you should know how the lessons which have been learnt in this war at such cost have been neglected. We *were* in a position to make this the turning point in the war, and I still hope may do so, but naturally I feel annoyed at the lost opportunity.

We were all pleased to receive your kind telegram [presumably one of good wishes on the eve of the battle], and I am, yours very truly

D. Haig

The responsibility for the failure to turn the battle of Loos into a decisive victory is here placed firmly at the door of Sir John French, who had misread the situation and been quite unable to cope with a development which required a fast and flexible thinker. Joffre, with his grandiose plans based on incomplete intelligence, is excused responsibility, and there is no mention of his deplorable behaviour after the failure of the French 10th Army, though by this time Haig must have known exactly what had happened. Nor did he comment on the fact that, even though the reserves were still under-trained by regular Army standards, they had performed magnificently at Loos under impossible conditions. Haig had undoubtedly lost any confidence in Sir John French which he might ever have possessed, and realised that others had as well. In October 1915 he wrote in his diary:

> I had been more than loyal to French and did my best to stop all criticism of him or his methods. Now at last, in view of what had happened in the recent battle over the reserves, I had come to the conclusion that it was not fair to the Empire to retain French in command. Moreover, none of my officers commanding corps had a high opinion of Sir John's ability or military views: in fact, they *had no confidence in him*.

It would not be correct to say that Haig was condemning his Commander-in-Chief solely because he wanted his job. He was condemning Sir John French because he believed he was hopelessly unsuited for his task.

On 9 October, Haig's old friend Haldane arrived at 1st Army's headquarters with a brief from the Cabinet to find out why the battle had been lost and why it had been so appallingly costly in lives. Haig added several more details to the comments he had made in the letter to Kitchener. He emphasised the fact that the two most inexperienced divisions had been allotted the task of making the breakthrough; they had arrived on the battlefield tired and hungry, which would not have happened if they had been brought forward earlier. Haig considered that, in place of 21st and 24th Divisions, the 12th and the Guards Divisions should have been used.

By this time the suitability of Sir John French as Commander-in-Chief was being widely debated. He was sixty-three, and the strain of warfare and of his complicated private life had taken their toll: his heart was beginning to give him trouble. He had spent over a year fighting an ingenious, determined and well-trained enemy, and in doing so had been handicapped by shortage of that vital component of modern war: artillery. At the same time he had had to co-ordinate his efforts with an ally who was unpredictable and not always co-operative.

Perhaps the best indication of his unsuitability came from 'Wully' Robertson. Robertson had all the realism which came from having risen from the ranks, and was also the most intelligent and best-informed of the senior officers in spite of being self-educated. He did not want the post of C-in-C BEF himself, and was well content with the much less prestigious post of Chief of the General Staff. But by November Robertson was firmly convinced that French should go. Soon afterwards the Cabinet came to the same conclusion, and on 25 November Robertson was the first to tell Haig of their decision.

A month after the battle of Loos had ended the Cabinet sent out Viscount Esher to tell French he was being relieved of his command. In order to soften the blow – if blow it was – it was suggested that he should resign voluntarily. He would then be rewarded with a viscountcy and be appointed Field Marshal Commanding-in-Chief, Home Forces.

On 17 December he resigned his post as Commander-in-Chief, BEF, but from then onwards he began to brood quietly over what might have been and whether in fact he had been the victim of a treacherous plot. If the latter, he decided, it must all derive from Haig, abetted by Kitchener. Kitchener was drowned in 1916 when his ship was torpedoed on a mission to Russia, but this did not prevent French attacking him even as late as 1919. Six years later, French himself died. He was not, as has been seen, equal to the task he was given in 1914, but he was kind, courageous and generous. It has been said of him, perhaps fairly, that he was born a century too late. French might have been the character so neatly described in Siegfried Sassoon's poem 'The General':

Good morning; good morning! the General said
When we met him last week on our way to the line.
Now the soldiers he smiled at are most of 'em dead
And we're cursing his staff for incompetent swine.
'He's a cheery old card,' grunted Harry to Jack
As they slogged up to Arras with rifle and pack . . .
But he did for them both by his plan of attack.

The question of who should be the next Commander-in-Chief, BEF, had been on the minds of the Cabinet for several months, for doubts about French had already been openly expressed even before Loos. There were only two candidates with adequate rank and experience: one was Haig, the other Robertson. In hindsight, it might be felt that Allenby and Plumer should also have been in contention, but by now they were too far behind in seniority. Haig was clearly the stronger candidate and on 8 December Asquith wrote and offered him the post: he took over officially on the 19th.

Robertson, for his part, became Chief of the Imperial General Staff in London; it was a post which suited him well, and he remained fiercely loyal to Haig. Sir Launcelot Kiggell, who spent his entire military life in staff appointments of one sort or another, became Chief of the General Staff in the BEF – perhaps the least satisfactory change in the general shuffle which took place at this time. French's former Directors of Operations and of Intelligence, Brigadier Generals F. B. Maurice and G. M. W. Macdonogh, departed for London to become Director of Military Operations (DMO) and Director of Military Intelligence (DMI) at the War Office and were replaced by Brigadier Generals J. H. Davidson and J. Charteris. Lieutenant General Sir Charles Monro now took over 1st Army; Plumer was commanding 2nd Army and Allenby 3rd. Haig would have preferred Rawlinson to take over 1st Army, but had been over-ruled by Kitchener; however, Rawlinson commanded it temporarily while Monro was sent to the Dardanelles to make a report on the situation there. After these changes, and the arrival of fresh troops on the Western Front, the outlook for 1916 seemed more promising.

II

Commander-in-Chief

WHEN HAIG TOOK over as Commander-in-Chief of the BEF in December 1915, he became the commander of the largest expeditionary force that Britain had ever put into the field. At the outset he was commanding three armies, but in the near future that number would be increased to five. In 1914, when he had commanded a corps, he had known at first hand what its various components were doing, but from 1916 onwards his contacts would inevitably be limited to the upper ranks of his vast command. He would, for the first time in his life, be completely reliant on the opinions of others, for he would have no time or opportunity to make his own assessments.

Thus far the war in France had been mainly a holding operation, checking the German tide and looking for opportunities of making a breakthrough. This latter rôle had culminated in the disappointment of Loos. Within the next year Haig would need to direct the Army so that it would be able not only to counter any threat from the enemy but at the same time prepare to make a decisive thrust of its own. By now the expectation, both in the Army and at home, that the war would be over first by Christmas 1914, then by Christmas 1915, had disappeared; in its place was the realisation that Britain must now brace itself for a long, hard struggle. Optimism had been replaced by realism on all fronts: there was little good news, but plenty of bad. Naturally enough, Haig would welcome any event which drew German troops out of France to fight elsewhere, but not if these other fronts were also going to make demands on his own Army.

Nothing of lasting good could be attempted in France, however, until the settling of what had come to be called the Munitions Crisis. Progress had been made in the supply of ammunition and arms to the British front, but there was still a long way to go. In order to co-ordinate and assist the factories in manufacturing ammunition of various kinds a Ministry of Munitions had been formed, but it was soon clear that producing enough war material was going to be a lengthier and more complicated process than turning civilians into soldiers. Demand for guns and shells was going to be vastly in excess of any quantity which had been remotely contemplated before 1914. The estimated time required to produce the quantity of arms which would be anywhere near what was needed was two years, and that estimate did not allow for any unexpected delays. Unless production was properly co-ordinated there would be shells without guns, guns without shells, or soldiers without either.

One of Haig's first and most welcome duties in January 1916 was to receive a visit from Lloyd George and Bonar Law, both future Prime Ministers, to discuss the whole problem of munitions supply. It was Haig's first meeting with Lloyd George, and he made a shrewd comment in his diary: 'Mr Bonar Law strikes me as being a straightforward honourable man. Lloyd George seems to be astute and cunning with much energy and push; but I should think shifty and unreliable.' He was obviously going to dislike Lloyd George, but realised he would have to work with him. Happily this initial antipathy was not reciprocated by Lloyd George, who subsequently commented: 'Things are much more businesslike than in French's time. There is a new spirit. Haig seems very keen on his job and has a fine staff.' Lloyd George had taken the opportunity to take his two sons with him on the trip and was very favourably impressed by the kindness that Haig showed to them. In writing to Haig to thank him for receiving his party, Lloyd George added: 'The visit, if you will permit me to say so, left in my mind a great impression of things being *gripped* in that sphere of operations; and whether we win through or whether we fail, I have a feeling that everything which the assiduity, the care, and the trained thought of a great soldier can accomplish, is being done.'

'Whether we win through or whether we fail' was not defeatism on Lloyd George's part, but realism. He knew that ultimate victory was not by any means certain, and Haig held the same view. In retrospect it is often assumed that all the First World War leaders confidently anticipated victory once a few minor details were settled. That view is totally mistaken. In the early part of 1916 the Allied leaders had no illusions about the difficulty of the task ahead of them. The Germans still had the initiative on all fronts, and they too had their plans on how the war should and could be won. The problem now confronting the Allied strategists, of whom Haig was the foremost, was no different from the one they had faced in 1914 and 1915: how to defeat an enemy whose motivation equals your own and whose resources seem unlimited.

The Allied master plan, which was to bring ultimate, and perhaps speedy, victory, had been settled at a conference between Sir John French and Joffre at the end of 1915. It was to launch a massive co-ordinated attack on all fronts in 1916: Russians, French, British and Italians would assault the Germans simultaneously. The conception of the campaign for France bore all the trademarks of Joffre's grandiose enthusiasms. Joffre, of course, had no authority over either Sir John French or Haig, but both had been given instructions from Kitchener to co-operate with him to the best of their ability. In the event, every part of the master plan ended in disaster: the French were effectively prevented from playing their part in the offensive because from February onwards they were involved in the gruelling defensive battle of Verdun; the Russian offensive, which began on 5 June 1916, opened with initial victories and high hopes, and ended in losses estimated at one million; the Italians' offensive eventually left them in a worse strategic position; and the British Army under Haig was left with no alternative but to battle on in France virtually alone.

During times of great danger, the religious beliefs of soldiers tend to fall into two separate categories. Some pray earnestly for salvation and delivery from the dangers confronting them; others feel that if the all-powerful God has allowed such slaughter and misery to occur, he is unlikely to wish to show any mercy to any particular soldier. Not surprisingly, in view of the enormous weight of his responsibilities, Haig began to turn his mind more seriously to religion in 1916. As described earlier, he had been brought up in a strongly religious atmosphere and had never gone through the period of agnosticism which was a common experience of many young men of his type. However, he had something of the Cromwellian spirit and attitude. At Loos, when matters were not going well, he had reminded Gough, he recorded, 'We shall win "Not by might, nor by power but by *my spirit*," saith the Lord of Hosts.' On 2 January 1916 he attended the Presbyterian service at his headquarters in St Omer. Previously he had gone to Church of England services, which were large and formal occasions; the Presbyterian service was held in an upstairs room in a school. The chaplain, a young Scotsman named George Duncan, was at first somewhat taken aback by the presence of a man of such exalted rank: his normal congregation consisted of a few private soldiers. Although Duncan felt overwhelmed by the occasion, he was gratified to learn later that Haig had subsequently written in his diary:

A most earnest young Scotsman, George Duncan, concluded the service. He told us in our prayers we should be as natural as possible and tell the Almighty exactly what we feel we want. The nation is now learning to pray and nothing can withstand the prayers of a great united people. The congregation was greatly impressed, and one could have heard a pin drop during the service. So different from the coughing and restlessness which goes on in church during peace time.

Here, Haig shows a lack of imagination. Church parade was compulsory in the army. Every soldier was asked his religion, which was then stamped on his identity disc. Any man who was under the impression that he could avoid church parade by saying he was an agnostic or atheist, or who belonged to some religion not represented by a church within the camp, was promptly given long and exhausting fatigues, such as cleaning latrines, which lasted well beyond the time allotted for church parade. When jeered at by their companions for being so foolish, many discovered they belonged to one of the standard religions after all. The soldiers in Duncan's congregation were probably less moved by the sermon he preached than by the awesome presence of the C-in-C, flanked by two ADCs.

Duncan initially assumed that Haig's presence at his service was a token gesture; he was therefore astonished to see him in the congregation again the following Sunday. He was told by the C-in-C's staff that it was unlikely to be a regular occurrence. However, on the following Sunday Haig was there again, and continued to attend every Sunday except when duty compelled him to be elsewhere. In March 1916 Haig transferred his headquarters from St Omer to Montreuil. To his surprise, Duncan found that he too was posted to Montreuil.

Montreuil was a smaller area than St Omer, and the only units there were connected with GHQ. The church was now a small wooden hut. Nevertheless Haig continued to attend, and would take his place without formality in a congregation of about twenty, most of whom were private soldiers. From time to time officers from Haig's personal staff would accompany him, but these were never more than a handful. Duncan had no duties to occupy him during the week, so he took advantage of the free time to visit units in or near the line. On several occasions during the next two years Duncan pointed out that he had been the GHQ chaplain for a long time and should perhaps be posted to a more active area. Haig's response was that he could go where he wished during the week, but added, 'If you are of help to me, I hope you will be satisfied.' Duncan let the matter drop.

George Duncan, who never rose above the rank of captain, which was allotted to the lowest grading of chaplains, kept in touch with Haig after the war. Once he received a letter which said: 'I had a hard time before I came across you at St Omer.' From this Duncan assumed that Haig, who had previously attended the formal Church of England services, had turned to the little Presbyterian church as a haven where he would not feel on parade. 'Denominational loyalties in themselves had little meaning for him,' reported Duncan. Although most of Haig's upbringing had been with the Church of England he later associated himself with the Church of Scotland and became an elder first of St Columba's Church, Pont Street, London, and then of the parish church at Bemersyde.

As may be imagined, Duncan was a fervent supporter of Haig and strongly resented criticism made by those who never met the Commander-in-Chief. He quoted in a book, *Douglas Haig as I Knew Him*, a tribute by a major, Neville Lytton, who had been wounded in the battle of the Somme: 'Haig's qualities are much more moral than intellectual; what intellectual qualities he has have been used up almost entirely in his own profession but he exhales such an atmosphere of honour, virtue, courage and sympathy that one feels uplifted.'

However, as Haig's criticis have not been slow to point out, one needs many more qualities than virtue, honour, courage and sympathy to be a successful commander-in-chief. Field Marshal Lord Montgomery was undoubtedly a successful C-in-C, although his personal qualities were not widely admired. Unlike Montgomery, Haig was no expert in the art of handling politicians, for like many soldiers he had an instinctive distrust of people whose climb to power had been achieved through skilful use of their tongues. There were, of course, politicians who had distinguished themselves in other places than the hustings – but even these men, he felt, were essentially not trustworthy. In spite of unfortunate experiences, Haig liked to believe that people would not deliberately lie, and that they meant what they said. He was inclined to be equally naïve in his dealings with the French: when he went to see Joffre, he wrote: 'The old man was evidently very much pleased with my visit, and came and saw me into my car at the entrance to the garden. He shook me by the hand most warmly twice, and held it so long I thought I was never to be allowed to go. Altogether it was a very satisfactory interview.' It was not, of course. Joffre had told Haig that he expected to drive the Germans back in April. By then, though, the French would be fighting for their lives at Verdun.

Fortunately for Haig he had the unstinted support of Robertson. The new CIGS was a realist who combined the virtues of patient tolerance with the ability to persuade. Although in theory a simple soldier surrounded by politicians, the clever and quick-witted products of a social class far above his own, he was more than a match for the best of them. When it was worthwhile to lose his temper he did so, but he used that ploy very sparingly.

There was an incident in January 1916 which, although humorous, showed the lofty irresponsibility which could characterise even members of the government. The Attorney General, Sir F. E. Smith (the future Lord Birkenhead), had been invited to stay with Winston Churchill, who, following the Dardanelles disaster, had joined the Army and was serving in France. Smith, who was wearing the uniform of a lieutenant colonel for no very clear reason, had arrived in Boulogne and bluffed his way past the sentries without the necessary pass. When the sentries reported that an unknown lieutenant colonel had moved into the operations area, the Adjutant General issued orders to arrest him. Smith was therefore apprehended and placed under close arrest in St Omer.

Bonar Law and Lloyd George, who were also in France at this time, promptly approached Haig and pointed out how embarrassing it would be for everyone if it became known that a Cabinet minister was in jail. Fortunately by then the Adjutant General had realised the explosive potential of having arrested the British Attorney General and had him released. Everyone was very grateful to Haig for having defused the situation, though in fact he had had little to do with it. He invited Lloyd George, Bonar Law and Smith to have lunch with him and later told Dorothy, as she recorded in her book, that he was 'rather shocked at the amount of his best brandy Sir F. E. consumed'. He would not be the only person to express astonishment at F. E.'s tolerance of alcohol. The story, despite being carefully suppressed, appeared in the *Evening News* the next day; one of the politicians had disclosed it on returning to England.

Haig had hardly had time to take up his appointment when he found himeslf differing from Joffre in discussions over planning. Joffre suggested that Haig should wear down the Germans by a series of local attacks prior to launching the full summer offensive. Haig thought that such a policy would be not merely pointless but also counter-productive, as it would give neutrals the impression that the Allies were unable to penetrate the German lines. Another point of difference was the place for the main attack. Joffre thought it should be over the River Somme. Haig preferred to attack further north and perhaps turn the German flank there.

Shortly afterwards Haig was given the disconcerting news, in a despatch from Joffre himself, that France was now so short of men that 'the French army could not do much more hard fighting'. This was a preliminary to Joffre suggesting that the British should take over that part of the front which at the time was held by the French 10th Army. Haig politely but firmly refused. However, scarcely had he made the position clear when the Germans launched a mass attack on the French forces at Verdun on 21 February. Although Haig suspected that this offensive might be accompanied by a smaller attack on the British sector, he felt that while the French Army was battling for its very existence he could not refuse; and on 27 February he told Joffre he had decided to fall in with his wishes. The decision was made easier by the fact that the British 4th Army, commanded by Rawlinson, was now in existence, created from conscripts, TA regiments and transfers.

However, the enormous pressure which the Germans were now putting on Verdun made it necessary that Britain should take more decisive action than merely taking over a sector of the French Line. During the planning for the summer offensive, instead of attacking in his chosen area north of the River Lys, Haig was now persuaded by Joffre to focus his attention further south, near the Somme.

Although its nightmare qualities do not fade, the First World War now tends to be regarded by armchair military historians as a series of major battles only. This is far from the truth. Although the slaughter in the great battles of Loos, the Somme, Arras and Passchendaele was appalling, it needs to be remembered that some degree of activity was taking place all along the Western Front throughout the war – even in the 'quiet' sectors. People tend to think of 1916 as the year of Verdun and the Somme. But the latter did not begin until 1 July, and running concurrently with the major fighting at Verdun in the first six months of that year there was also a series of lesser actions. Falkenhayn, who was now the German commander, had decided that the Allies should not be left unharried elsewhere. The first of several German attacks came on 14 February in the Boesinghe sector on the extreme left of the British front. It penetrated the British line, but was then driven out.

Two miles south of Ypres the soil from the excavation of the Ypres-Comines canal had been piled into a heap which was named by British troops 'the Bluff'. It was about thirty feet high and, being just inside the British lines, gave invaluable observation over the Germans opposite. After a fierce artillery barrage, successful mining and heavy attacks, the Germans captured the Bluff. It was recaptured by the British in March, after desperate fighting, by which time both sides had casualties running into many thousands.

In April the Germans attacked Hulluch, near Loos, using gas. After heavy fighting the German gas suddenly blew back over their own lines, and as the troops ran backwards to escape it they were caught by a British artillery barrage. The gas cloud destroyed all vegetation down to the last blade of grass.

This setback did not prevent the Germans using gas again at Wulverghem at the end of April, though this attack too was unsuccessful. However, in the Hohenzollern Redoubt area they had more success and occupied a small feature known as the Kink. More serious was the fact that the Germans had captured from the French, in a surprise attack, the Pimple, a knoll on the northern end of Vimy Ridge. Vimy Ridge is nine miles long and extends from the valley of the Scarpe in front of Arras to the valley of the Souchez; on the other side of the Souchez Valley is the Lorette Ridge.* The Germans held the entire summit of the

* The memorial chapel of Notre Dame de Lorette now stands on top of the ridge.

ridge except for the northern end, on which the two lines of trenches faced each other.

The general aggressiveness of the Germans all along the front, combined with their possession of many excellent observation points, gave little comfort to Haig as he continued to plan the summer offensive. Meanwhile, as the French were pouring more and more troops into the slaughterhouse of Verdun, their potential share in the coming Somme offensive continued to diminish. Their attacking front shrank from twenty-four miles to eight, and the number of divisions they allotted to the attack to sixteen. In the event on 1 July only five French divisions were available.

Haig was only too well aware of the problems the French were facing and sympathised; he realised they were under such pressure that they would be unlikely to mount another offensive for a long time to come. In consequence the battle of the Somme, which would now be fought over terrain he would not himself have chosen, would be an almost all-British effort.

However, even in his most pessimistic mood he could not have guessed that during the next two years he would not merely have to mount the main offensive continuously with British troops alone, but also have to divert German interest from what was happening in the French sector. His options, which at the beginning of the year had seemed numerous, were fast vanishing.

Nevertheless, Haig never lost sight of the fact that, however great his own trials seemed to be, his position was infinitely preferable to that of the soldiers in the trenches. Charteris recalls an occasion:

There is a picture that will always remain vivid in the minds of those who were present when Haig chanced to meet, returning from the trenches, a battalion in which almost every man was suffering from trench foot. They could only move a hundred yards or so and then rest for some minutes, but with unconquerable spirit they were singing and whistling as they struggled onwards.

He stopped the column, and passing slowly down the ranks

exchanged a few words with each man. Then mounting, he watched the men resume their weary march. He was deeply moved. 'What right have we,' he said, 'to any credit when these men are enduring so much.'

Charteris noticed that the word 'endure' had become a common word in Haig's vocabulary. He was still using it at the end of the war, as a letter to Rawlinson, written in 1918, showed: 'It is due to the generous support which you and the other high commanders have given me, that I have been able to endure to the victorious end.'

Charteris's observations on Haig, with whom he had close contact throughout the most criticial years of their lives, reveals the Charteris tendency to exaggerate and generalise, a tendency which would make his intelligence summaries dangerously misleading. It seems unlikely, for example, that Haig can have spoken to 'each man' in a battalion, which, even though consisting of walking wounded, probably numbered some eight hundred men. Other Charteris stories about Haig seem to be designed simply to mock: the one in which he describes Haig speaking to a soldier on a different occasion and saying, 'Where did you start the war, my man?' and receiving the shocked reply: 'I didn't start the war, sir. I thought the Kaiser did,' is, in fact, a rehash of a cartoon joke. However, in between examples of such obvious nonsense are extremely valuable points:

He had an amazing power of keeping discussion on relevant topics.

Any tendency to undue excitement in anyone – high or low – with whom he came in contact, called forth a frigid, 'Don't fuss.' He had a few favourite aphorisms which he frequently used, 'It is the spirit which quickeneth.'*

It is better to command in chief than to be concerned in all.

Aim high, perchance you may attain.

* Charteris seemed unaware that this was Haig's old school motto.

The deep underlying sympathy with humanity in all its weakness and frailty was continuously evident. He was ruthless in removing those whom he considered incompetent for the task required of them, but he would be at great pains to soften the blow by a kindly word. 'You have done your best, none of us can do more.' 'There is work elsewhere that you can do and will do well; wherever you may be you will be helping to win the war.'

Haig had a pawky sense of humour which made him enjoy occasionally mingling unrecognised among ordinary soldiers, usually in the dark, with an overcoat covering his badges of rank. Usually he let them know later who had been among them. Sometimes, on a journey, he would stop to give a lift or other help to one of the 'walking wounded', who had been despatched from the casualty clearing station to make his way to a hospital further back but was having considerable difficulty in doing so.

But chance encounters were not invariably happy. He had a prudish, rather priggish, attitude to nudity, as when he rebuked an officer for allowing his men to strip and bath themselves in view of appreciative French girls. On another occasion, when he came across a battalion marching along singing a coarse version of a song, he rode up to its commander, 'a big, jolly-looking, fat man', and told him the tune was good but the words 'inexcusable'. The colonel, alas, was singing them as lustily as anyone.

Secrett wrote:

He was a great stickler for discipline and correctness in detail. I know he put the men's comfort before their appearance, but still, he liked to see smart parades. On the line of march, when the men were tired or weary or hot, he didn't mind at all the 'March Easy' order. But he never quite accustomed himself to seeing officers negligently dressed.

The late Field Marshal was most careful to avoid any possible ground for scandal in connection with the women workers.

The leaders of the WAACs (Women's Auxiliary Army Corps) were invariably women of considerable standing and, in every sense, above reproach . . . Nevertheless, for all the rules of the Powers-That-Be, the WAACs met soldiers at out-of-the-way places and many a romance between members of the two branches of the service began in France.

Sir Douglas Haig was such a stickler for the absolutely conventional that I am certain that if he had had his way there would have been no WAACs within reach of the Tommies at all.

On one occasion when Haig was passing by a large WAAC camp he saw two men go up to the military police sentries outside and speak to them. Then 'something was passed into the hands of the police and the men went inside'. Soon these were followed by others. Haig returned to his HQ and told the provost-marshal to conduct 'an inspection'. The result was the arrest of five officers, seven sergeants, three corporals and twenty-one privates. At the enquiry every man had a different story, each being completely plausible. Eventually the enquiry decided to accept the story that they had been attending a birthday party, and they were let off with a warning. Later, Secrett heard that their hostesses fared far worse, commenting, 'But women are always notoriously harder on the affairs of young people than men.'

This sort of story gives the impression that Haig had the attitude of a repressed spinster, but there was probably more to it than that. The girls were all volunteers, and the scandal which would have ensued if there had been a wave of pregnancies would undoubtedly have been enjoyed by the press. Haig had enough to contend with without being accused of establishing brothels stocked with patriotic English girls.

In spite of the widely held belief that Haig, like most of the other generals, never went near the front line, he did so on a number of occasions, to the horror of his staff. High-ranking officers are never welcome visitors to forward areas, for the enemy often observes that unusual activities are taking place and arranges an artillery strike which lasts until well after the visitor has left. Secrett described Haig as 'absolutely fearless', but compassionate towards those whose nerves gave way.

Charles Carrington, who fought through the First World War from beginning to end in the infantry, and who subsequently became a professor of international affairs and a distinguished author, made the following comments on the Higher Command in both world wars:

The simple rule, 'blame the Corps Commanders', would pass when one was young and ignorant, but won't do as an historical verdict. In their station of life, I now suppose, they did their best. Above the Corps Commanders whom we condemned on insufficient evidence, and above the Army Commanders of whom we knew nothing, was the C-in-C. I wish to place it on record that never once during the war did I hear such criticisms of Sir Douglas Haig as now are current when his name is mentioned. There are channels of communication between human beings which the psychologists have not yet identified, and this silent man made himself known to his two million soldiers by telepathy. He was trusted and that puts an end to discussion. Looking back I convince myself that I can see faults in his character and errors in his judgement – which is only to say that I have now enough knowledge to consider him as a human being.

In those days we used to envy the generals for the splendours of the chateaux in which they lived while we grovelled in the mud, but, having been a staff officer in the Second World War, I've shifted my point of view. Sir Douglas Haig lived in a modest country house near Montreuil, with a staff, I believe, of 200 officers. He rode every day for exercise and a fine sight he was, as I saw him once near his advanced headquarters at Beauquesne, with a trooper riding in front bearing his Union flag, a group of red-tabbed officers at a decent interval, and an escort of lancers with fluttering pennants. I do not think he enjoyed pomp – a simple, thoughtful man. It is when I compare Haig's GHQ with Eisenhower's SHAEF that front-line jealousy begins to rise in me. While Eisenhower was still in Algiers the current joke was that he had more officers on his staff than Washington had soldiers at Valley Forge, and the Byzantine luxury of the successive resting places of SHAEF as it traversed Western Europe was disquieting.

Carrington makes the point that, though most of his soldiers knew the name of their brigade and divisional commanders, that of their corps commander was unknown – he recalled that he served in both 3rd and 4th Armies for months without ever catching a glimpse of either Allenby or Rawlinson. Nevertheless, every man knew the name of Haig: 'The BEF in France was so huge and ponderous a machine that no one except Haig could impose his personality upon it, or at least no one did.'

Carrington described the enormous complexity of the tasks involved in the administration of the BEF:

The feeding and clothing and housing of two million men who were continuously on the move, grouping and regrouping themselves in ever-changing patterns of concentrations, and who every few months were faced with a catastrophe on the cosmic scale like an earthquake or flood, precluded sudden changes of plan. The build-up for a battle required such masses of supplies and munitions, such elaboration of movements by road and rail that it could not be concealed, and, once set on foot, could change direction only at the cost of chaos. As a feat of organisation the staff work of the BEF was surprisingly efficient, far more so than the armies of our allies.

Carrington considered that 'the comical assertion [by critics of Haig] that the British generals were "donkeys" does not stand up to a moment's criticism.' He considered that:

If they had really been donkeys, their men would have refused to follow them: this, of course, was what happened in both the German and Russian armies at the end of the war ... *

---

* The description of the British generals as donkeys occurred originally in Falkenhayn's *Memoirs*, where the following conversation is reported:

Ludendorff: The English soldiers fight like lions.

Hoffmann: True. But don't we know they are lions led by donkeys.

Hoffmann succeeded Ludendorff as Chief of Staff on the Russian Front in August 1916.

Attempts to make scapegoats of Haig or Gough break down on the fact that no one else could do any better, certainly not the German generals. The sideshow in the Mediterranean by which Lloyd George hoped to find an easier way to win the war produced similar massacres and deadlocks without bringing about a decision . . . There was no easy way out, no escape from a simple dilemma – fight your way through or stop fighting.

12

The Battle of the Somme

THE SOMME BATTLE concentrated on the area between Gommecourt in the north and Maricourt in the south. The river itself flows in an east-west direction south of Maricourt, and turns sharply south at Peronne. South-east of that town lies St Quentin. The battles for which the Somme is best known were mainly for the possession of the high plateau ('high' being for the most part 130 metres) which, midway between Gommecourt and Maricourt, is divided by the valley of the River Ancre, on the northern side of which lie the villages of Beaumont Hamel and Serre, and on the southern side Thiépval. Approximately seven miles north-east of Thiépval is the strategically important town of Bapaume. South-south-west of Thiépval lie High Wood, Delville Wood and Ginchy. The area contains many small villages, hillocks and ridges, each of which would be captured at the cost of much blood.

Until June 1916 the Somme area had been relatively quiet. The range of low hills which the British wished to capture had been in German hands since October 1914, giving them a series of observation posts which enabled them to take note of all that was happening for a considerable distance behind the Allied lines. While the French had occupied this sector, activity had been limited by a form of mutual tolerance which could not last for ever but which saved casualties as long as it did. This attitude to the war favoured the Allies more than the Germans, for the latter, as already explained, had better tactical positions, more guns and

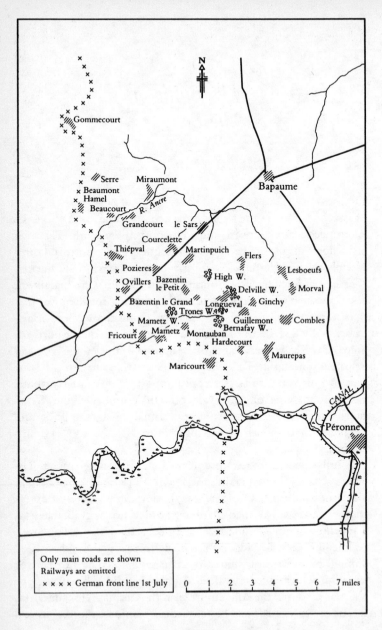

THE BATTLE OF THE SOMME, 1916

more ammunition. The situation began to change in July 1915 when the British took over the sector from the French, but for the remainder of that year it was still possible, according to the eminent military historian Liddell-Hart, for British battalions 'to drill undisturbed in full view of the German lines whereas six months later billets several miles further back were harassed by gunfire'.

The Germans soon became aware, of course, that a huge offensive would be launched at them in this area; it would be more appropriate to call it the battle of the Ancre than the Somme, which in fact lies to the south. Even if the Germans' observation of the activity behind the British lines had left them in any doubt about the scale and imminence of the assault, this would have been dispelled by the error of a British censor who had passed for publication the text of a speech made on 2 June by Arthur Henderson, the Minister for Labour, encouraging the munitions workers to greater efforts. It is said, however, that Falkenhayn thought the preparations so blatant that until mid-July he suspected they must be either a preliminary or a deception for a much stronger blow to be launched in the north. Meanwhile the British were establishing ammunition dumps, bringing up rations, improving water supplies, establishing elaborate communications (7,000 miles of buried cable and 48,000 miles above ground, as well as pigeons and dogs), and carefully preparing and camouflaging the front line trenches from which the attack would be launched.

Haig's battle plan was essentially simple, as all good plans should be. It was to destroy the enemy defences with a massive artillery barrage and then to occupy the area with infantry. Joffre, who had persuaded Haig to choose this area for his 'big push', had in fact visualised a slow battle of attrition, not an attempt to make a breakthrough. Rawlinson, commanding 4th Army, was inclined to Joffre's view and requested a long bombardment, which effectively disposed of any chance that the Germans might be taken by surprise. Haig, having given in to Joffre about the site for the battle, now took an optimistic view of obtaining a breakthrough: given the massive amount of preparation and the fact that the necessary quantity of shells had at long last been delivered, the battle should be a walkover.

What the British did not appreciate was how thoroughly and imaginatively the Germans would fortify this sector once they realised it would soon be under threat from an Allied attack. In doing so, they were greatly assisted by the chalky nature of the soil, which enabled them to make dugouts and galleries deep below the surface and therefore impregnable to shellfire. In the event, the Germans were even better off than they had anticipated, for the bombardment was so widely dispersed that many of their strongpoints and machine gun posts were never touched.

Yet so great was the British Higher Command's confidence that gas was not employed, except for a few token shells, and the attack, which should have taken place in darkness or at least no later than dawn, was postponed until 7.30 a.m. The timing was apparently in response to a request by Joffre, who had already had the whole attack put back two days from 29 June. In Joffre's own area the postponement was apparently justified, for the small French sector was one of the most successful on the first day. However, it meant that the front wave of British troops had to wait an extra forty-eight hours in their own trenches, being deafened by gunfire and drenched with torrential rain, before going over the top in full daylight.

A point of some interest, which is not well known, is a suggestion made by Haig during June. He thought that after the preliminary bombardment, which lasted from 24 June to 1 July, small parties should be sent forward before the main assault was launched to ascertain whether the wire had been satisfactorily cut. But this suggestion was pronounced unnecesssary by his corps commanders, and abandoned: they were relying on their own observation from a distance, and also on reports from Royal Flying Corps pilots who had flown over the area. What no one realised was the huge extent of the area which the Germans had wired and the fact that they had established not just a defensive line but a whole series, one behind the other.

On 1 July itself the earlier rain had stopped and was replaced by brilliant sunshine and broiling heat. When the attack began the battalions went forward in waves, the men shoulder to shoulder, upright and at a slow walk. They could not move much faster, for each man was carrying 66 lb, mostly ammunition. The sheer bulk of the soldier's load made it impossible for him to climb out of a trench quickly, to get up or lie down quickly, or to run. As the men had to cross open ground in the face of perfectly positioned machine gun fire the inevitable result was that the infantry fell in swathes, like hay after a reaper. Shell-holes and uneven ground made progress difficult. Those behind had the additional problem of stepping over their dead comrades.

Undoubtedly much of this slaughter of the British infantry had been the result of a combination of stupidity and over-confidence at a much lower level than that of the Commander-in-Chief. Divisional and brigade commanders had decided that, since enemy resistance would have been virtually wiped out by the artillery barrage, smoke would not be necessary to cover the advance of their own troops; in fact it was thought that to use smoke would be counter-productive, as it would cause difficulties in finding allotted objectives. The distance the doomed soldiers had to cover was, on average, five hundred yards: in some areas the lines were as much as eight hundred yards apart but in a few narrowed down to about fifty. Even so, fifty yards of open ground exposed to traversing machine gun fire was enough to account for hundreds of men long before they reached the uncut wire in front of the German trenches. In some areas the original formations, advancing like lines of eighteenth-century infantry, were broken up by casualties into small groups, which then advanced by hopping from shell-hole to shell-hole. These were, of course, the tactics which should have been adopted from the beginning, and at night or under the cover of darkness or smoke. But so great was the confidence in the British Army's material superiority that such cautious tactics had been deemed unnecessary and time-wasting. It was then argued that it would take too long to infiltrate sufficient men to occupy a position and hold it against the inevitable counter-attack.

There were excellent reasons for doing everything which was done on the first day of the Somme: it was reasonable to rush forward and occupy as much of the German position as possible before its defenders had recovered from the massive British artillery barrage; it was reasonable for the British infantryman to be encumbered with bulky equipment, for he would need it all when he consolidated himself in his newly captured position. But by nightfall on that day the fallacy behind the reasoning was shown by the evidence of twenty thousand dead bodies on the battlefield.

But it was not all failure. In the south, between Fricourt and Maricourt, 13 Corps reached as far as Montauban, which was its given objective. Mametz was also captured. Third Corps in the centre, however, tried without success to capture Ovillers; and 10 Corps, allotted the capture of Thiépval, found their task absolutely impossible.★ One of the great success stories was that of 36th Ulster Division, which had been allotted Grandcourt, north of Thiépval. Fighting with almost superhuman courage and tenacity, it penetrated to Grandcourt. This achievement presented a magnificent opportunity to extend the gap in the German line and come in behind the positions which would cost so much blood to capture later. Unfortunately the Corps Commander, who should have reinforced the Ulster Division at that point, chose to use his reserves to help a division which had made no progress at all. The result was that the battered 36th had its advanced position cut off in a German counter-attack. Eighth Corps had been allotted Beaumont Hamel and Serre; and here very little progress was made. Seventh Corps in the extreme north at Gommecourt did well initially, but then was brought to a halt.

The cost in casualties was stupendous. The corrected figure for the first day alone was 57,470, of which 19,290 were killed, another 35,493 were wounded – many sustaining injuries of which they would die later – and a further 2000 were listed as 'missing'; 'missing' in the battles of the Western Front often meant that a

★ Thiépval village, which was totally destroyed, was eventually captured by the 51st Highland Division at the end of September 1916. By that time, thousands would have died on both sides: the Memorial Arch to the Missing gives the names of 73,412 men; other memorials to the known and unknown dead are nearby and contain thousands more names.

man had been blown to pieces, none of which could be identified. The graves of many of the 'missing' are marked with a simple inscription 'Known unto God'; sometimes a strip of uniform enabled this description to be prefixed with the words 'To an Australian [or perhaps Canadian or New Zealand or British or American] soldier'. In France one in four soldiers killed was unidentified; in Belgium the figure rose to one in three.

Although many German prisoners had been taken, and penetrations had been made in several sections of the German line, the first day of the battle of the Somme had been a ghastly failure. The might of the British Army had been held and massacred by a numerically inferior German force. Certain truths had been learnt and re-learnt at terrible cost. The British Army, which consisted of civilians in uniform with minimum training, had performed with unequalled courage and tenacity. Most armies would have been totally destroyed by the experience; this one paused, waiting to renew the battle.

One of the greatest tactical shortcomings was demonstrated when 36th Ulster Division were not reinforced in time to exploit their previous success. This was an even greater mistake than the delay in the use of the reserves at Loos. But perhaps the most significant lesson learnt from the opening hours of the Battle of the Somme was that although Haig had agreed to the site, the timing and the method for the actual battle, once an organisation, in this case an army, goes beyond a certain size it is beyond the control of any individual. The commanders of the First World War faced huge and unexpected problems by virtue of the vastness of the forces they commanded. This was only too obvious at corps and army level, but even though Haig's air of self-confidence gave the impression that difficulties of this kind did not apply to him, such a huge army proved ungovernable by one man, even with the aid of modern methods of communication.

According to Duff Cooper, in his biography, Haig was full of original ideas for breaking through the German lines in the battle of the Somme, but at each juncture he was thwarted by his need to obtain the agreement of the French. Duff Cooper asserts that Haig had originally made secret plans for advancing 'along the coast from Nieuport to Ostend, which was to be combined with the landing of additional troops and naval support. Such an operation,' continued Duff Cooper, 'if successfully conducted, would have turned the flank of the enemy and, in the opinion of those best qualified to judge, such as the Official Historian, might have produced a decisive result in 1916.' To which one can only add that the Official Historian should have studied the Gallipoli campaign and other combined operations of the past and refrained from speculative comment.

Haig had wanted to begin the battle with tanks but was told that these would not be available for another three months. It is not unlikely that if tanks had emerged from the British lines on 1 July the Germans would have abandoned their positions, however well fortified against infantry, and run for it as they did when they first saw them later. Even a charge by horsed cavalry across the exposed area of No Man's Land would have fared better than the slow-moving infantry, and in fact cavalry was used on the 14th, but in a less suitable situation.

Liddell-Hart was surprised that after the disastrous results of the first day's attack on the Somme area Haig did not call off the battle and switch his efforts further north – to the other side of the River Lys towards Messines, where he was to attack successfully in 1917. However, he concludes that Haig's decision to continue the battle was based on two factors. One was his bulldog determination not be shaken off once battle had been joined, and the second that he had probably been misled by over-optimistic reports from divisional and corps commanders, who were elated by the gains that had been made but were so far unaware of the fearful costs of the day.

However, Haig took the precaution of limiting the attack on the second day to those areas where some success had been gained on the first. Most of these lay in the 4th Army area, though its commander, Rawlinson, now took a cautious approach. Thirteenth Corps advanced beyond Mametz and reached Bernafay Wood, but were then told to dig in and consolidate the position. This advance meant that they were well on the way to Guillemont and, if reinforced, would no doubt have reached it and gained a good tactical position. On the southern bank of the River Somme, the French were continuing to advance; they captured the German second line of defence and moved on to the high ground overlooking Péronne. Haig now wished to leave the north – where Gough had been given command of 10 and 18 Corps, although these were part of 4th Army – and to concentrate on reinforcing success in the south. The French, however, objected. Joffre thought that Haig should continue the attack further north, where the British had been so bloodily repulsed. When Haig persisted that he would prefer to try to push on to Longueval and Ginchy, Joffre told him he would have no success in that area. Joffre, then presuming on his friendship with Haig, gave him a direct order to make further attacks in the north. Haig, although well disposed towards Joffre, considered him fast approaching senility – he often referred to him as 'the old man': Joffre was sixty-four,* Haig fifty-five – and told the French Commander-in-Chief he had no authority to give orders to the British Army. The only orders that he, Haig, was prepared to listen to would come from the British government.

Fourth Army therefore pressed on towards Longueval, but was held up in Mametz Wood, north of Mametz itself. As the line between Pozières and Mametz was now very strongly held by the Germans, the stage was set for a series of dogged, bloody battles for the possession of such features as Trones Wood, Delville Wood and High Wood.

Although the cost of the gains on the first day had been enormous, it was necessary to continue the successful advance with all possible speed before the Germans could build second and third lines of defence as formidable as the first. On the other hand, the disasters of the first day must never be repeated. Rawlinson therefore decided on an advance by night, followed by a swift and devastating bombardment and finally a dawn attack. These were the tactics which should have been adopted on the first day, but

* Joffre was now nearing the end of his long period of active service, and in December 1916 the French government would replace him with Nivelle.

had been ruled out by the Higher Command on the grounds that the new troops were too inexperienced to engage in night operations, difficult manoeuvres in which it was all too easy to mistake friend for foe. Haig considered that the project was more likely to end in total disaster than limited success, and the French also expressed considerable doubts. However, Rawlinson persisted and the assault was fixed for 14 July. At a time when every day counted, for the Germans were, as usual, frantically reinforcing every position, the postponement of an attack by just one day could be crucial.

The plan worked. On the left, 21st Division gained Bazentin-le-Petit Wood; 7th gained Bazentin-le-Grand Wood; 3rd Division captured Bazentin-le-Grand itself, while 9th Division reached the outskirts of Delville Wood after a difficult battle for Longueval. Of these gains, that of 7th Division was the most important. The Germans had not expected the British to reach this far and were thoroughly demoralised: if 7th Division had been adequately reinforced – or even replaced – there was a never-to-be-repeated opportunity of breaking right through to the northeast and turning the German lines in both directions. The terrible cost of the first day would have seemed justified if this vital breakthrough could be made. Seventh Division had already performed prodigies of valour and still had the will, though desperately tired, to press on. On the night of the 14th they took possession of High Wood except for the northern outskirts. There were no reinforcements available for them, other than two squadrons of cavalry. Meanwhile the German reserves were hurrying forward to the line: if the attack had begun a day earlier, as originally planned, they would not have reached the area in time. However, they did, and the numerical strength of the defenders was thus increased by thousands. In consequence, after 14 July the Germans were able to mount a massive counter-attack which pushed 7th Division back out of High Wood. It would not be recovered by the British until 15 September, and only then at the cost of many more lives.

During the next four days Delville Wood was the scene of some of the bitterest and most bizarre fighting of the war. On 15 July the South African Brigade fought its way into the wood, where the trees were burning in spite of torrential rain. At the beginning of the action the South African Brigade numbered 3153, all ranks. By 20 July, only 780 were left.

During the next few weeks casualties mounted steadily all along the front. In the northern sector, Gough was trying to extend a small gain which the British had made on the southern side of the Thiépval Ridge. This meant attacking towards Pozières, and for this purpose the Anzac Corps was allotted to his 5th Army. In the attack on 23 July, which was launched in partnership with three corps from Rawlinson's 4th Army, the only success was gained by 1st Australian Division. During the following week the Anzac Corps probed relentlessly at the Germans in the Pozières region, gaining a mile for the cost of twenty-three thousand casualties. The Australians who suffered these losses were all volunteers. Like those soldiers in the British sectors they represented the very best of the nation, the young, adventurous, courageous idealists, who would have been invaluable as leaders in the future.

During July and the following month, the tactics used to advance were based on the idea that a quick breakthrough was not possible and that progress would only be made by 'nibbling' at the German defences. This meant a prodigious shelling followed by limited-objective attacks. However, the Germans were determined not to give up an inch of ground without making strenuous efforts to recapture it if they did. In consequence, every gain made by 'the British' (a term which included Canadians, Australians, New Zealanders and South Africans) was immediately followed by a German counter-attack. If the first counter-attack was unsuccessful, it would be followed by two or three more. Nevertheless, the British crept forward. Thiépval still held out, but further east Ginchy was finally captured on 9 September. These gains presented the prospect that a large-scale break-out might now be made in the direction of Bapaume. Most of the Somme Ridge was in British hands, and what was still held by the Germans was tactically unimportant.

Haig had been reluctant to try to impose his ideas on the Army commanders during the recent battles, feeling that the 'man on the spot' (if that could be said of the Army commanders) knew best;

but now he felt that there was a chance for a decisive blow, whether they agreed or not. In consequence, a last great effort was planned for 15 September. Fourth Army was to break through the German line between Le Sars and Morval, while the French 6th Army drove up on their right. This would make a pincer movement and should isolate Combles. The British assault would then turn north and capture Courcelette and Martinpuich. The preliminary bombardment began on 12 September and lasted three days. Then, on the 15th, the great attack, and even greater surprise, was launched. The new British secret weapon, the tank, appeared on the battlefield for the first time.

Tanks had been a well-kept secret. The prototype had been built fifteen months earlier, but the teething troubles of the revolutionary new weapon had been numerous, and in consequence only one hundred and fifty had been made by autumn 1916. Sixty of these had been taken to France, but only forty-nine were available for the first day of the offensive. That number was again reduced by mechanical breakdown, and only thirty-two were available for this critical battle. When the attack was launched, nine tanks did well, nine were too slow to keep pace with the infantry they were supposed to be supporting, nine stopped through mechanical failure and five were bogged down on the battlefield.

Nevertheless, overall, the tanks were a success. Haig has been criticised by military historians such as Liddell-Hart and General J. F. C. Fuller for not giving orders that they should be used as a massive, collective armoured spearhead, but whether he actually failed to do this or left the decision to his army commanders is open to question. There is no doubt that Haig had great faith in the tanks and was greatly disappointed when they failed to achieve the dramatic result he had hoped for. Nine tanks was too small a number to achieve more than a local effect, devastating though that was. German sources later revealed that the arrival of these apparently invincible ironclads on the battlefield had an effect out of all proportion to their number: if enough of them had been available there seems little doubt that the long-sought breakthrough would have been achieved.

Overall it was a desperate, hard-fought battle. East of Flers, 14 Corps had heavy losses before it reached Lesboeufs and Morval. Third Corps also found the going difficult. High Wood, where thousands had died, was at last cleared by 47th Division. Martin-puich and Courcelette, midway between Thiépval and Flers, were also taken. These successes still left the eastern crest of the ridge in German hands but that too was captured on 25 September. On the 26th, Gough's 5th Army broke into Thiépval after the sudden appearance of three tanks had caused the Germans in the front line to fall back in dismay and leave a slight gap.* The subsequent battles were still being doggedly fought in mid-November, but by that time the Somme Ridge was in Allied hands. Two of the last important German fortifications to fall were Beaumont Hamel and Beaucourt, on 13 November, though Serre was still holding out in spite of numerous attacks. Beaumont Hamel and Beaucourt were both protected by heavy machine gun fire from 'the Bergwerk' (the mine), which contained a system of caves and underground galleries as a result of ancient chalk mining. On 1 July one of the last of the Public Schools Battalions,† the 16th Middlesex, had been virtually wiped out here, advancing against uncut wire, and the position had held out for four months longer under almost continuous attack.

In his despatches Haig described the battlefield in the final stages in these words:

The ground, sodden with rain and broken everywhere by innumerable shell-holes, can only be described as a morass, almost bottomless in places: between the lines and for many thousands of yards behind them it is almost – and in some localities, quite – impassable. The supply of food and ammu-nition is carried out with the greatest difficulty and immense labour, and the men are so worn out by this and by the

* There were only eight tanks available for the entire operation.
† The name given to regiments consisting of public schoolboys, who would have been better employed as platoon commanders in other units. This was just one example of future leaders being used as cannon fodder, a situation avoided in the Second World War.

maintenance and construction of trenches that frequent reliefs – carried out under exhausting conditions – are unavoidable.

In the front trenches there had been no opportunity to provide adequate cover against either fire or weather. Between the front and the reserve positions on the reverse slopes of the Bazentin Ridge – Ginchy, Guillemont, Longueval, the Bazentins, Pozières – stretched a sea of mud more than two miles in extent, and the valley of the Ancre was a veritable slough of despond. Movement across these wastes was by way of duck-board tracks, which, exposed as they were to hostile shellfire and the disintegrating action of the mud and rain, could only be maintained and extended by arduous and unending labour. Stretcher bearers, with never less than four men to a stretcher, made the journey down from regimental aid posts through mud which no wheeled carrier could negotiate . . .

Frostbite, trench foot, nephritis* and dysentery took a heavy toll to add to the casualties from shellfire, and these horrific conditions would be seen again at Passchendaele on an even wider scale a year later.

Combined Allied losses on the Somme, of which the bulk were British, amounted to 630,000. German losses in the same period totalled 680,000. After the war German historians considered that the casualties sustained by their Army on the Somme had made eventual defeat inevitable.† The very high figure for German casualties was entirely unnecessary for they had begun with the advantage of superior defence positions. However, on 2 July Falkenhayn had ordered that any ground lost must be retaken whatever the cost. Any officer who gave up an inch of ground, even for tactical reasons, was to be court-martialled immediately; the order certainly encouraged a dogged defence, but it also ensured that the survivors would die in the counter-attacks.

The main criticisms of Haig's conduct of the war centre round his handling of the Somme battle in 1916 and the Passchendaele

* Kidney disease, brought on by exposure to cold and damp.
† The damage to morale was perhaps even more important.

(Third Ypres) battle in 1917. He has been taken to task, not surprisingly, for launching the offensive on 1 July without being clear in his own mind that this was the best and only course of action. He had accepted the assurances of his Army commanders that, although there was much open ground to be covered, the lengthy preliminary bombardment would have cut the wire and destroyed the German front-line trenches. But it did not; the result was catastrophic, and as Commander-in-Chief he cannot escape the blame.

In the later stages of the battle, when the main objective, the crest of the ridge, had been captured, he is criticised again for allowing the battle to drag on into the winter in such appalling conditions. He did so because, once again, he was acting in deference to the wishes of the French generals, Joffre and Foch. When he closed down the battle in mid-November he was blamed by Joffre for not continuing until he had achieved a decisive victory. The French were convinced that a breakthrough was there for the taking, and had demonstrated the point by launching an attack at Verdun on 15 December: it made considerable territorial gains, inflicted heavy losses, and captured 11,000 prisoners and 115 guns. It was ironic that the greatest gain from the Somme offensive, which had originally been launched in order to take the German pressure off Verdun, should have been such an indirect one.

As with all the objections to Haig's policies, it is difficult to think of credible alternatives. If he had decided to stay on the ridge instead of advancing towards Bapaume, he would merely have been giving the Germans several months in which to improve their defences. Having fought the Somme battle, he had little alternative but to try to exploit his victory, even though that left his armies exposed on forward slopes in full view of the enemy and in appalling climatic conditions. The Somme Ridge was of no value to him once it had been captured; it had been an invaluable asset to the Germans, for it was a formidable stake in French territory, but its possession by the British only meant that they were committed to continue fighting in an area which Haig had not favoured in the first place. And because winning the battle had taken so long, the unfortunate British troops were doomed to spend the winter there in flooded, muddy trenches.

Charles Carrington considered that Haig accepted the views of the army and divisional commanders too easily – on one occasion, for example, he had a sharp difference of opinion with Rawlinson over tactics. Haig preferred to probe with fighting patrols, but Rawlinson wanted an all-out attack by waves of infantry; Rawlinson had his way, and it was a costly concession. Carrington considered that Haig was not good at choosing his deputy commanders and that he made the situation worse by being too loyal to them when they had proved unsatisfactory. Hunter-Weston, nicknamed 'Hunter-Bunter', was a case in point. He looked and behaved like a music-hall general, and Carrington, who met him after the war, doubted if he was completely sane. Gough was another choice over which many had doubts. At forty-seven he was the youngest of the Allied Army commanders, and Haig may have felt some special loyalty to him because his brother, as mentioned earlier, had been Haig's Chief of Staff before being killed by a sniper. The official historian considered that Gough would have been an ideal commander for open warfare, but was too impetuous and impatient for the siege conditions of the Western Front.

Although it is almost impossible for British and Commonwealth readers to contemplate the battle of the Somme without feelings of horror at the waste and futility of it all, it is worth taking note of the German view. Captain von Hentig, of the German General Staff, wrote in his *Psychologische Strategie des Grossen Krieges*:

> The Somme was the muddy grave of the German field army and of its faith in the ability of the German leaders. The German Field Command, which entered the war with enormous superiority, was defeated by the superior technique of its opponents. It had fallen behind in the application of destructive forces, and was compelled to throw division after division without protection against them into the cauldron of the battle of annihilation.

The same point was made by Colonel Gudmund Schnitler, the Norwegian Military Attaché with the German Army, in *Der Weltkrieg 1914–18*:

> If the battle of the Somme in the tactical and strategic sense had no direct importance, its consequences nevertheless were great, particularly from the morale aspect. It gave the Western Powers confidence. Their armies had accomplished in common an achievement that gave good promise for the future. The confidence of the German troops in victory was no longer as great as before. The old steadfast highly-trained body of the German army, particularly in the infantry, had for the most part also disappeared. A great part of the best, most experienced and most reliable officers and men were no longer in their places. Within the German army a remarkable decrease of moral force had manifested itself. This was the more marked as the heavy losses had made it necessary to send to the front a great number of young soldiers whose training was defective.

Reading these comments, one is immediately struck by the contrast with the British Army which, when it had lost its 'Old Contemptibles' in 1914 and 1915, was able to replenish its ranks with volunteers from 'Kitchener's Army'. These, though regarded somewhat disdainfully by the survivors of the pre-war Army, had beaten the best of the German forces by dogged courage. One recalls the Duke of Wellington's remark at Waterloo in 1815: 'Hard pounding this, gentlemen, let's see who will pound longest.'

The German Official History echoed these sentiments:

> The heavy loss of life affected Germany much more heavily than the Allies. The enormous tension on all the fronts compelled the Supreme Command to leave troops in the line until they had expended the last atom of their strength and to throw division after division into the same battle. In the circumstances it was inevitable that the demoralising effect of the defensive battle should affect the soldier more deeply than was consonant

with the maintenance of his lust for combat and his power of devotion, but more serious still was that the demand for self-sacrifice greatly exceeded what could be expected of the average man, with the consequence that the fighting was largely left to the best of the troops and not least to the officers. The result of this was again a terrible death-roll of the men fully-trained in peace time and the finest soldiers, the replacement of whom was impossible. It is in this that the roots of the tragedy of the battle lie.

Although the German losses were greater than those of the Allies, they were not substantially different. As the writings of the Germans show, though, the effect of their heavy losses was very serious, for they lost the core of their old Army. However, for the British it was the death of a volunteer army, and perhaps, in the longer term, that was worse.

The hard fact that emerged by the end of 1916 was that the war had still to be won by the Allies. If peace had been negotiated then, there would have been no long-term solution. Woodrow Wilson, President of the United States, was drawing up peace proposals at the end of 1916. At that time the German Imperial Chancellor, Bethmann-Hollweg, was the representative of a number of Germans who were seeking a peace formula and deplored unrestricted submarine warfare, which the German Navy was claiming could end the war in six months. On 12 December 1916 the Central Powers (Germany, Austria, Hungary, Turkey and Bulgaria) presented a note to the neutral states and the Vatican saying they were willing to negotiate a peace. This pre-empted Wilson's note, which was only delivered on 10 January 1917. The German proposals were that:

1. Their colonies, except for those in the Pacific, should be returned to them.
2. They should receive the Congo Free State from Belgium.
3. They should retain the Briey-Longwy basin which, linked with Luxembourg, should become a state of the German Empire.

4. Germany should be granted either (a) direct influence over Belgium or (b) possession of Liège.
5. Courland (Latvia) and Lithuania should become part of the German Empire.
6. German influence should be extended in the Balkans.

Clearly there was no reason to suppose that the German nation had lost its appetite for conquest. It was learning hard lessons, but was not yet ready to make any concessions.

13

Enemies on All
Sides

EVEN AS THE Battle of the Somme was drawing to an end, another, of a different type, was beginning. This time it was a political one, in Britain, and it would eventually have a great effect on Haig and Allied strategy on the Western Front.

On 15 November there was a conference at Chantilly which was attended by Haig, Joffre, and representatives of the Russian, Serbian, Romanian and Italian armies. The four countries were all anxious for more troops to be sent to beleaguered Salonika. At Chantilly the representatives were all military men, but the next day, when the conference adjourned to Paris, it continued with civilian additions who included Asquith, Lloyd George and the French Prime Minister, Briand. Lloyd George was in favour of sending more troops to Salonika, but this was resolutely opposed by Joffre and, less vigorously, by Haig. Further talks occupied the next few days.

There was now considerable dissatisfaction in Britain with the conduct of the war, which seemed to have reached a state of casualty-provoking deadlock. There were mutterings against the Higher Command, and there was open criticism of the government. People were asking how much longer their husbands and sons would be asked to die for no apparent gain. It became known that the Germans were making peace proposals, but not so well known that these would have left the enemy with the spoils of war while inflicting great injustice on the Allies. There was already a movement to replace Asquith as Prime Minister; this did not please Haig, who had a high opinion of Asquith, though at that time he was also on reasonably good terms with Lloyd George, who was Asquith's likely successor.

On 7 December Asquith was replaced by Lloyd George at the head of a new coalition government. The positions of Haig and Robertson remained unchanged, but Lord Derby became Secretary of State for War, Balfour became Foreign Secretary and Sir Edward Carson First Lord of the Admiralty. Across the Channel Joffre was appointed a Marshal of France, which gave him great honour but deprived him of power, and General Nivelle replaced him as Commander-in-Chief of the French armies. Marshal Lyautey, much of whose service life had been spent in Morocco, was the new Minister for War.

Haig was favourably impressed by Nivelle when they met, though he realised that there was a long way to go before he reached the warmer understanding he had had with Joffre, despite their occasional differences. In his wildest nightmares he had no conception of the trouble Nivelle was going to cause him. Even less did he expect that his own Prime Minister would soon be opposing him in every way possible: although his position as Commander-in-Chief was probably unassailable, there were ways of making it almost intolerable and Lloyd George knew them all.

The news elsewhere was not encouraging. Romania, which had come into the war on the Allied side on 25 August, had soon been overwhelmed by the Germans. As an offensive thrust from Salonika had failed to prevent that happening, Haig saw little point in continuing to keep valuable Allied troops locked up in the great 'internment camp' there. The Russian offensive had come to a standstill. The only encouraging note had been in Greece, where France and Britain had decided that the pro-German attitude of King Constantine was too great a threat: in December they took control of the country. Six months later, Constantine would be deposed and Venizelos made Prime Minister. Greece then joined the Allied side.

The winter of 1916–17 in north-west Europe was bitterly cold and uncomfortable; it was said to be the worst for twenty years.

Hard frost and intermittent snow lasted until mid-April. The snow and the damp made life in the trenches slightly more unpleasant even than usual, though the frost was welcome because it hardened the mud and made movement much easier.

At the other end of the military scale, plans were being made on both sides for a quick ending to the war. Although uneasy about the reliability of Lloyd George, Haig had had his self-confidence reinforced by being appointed a field marshal. This was at the instigation of King George V and took place in late December. It was unusual for such a prestigious title to be awarded at that stage in a war; but the King was aware that his favourite general had enemies, so he was determined, if possible, to put him further out of their reach.

Haig still adhered to his belief that the most likely place to break through the German line was in the northern, and not the central, sector, but he soon discovered that the preference of the newly appointed Nivelle for an attack in the centre was attracting more support. Furthermore, whereas Haig had under his command a total of 61 divisions and 1157 large guns (including howitzers), Nivelle had 115 divisions and artillery to the number of 4970. In the circumstances it seemed that sheer weight of numbers and metal must make the French the senior partners. Nivelle was an artillery officer with a good fighting record, his mother was English, he was fluent in both languages and he had considerable charm. He knew exactly how he proposed to win the war, for in the previous year he had succeeded Pétain in command of the French 2nd Army at Verdun, and had won two impressive victories by his use of concentrated firepower. Although concentration of effort could scarcely be said to be a novel concept in warfare, it gained the enthusiastic approval of the politicians who had previously become resigned to the fact that the war would last for years and even then only be won when one of the belligerents was marginally less exhausted than the other. Nivelle's plans offered the exciting prospect that, if he succeeded, the Germans, urged on by President Woodrow Wilson of America who had already launched two peace plans, might come to sensible terms. In the following April the United States declared war on

Germany after three US merchant ships had been torpedoed by U-boats.

Haig was relieved to find that the French were now planning to shoulder the major burden, instead of leaving it to him as had happened in the battle of the Somme. The Nivelle plan merely required the British to attack north of the Somme and to the south in the sector which had previously been occupied by the French 6th Army. But Haig was not pleased to see that the British effort was to be divided in order for the French to be able to focus theirs: he was not unmindful of the fact that the French had had grandiose plans in the past, and they had ended by leaving the British to incur heavy losses in supporting or diversionary attacks. Once again, the main French attacks were to be made in Champagne, where they had previously been unsuccessful.

Haig would not have chosen to attack in the Arras sector, which he was now allotted. However, he did not feel he could refuse to do so, as his attack there was designed to draw in the German reserves so that they would not be available to the enemy when Nivelle made his successful break through the Champagne sector. If, for some unexpected reason, the main French attack failed, Haig was promised full support for an attack through Belgium. A breakthrough in this area had always seemed to Haig to be a much more practical proposition than the attack further south and, if successful, would have the additional benefit of liberating the Channel ports, notably Zeebrugge and Ostend, which were thought to be the main U-boat bases.

U-boat attacks on merchant convoys had become increasingly successful and dangerous, and the Admiralty was beginning to make it clear that, unless the ports along the Belgian coast were captured, they might lose the U-boat war. The naval war was very complicated, and lies outside the province of this book; however, the assumptions made by the Admiralty at this point would have a strong influence on British land strategy later. The Navy had, as Haig was well aware, performed miracles by ferrying millions of soldiers back and forth across the Dover Straits, in spite of strenuous German interference, so Haig felt under a moral obligation to assist the Senior Service in any way possible. The French, who had internal lines of communication, paid little attention to the threat to merchant shipping.

The friction with Lloyd George began briskly. On 15 January, Haig was summoned to a meeting at Number 10 Downing Street to explain to Lloyd George and the inner War Cabinet what Nivelle had in mind and what part British troops would have in the forthcoming offensive. He was surprised to find that Lloyd George considered that the French were fighting the war much more intelligently and successfully than the British. In support of this statement the Prime Minister observed that the French had achieved more, and incurred fewer casualties, in the battle of the Somme. Haig pointed out firmly that there was no comparison to be made here, for the British Army had agreed to attack on the Somme because of the desperate need to relieve German pressure on Verdun – which it had done successfully. He added that the only reason the French attacks had been successful in the Somme area was that the Germans had been taken by surprise by being attacked in the south: once they realised that was happening, they had soon taken the measure of the French. Lloyd George was unresponsive to this or any other argument from Haig and stated firmly that, in his view, it was a waste of time and lives to try to beat Germany by attacking on the Western Front: there were better options elsewhere.

The following day Haig and Nivelle attended a meeting of the War Cabinet, after which Haig was told by the Prime Minister that he must co-operate fully with Nivelle and agree to his requests. The fact that both Haig and Robertson had considerable doubts about Nivelle's ability to do all that he said he could merely confirmed Lloyd George in his opinion that the two were bankrupt of sensible strategic ideas: he would have liked to rid himself of two such obstructionist colleagues, but realised that public opinion would not allow it.

At this point Haig was made to look foolish through a careless lapse by Charteris. Like many inarticulate men, Haig had a great admiration for fluent speakers, unaware perhaps that words could sometimes flow faster than the thought and discretion behind them. Charteris had been promoted to brigadier general and was head of the Intelligence Branch at GHQ in France. Being a natural optimist, he felt it was part of his duties to raise Haig's morale by putting the best possible construction on the news in the intelligence reports, which came from a wide variety of sources. He was, however, sensibly aware that it was necessary to warn Haig of the dangers facing him. He had strong doubts about Nivelle:

> In marked contrast to Haig, who never acquired the art of lucid verbal explanation of his plans, and who at times was almost inarticulate, Nivelle had a great – for a soldier exceptional – gift of exposition. He spoke fluent English: he was ready to make great promises. It is doubtful whether any of the British Cabinet possessed sufficient knowledge of military affairs to test these promises and to judge how far they were capable of fulfilment, and Nivelle appears to have experienced little difficulty in converting them to that view.

Knowing that, Charteris seems to have been astonishingly careless in not preventing Haig giving a personal interview to three French journalists in February 1917. Misguidedly Charteris had indicated to Haig that he should strike an optimistic note and inform the journalists that the Allies were on the brink of victory, that their coming breakthrough would be exploited by the cavalry, and that the war would come to a successful conclusion within the year. Charteris was on leave in England when the interviews took place, and when the British officer in charge of foreign press correspondents submitted the French articles to him for comment, he spent less than ten minutes looking at them. The censor had already blue-pencilled certain lines, and Charteris confirmed that these should be erased. Apparently he believed that either Haig or Robertson would scrutinise them carefully before passing them for publication. This did not happen. Charteris should have known very well what occurs when imprecise orders are given, and in consequence should not have been surprised when the articles appeared without further amendment in the French papers and, even worse, in a bad translation in *The Times*. The glib assurance of the articles infuriated the Cabinet and convinced Lloyd George that Haig, as the originator of such over-optimistic nonsense, must be losing what few mental powers he credited him with having: it was now clear to the Prime Minister that the British Commander-in-Chief was quite unfit to influence strategy. Lloyd George therefore made his plans.

On 26 February, a conference took place at Calais for the ostensible purpose of discussing the improvements necessary in the French railway system before another major attack could be launched. Haig had suggested the idea of this conference in the hope that the result would be an immediate drive to improve the whole system. The French Prime Minister would be there, as would Nivelle, Lloyd George, Robertson and Sir Eric Geddes, the British Director of Transportation at GHQ. Lloyd George did not seem particularly interested in the French railways and soon moved the discussion on to general strategy. He then asked the French to produce a plan for a command system for the forthcoming offensive and hand it to the British later for discussion. The paper, which was given to Robertson, though not to Haig, that evening, included in its first paragraph the remarkable statement that:

> with the object of assuring unity of command on the Western Front, the French Commander-in-Chief will, as from March 1st, have command over the British forces operating on this Front in all matters affecting the conduct of the operation.
>
> And in particular
>
> The planning and execution of offensive and defensive action
> The grouping of forces in Armies and Groups of Armies
> The boundaries between these large units
> The distribution of supplies, materials and resources between the Armies.
>
> The French Commander-in-Chief will have a British Chief of Staff who will reside at GHQ. This Chief of Staff will have under his orders:
>
> a. A general staff charged with studying questions of operations and the relations with the British War Cabinet.
> b. The Quartermaster-General. It will be his duty to keep the

British War Cabinet informed of the situation of the British Armies, and to transmit to it the demands made by the French Commander-in-Chief in regard to the needs of those armies.

The reactions of Haig and Robertson to this remarkable document may be imagined. Even if Nivelle had been a universally acknowledged master of warfare, instead of a rapidly promoted artillery officer, the terms would have been absurd. Not only were the British armies to be under unchallengeable French command, they were also to have their supplies allotted as the French decreed. If Nivelle decided that the British should be deprived of their artillery, there was no room for argument. Grimly the two men requested to see Lloyd George, who received them at 10 p.m. However, Lloyd George was not to be budged. As he points out in his *War Memoirs* in a somewhat verbose and circumlocutory way, he had decided that the situation required 'a fresh mind unhampered by commitments or traditions' – and that mind was Nivelle's. Lloyd George's only regret was that the French government had not seen fit to put Nivelle in charge of the whole war. Far from compromising at this fateful meeting, Lloyd George also informed Haig that Nivelle had demanded that Wilson should be the British Chief of Staff at the French GHQ. Whether Nivelle had ever made this demand seems doubtful, and it probably owed more to Lloyd George than Nivelle, but it served to infuriate Haig, who considered Wilson to be pro-French to the point of being anti-British. Lloyd George brushed aside the objections raised to the new proposal and added insult to injury by ordering the two generals to produce a plan implementing the scheme by 8 a.m. next day.

Robertson's first reaction was to seek out Nivelle, whom he confronted soon after dawn, and ask him why he had given no earlier inkling of this impending thunderbolt. Nivelle was quite incredulous when he realised that Lloyd George had not settled the whole business with Haig and Robertson before they even met at Calais.

Another person to have had a busy night was Lieutenant

Colonel Maurice (later Lord) Hankey. Hankey had recently been appointed Secretary to the War Cabinet, and had considerable diplomatic aptitude, as his later career would show.* He produced a compromise solution to the immediate problem by suggesting that Haig's period of subordination to Nivelle should be limited to the forthcoming offensive. If that proved successful, then presumably the experiment would have been justified; furthermore, the end of the war would be in sight. Haig and Robertson accepted this for the sake of Allied harmony, but it soon become clear that the only harmony which Nivelle had in mind was instant compliance with whatever orders he sent to the British.

Although the Nivelle strategy subsequently ended in total disaster, Lloyd George did not apportion any blame for this to the French in his memoirs:

> It was largely due to the workings of a divided command. This was my first attempt to establish a unity of command. It was resisted viciously by Haig and Robertson so that the delays caused by the time spent in allaying suspicions and adjusting differences destroyed the effectiveness of the plan . . . As it was, the Armies were never given a decent chance. The stubborn mind of Haig was transfixed on the Somme. When a change of terrain was suggested it took him a long time to extricate his mental top boots from the Somme mud. He always moved slowly and heavily when rapid and agile movement was essential . . .

Lloyd George had a fixation about Haig's boots, stating on another occasion that the C-in-C's intelligence did not rise above the top of them.

There were two reasons for the failure of Nivelle's offensive: a captured French prisoner gave the plan away to the Germans and caused them to act in a way which effectively blunted it, but when a German prisoner revealed the information that the German Army had strategy for luring the French to destruction, his information was ignored by Nivelle. In fact, the German strategic

* He became a cabinet minister in the Second World War.

withdrawal had begun even before Nivelle planned to launch his victorious campaign. To the Allied armies it was almost inconceivable. As explained earlier, on the Somme the German soldiers were not allowed to yield an inch of ground. However, that had been on the orders of Falkenhayn, and now he had been replaced by Hindenburg and Ludendorff. Ludendorff was the sharper thinker of the two, and he estimated that the Russian Army was tottering on the point of exhaustion and might soon be forced out of the war by a final German offensive. He was right, although he did not envisage a left-wing revolution following that collapse. When the Russian Army had been finally defeated, the victory would release German troops to reinforce the badly depleted armies on the Western Front – as noted earlier, the cost to the Germans of losing the battle of the Somme was 680,000; to that had to be added another 280,000 at Verdun. Ludendorff realised that the situation in France must be stabilised pending the arrival of the troops from the Russian front, but that could only be accomplished if the German Army withdrew to a naturally defensive position which could be strongly fortified. Russian prisoners supplied the heavy manpower for the building of the defensive wall; its official name was the Siegfried Stellung, but the German soldiers called it the Hindenburg Line; the Nazis were to build an even more extensive Siegfried Line in Germany in the Second World War.

The Hindenburg Line ran from Arras through Cambrai and St Quentin until it joined the old German line east of Soissons on the River Aisne. Previously the German line here had jutted out in a huge salient which in mid-1916 had encompassed the Somme, but which by the end of the year was back to Bapaume, Péronne and Roye. Shortening the line released fourteen German divisions for the Russian front. Nivelle seemed unaware that he would now need to cover nearly thirty-five miles before he encountered the full strength of the German Army.

Haig decided that he would accept Wilson's appointment as Chief of Staff, but insisted that the controversial first paragraph of the proposed agreement should be erased. He then inserted a paragraph stating that his co-operation was one of an ally and not a subordinate before signing it. Lloyd George, anxious to get the matter settled without further delay, agreed to the amendment.

Lloyd George was, of course, just as eager to win the war as Haig was, but he felt, not surprisingly, that there must be a better method than sacrificing the best of the manhood of Britain and the Empire in conditions of appalling suffering in a war of attrition. He himself had made an enormous contribution to the Allied war effort by his brilliant performance as Minister of Munitions, and he now felt that, as Prime Minister, he could probably achieve as much in the strategic side of the war.

Haig had good cause for gratitude to Lloyd George, for in the forthcoming battle the British would enjoy a three-to-one superiority in heavy guns and howitzers. With this, Haig could not merely divert attention from Nivelle's offensive; he would be able to deliver a massive blow in his own right. Three armies would be used in the attack: 1st Army, now commanded by General Sir Henry Horne, would attack in the northern sector and in the process capture the long-coveted Vimy Ridge. Third Army, now under Allenby, would push past Arras and capture Monchy-le-Preux, and 5th Army, under Gough, would attack Bullecourt. Sixty tanks were available, but these were distributed evenly instead of being concentrated in one sector. Four cavalry divisions, one in reserve, were ready to exploit any large breakthrough.

An advantage now enjoyed by Haig was one which had been available to the enemy in the Somme battle. There were old chalk workings under the area designated for attack, and these were now extended and equipped to an extent which even the Germans would have envied. They were large enough to shelter about thirty thousand men.

The battle began on 9 April in the unpleasant weather conditions, including sleet and snow, which so often occur suddenly in mid-April. In contrast to the first day of the Somme, it was remarkably successful, one of the major achievements being the Canadian seizure of Vimy Ridge which had previously resisted numerous French attempts to capture it. In this and other sectors of the front, eleven thousand German prisoners and large numbers of guns were taken. Two days later the offensive came to a halt at

Monchy-le-Preux and Bullecourt, on the outskirts of the Hindenburg Line. However, the British had advanced five miles. So far Nivelle's great offensive had not begun, and was not due to do so till 16 April. This was the point at which the Arras battle had served its purpose and should have stopped. However, Haig felt he was under an obligation to Nivelle to continue; he launched another attack on 23 April, but progress was slight.

By then Nivelle's offensive had proved an almost complete disaster. The first part of the advance had been over ground on which everything usable had been carefully booby-trapped or poisoned by the retreating Germans. The French lost 96,125 men; the Germans 83,000. In spite of Nivelle's often-repeated promise that the battle would be over in two days, it was still grinding on on the ninth day, with steadily mounting casualties. The high-cost failure proved all too much for French morale. Along the entire French front men refused to continue the battle; in some sections there were actual mutinies and soldiers began to desert, leaving huge gaps in the French line. Nivelle was not dismissed, but Pétain was appointed Chief of the French General Staff with the mission of restoring the morale of the French Army.

The full extent of the French mutiny was concealed. No one in the French Army dared state the full facts, or the Germans would have taken the opportunity to walk through unopposed and continue until they reached Paris. Haig, of course, knew, but dared not communicate the information to Lloyd George for security reasons; he knew only too well what happened when politicians were given information in the strictest confidence. The French government was also kept in the dark about the true state of the French Army; it realised the Army was incapable of withstanding further losses, but had no concept of how bad the situation was. In consequence the French politicians assumed that the Army had been brought to a halt but would recover to fight again later.

Haig had been one of the first to learn the truth in early May, from his intelligence officers. With that knowledge came the realisation that under no circumstances must the news be allowed to travel beyond the battlefield. Miraculously, the Germans did not realise how events had turned everything in their favour. It was the second time that such an opportunity had occurred – the first had been after their use of gas at Ypres in 1915 – but this time the danger to the Allies was far greater. Haig, on the pinnacle of power, was now more alone than ever. He would have to take unpopular decisions without ever being able to explain why he was doing so. He no longer had a choice of policies, and the only course he could pursue was to attack the Germans as often and as hard as he could so that the German generals would not be able to let their minds toy with the idea of further offensives in the French sector. For the moment they were unlikely to do so, for they knew that a wide band of scorched earth lay behind the French lines: it was one they had created themselves. But later they might reconsider the possibility, and if they were pressed too hard by the British, they might feel that a thrust at the French sector would provide a diversion and at the least prevent the French from supporting any British advances.

The French mutiny could not have come at a worse time. In Russia a revolution had begun, and it was known that the Russians were ready to accept peace at almost any price. The French government was also in disarray, and Briand had been replaced by Alexandre Ribot. Although the United States had declared war on Germany early in April, it was almost totally unprepared for any military action and for months would have to be supplied with weapons and aircraft by France and Britain. In the long run the USA would be an invaluable asset, but at the moment it was almost a liability because the Germans would make every effort to win victory before potential American strength could be put into the Allied side of the scales. Gloomily, Haig wondered whether the attitude of the French Army would spread to their government and Britain be left to fight the war on its own.

A week after the failure of his offensive, with his Army break-ing out in mutiny, Nivelle's confidence was still unimpaired. When he met Haig on 24 April he assured him that, after a successful offensive on the Aisne, he would have the resources to help Haig in a British drive through northern Belgium. However, by 15 May the French government had taken the measure of

Nivelle and replaced him by Pétain. Foch moved up into Pétain's former post as Chief of the General Staff, and no more was heard of Haig being put under French command. There was nothing to be cheerful about, however. The Arras battle, which had been undertaken partly for the benefit of the French, had made no strategic gains of real value but had added another 158,660 names to the British casualty list.

Haig had always believed that the best way to defeat the German Army would be to turn its flank by a thrust through Belgium, rather than to engage in slogging matches further south. Over-running Belgium would yield rich prizes. The first would be the liberation of those northern Channel ports which the Admiralty were convinced – wrongly, as it turned out – were the mainspring of the U-boat war. The second would be that, once a breakthrough had been made in this area, it could be exploited by cavalry and in consequence British armies would be able to drive into the heart of the German industrial area. With Cologne in Allied hands the Germans would, it was assumed, have no heart to continue the fight, though the experience of the Second World War suggests that this forecast for the First would not necessarily have been true.

Haig had reason to feel some confidence about fighting in the Ypres area. In 1914 his corps had taken an important rôle in halting the Germans there. Unfortunately this area, in which the first stages of a new offensive would have to take place, favoured the Germans. The earlier battle had left them in possession of the points from which Ypres itself could be observed and shelled, and their position on the semi-circle of hills meant that they dominated events on the low-lying plain below. The desired objective for the British forces was Roulers, which lay a few miles beyond the Passchendaele Ridge. Passchendaele was the name of a small Belgian village which sprawled across the summit of a low ridge which is hardly noticeable to the modern motorist but in the days of the First World War was of enormous strategic importance. Capturing the Passchendaele Ridge looked to be a minor problem in comparison with the difficulties of the Somme battle, where the Germans had so carefully prepared for the Allied attack. There were strongly fortified German pillboxes along the Passchendaele battlefield, but no deep caves: the nature of the country precluded that. An advance of some seven miles would bring the British forces to the crest of the ridge, from where they could sweep on to Roulers . . .

The capture of the Passchendaele Ridge was not a new concept. As long ago as the spring of 1915 a start had been made on mining operations under the Messines Ridge which was to the south of Passchendaele in the semi-circle of hills to the east of Ypres. Fighting had been continuous in this area since the beginning of the war and had involved mines on two previous occasions, one at Hooge and the other at Hill 60. Hard lessons had been learnt at Hill 60 in the spring of 1915. It was not really a hill at all but a heap of rubble, dug out to make a nearby railway cutting; it had settled down and had made a very good observation and artillery post for the Germans. Three tunnels had been dug underneath it with considerable difficulty by the British. On 17 April 1915 six mines had been exploded, blowing the top off the hillock. British infantry then surged forward to occupy what was left of the summit, and the Germans counter-attacked promptly and vigorously. The battle raged for several days, but finally the Germans clinched victory by using poison gas. The hill then remained in German hands until June 1917. When it eventually fell to the British it was once again as a result of mining. In April 1916 Canadian engineers had begun tunnelling once more, and in November that year they had been relieved by Australians who completed the task.

The Messines Ridge had also received the attention of miners since 1915. The problems here were greater than those at Hill 60 and required operations on a similar scale. This project was the brainchild of a mining engineer named Major J. Norton Griffiths, who had known Kitchener in South Africa and been summoned by him to the War Office. Norton Griffiths travelled everywhere in a 2½-ton chocolate and black landaulette Rolls Royce equipped with silk blinds and luxurious upholstery. He was a man who thought on a large scale. Previous mining had been done close to the surface and had involved scooping out a liquid mess and revetting the sides in the hope that they would not collapse. But although the surface of the land in the Ypres area was waterlogged and thus extremely unsuitable for mining, the ground deep below was blue clay and therefore excellent for mining operations. But the blue clay was some seventy feet below the surface, and disposing of the spoil without the Germans knowing what was happening presented a problem. The whole operation was immensely complicated and involved the construction of five thousand yards of underground tunnels, as well as enough accommodation to shelter ten thousand men.

On 7 June 1917, nineteen mines were exploded under Messines. A million pounds of ammonal had been put in place, and the result was an explosion which was heard as far away as London. The position which had dominated the southern end of the battlefield for two years was blown apart, causing hundreds of German casualties. The Messines area was under the command of Plumer (2nd Army), who was not a man to let a valuable prize slip from his grasp. This time no chances were taken with the counter-attack, and the British artillery and one hundred thousand infantry were ready for the aftermath of the explosion. The Germans, as expected, mounted a series of desperate counter-attacks but this time could not dislodge the Allies. Even so, the British (half of whom were Anzacs) sustained nearly twenty-five thousand casualties. The figure was approximately the same for the Germans, although the latter also lost seven thousand as prisoners.

Six weeks then elapsed before the next British attack, a delay which seems on the face of it inexplicable as well as inexcusable from a purely military point of view. However, there were reasons to support a more cautious view, and Haig was a man who liked to move slowly and with adequate preparation: he had not reached this stage in the war to throw away a vital chance in a hastily prepared operation. He knew from letters on captured German prisoners that conditions in Germany were now very bad. Luxuries had disappeared: basic necessities, such as food, were desperately scarce and the situation seemed likely to deteriorate even further. In this matter he felt that time was on his side. Time might also be on his side in the French crisis. Although the situation in the French Army was far worse than he dared admit to the British Cabinet, there were encouraging signs that the ring-leaders of a potential revolution within France itself had now been rounded up. With luck, the French nation and Army might be transformed into a formidable fighting force once more. But it was not a time to take a gamble, however tempting the prospect. Any failure at this stage would have far-reaching results. The French Army, which was now coming back into shape under Pétain, was still in a very brittle state and would react badly to a British defeat. Lloyd George, who had swung round to giving Haig his full support after the Nivelle disaster, could as easily swing back again. If the Passchendaele offensive failed and the Army did not succeed in capturing the Belgian ports, there was no knowing what burden this would place on the Navy: Admiral Jellicoe had told Haig privately that if the Army could not capture these ports the Navy would probably lose the war at sea.

There was a further danger. If the Passchendaele battle appeared to be going well, there was a strong possibility that Haig might be deprived of troops in order for them to be sent to Italy. Nobody doubted that the Italians needed all the help they could get, but what happened between them and the Austrians was not likely to have much influence on the outcome of the war. It still seems surprising, though, that Haig should now have entrusted the main assault to Gough's 5th Army. Gough himself was by no means confident that he was the right choice to be directing the main assault towards Passchendaele; Plumer was more familiar with the area, as well as being older and more experienced. However, Haig thought that Gough had the necessary qualities and now strength-ened his 5th Army by transfers from 2nd and 3rd Armies. The forthcoming battle required considerable redeployment of the Allied armies. Fifth Army was allotted the sector from Boesinghe in the north to Zillebeke in the south. Its right flank rested on Plumer's 2nd Army. On the left of 5th Army was the French 1st Army and the Belgian Army. Fourth Army (Rawlinson) was allotted the sector of the line between Nieuport and the sea. The main assault was to be in a north-easterly direction from Ypres to Passchendaele.

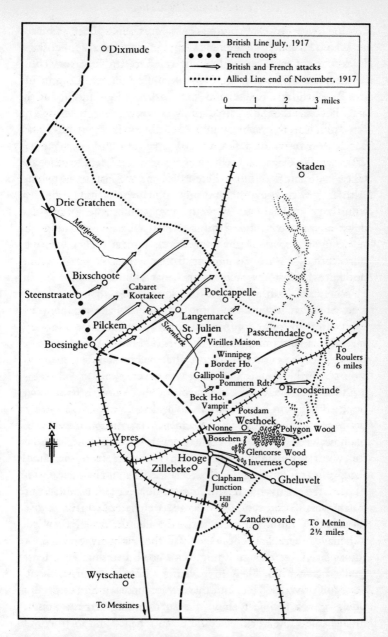

	British Line July, 1917
	French troops
	British and French attacks
	Allied Line end of November, 1917

0 1 2 3 miles

Dixmude

Staden

Drie Gratchen

Martjevaart

Bixschoote

Steenstraate

Cabaret
Kortakeer

Poelcappelle

Pilckem

R.

Steenbeek

Langemarck
St. Julien

Passchendaele

Boesinghe

Vieilles Maison

To
Roulers
6 miles

Winnipeg
Border Ho.

Gallipoli

Pommern Rdt.

Broodseinde

Beck Ho.
Vampir

Potsdam

Westhoek

Nonne

Polygon Wood

N

Ypres

Bosschen

Glencorse Wood
Inverness Copse

Hooge
Zillebeke

Clapham
Junction

Gheluvelt

Hill
60

Zandevoorde

To Menin
2½ miles

Wytschaete

To Messines

THE BATTLE OF PASSCHENDAELE AUG.–NOV., 1917

There were many who doubted the feasibility of the enterprise on which Haig was now embarking, not least among them Foch. Foch was not at all certain that any rapid or simple victory could be achieved by advancing across the hollow between Ypres and the Passchendaele Ridge, and had further misgivings about the area beyond the ridge itself, if and when Haig succeeded in capturing it. Roulers, he thought, was not likely to fall into Haig's hands as a result of a few cavalry charges. The Germans had extended the Siegfried Stellung which had defeated Nivelle, and taken it up into Belgium where it became the Flandern Stellung. Although Foch knew this and mentioned it to Wilson, who was still actively liaising between the two armies, the information never seems to have got through to Haig. Whether Charteris did not know it, or whether he knew but thought that Haig would be unreceptive to warnings coming from the French via Wilson, is not known. But the fact remains that Haig embarked on the Passchendaele battle without the knowledge that, even if he reached the ridge within the time provisionally allotted, he would soon afterwards be confronted with an even more time-and-manpower-consuming battle. In the end he did not reach the ridge in time to press forward before the winter rains set in, so the strength of the Flandern Stellung was never tested.

Liddell-Hart subsequently wrote: 'The Ypres offensive was doomed before it began – by its own destruction of the intricate drainage system in this part of Flanders.' As mentioned earlier, the plain between Ypres and Passchendaele is virtually at sea level and for centuries was an unusable swamp. However, from the Middle Ages onwards it was gradually reclaimed by an elaborate system of drainage canals and streams, mostly flowing from south-east to north-west. There are three large stretches of water, known locally as 'ponds': the Dickiebusch, Zillebeke and Bellewarde. Whenever there was a heavy rainfall the water lay very close to the surface, even though it might not be visible; thus any attempt to dig a trench was likely to leave not a hole in the ground but a pool full of water. Here and there were pieces of higher ground, often only a few feet above the surrounding territory but of inestimable value, for they could be entrenched and fortified. On some of these slopes were woods which have now grown up again, but which in 1917 were blown away by gunfire until only a few tree stumps remained. Many of them have poetic names: Glencorse, Sanctuary Wood, Nun's Wood.* Earlier in the war, the Belgian Roads and Bridges Department had sent a memorandum to the British GHQ, pointing out that if the drainage system of the area was damaged by bombardment the whole area would once more become a swamp. The memorandum was mislaid. The Belgians had also produced some interesting statistics about the weather, and pointed out that during the late summer and autumn it was unlikely that there would be more than a fortnight, or possibly three weeks, of fine weather. This useful piece of information was also mislaid.

There was considerable confidence on both sides during 1917. Haig thought that the Messines battle had been a good omen for the future, but on the German side of the line Crown Prince Rupprecht, the Army Group Commander, felt that it proved that if the British tried to press forward under less favourable circumstances it should not be unduly difficult to defeat them. The Germans, of course, being in possession of the ground on which the battle would later be fought, had established powerful blockhouses and gun positions on all the most favourable sites.

The preliminary bombardment lasted ten days and employed over three thousand guns: it was calculated that 4¾ tons of shells were thrown at every yard of the German front. The attack, which had been planned for 25 July, was postponed to the 31st at the request of the French General Anthoine, who said he needed the extra time to make his artillery preparations. It was important for French morale that their Army should be seen to be making a prominent contribution to this battle, which was certain to be a success. Gough was happy about the postponement, for his own preparations were not quite complete either. Haig, on the other hand, was far from pleased, for the weather reports were not

---

* Some of these names were translations of the original Flemish names, while others were conferred by British troops, often for sentimental reasons.

encouraging and rain was likely to be a more dangerous enemy than the Germans.

Gough had been instructed to direct his initial attack towards the Gheluvelt plateau, which would then be taken over by Plumer's 2nd Army as 5th Army moved forward. In the event Gough decided that it would be better to head straight for Passchendaele, assuming that the Gheluvelt plateau would fall into his hands easily as he did so. It never did. His reasoning, that to capture a salient, however low, would expose him to German fire on all sides, was accepted by Haig. In hindsight, it seems that Haig should have refused to change the order, but Haig was, of course, always reluctant to interfere with the man actively conducting an operation. Unfortunately the rain began on 30 July and continued until 4 August. Haig's apprehensions had proved all too correct.

Even so, the attack which began on 31 July was remarkably successful, the average gain being two miles. Fifty-two tanks had begun the battle, but the terrain was so wet and pitted with shell craters that thirty-three were soon out of action. Valuable objectives were gained, incuding a footing on the Pilckem Ridge, Westhoek, St Julien, Bixschoote and Steenstraat: the last two were reached by the French. The Gheluvelt plateau was left half in German and half in British hands. Areas over which the infantry had expected to advance without too much difficulty were found to be full of mud, broken trees and shell-holes. Continuous rain steadily turned the battlefield into a swamp, which separated the newly established front line from the rear areas; it was two miles wide and could only be crossed by the remains of a few roads which were under constant shellfire. None of the principal German gun positions had been touched, and the result was that they were able to shell the area behind the British front relentlessly. Clinging on to their newly won positions, the British infantry were cut off from food, water, reinforcements and ammunition. It was vital to renew the attack before the Germans could bring up even more reinforcements, but impossible to do so while the rain continued.

An attack had been planned for 2 August, but that had to be postponed. The casualties were now nearly forty thousand. The attack was renewed on the 9th, which was the first clear day, but after hard fighting the whole of the Gheluvelt plateau had still not been captured. Another attack was planned for the 14th, but that day brought another heavy thunderstorm and the plan was postponed until the 16th. By desperate courage the infantry made further limited advances, in spite of heavy German counterattacks. Casualties were mounting fast: they had now reached sixty-eight thousand.

At this rate Haig had doubts about continuing the battle at all unless the weather cleared. However, he was greatly encouraged by Charteris, who over-optimistically told him that not only were the Germans in Belgium at the end of their tether, but back in Germany defeatism and despair were everywhere. A new attack was therefore planned for 25 August.

Unexpectedly, fine weather appeared on the 17th. Since time was so important the earlier attack was continued and, several valuable strongpoints were over-run. Haig now decided on a change of tactics. It was obvious that 5th Army was not going to capture Gheluvelt as part of its general operations. In fact, it might find it difficult to hold ground already gained, for in some sections the British troops had been driven back to their start lines. Charteris commented that this was the wettest Belgian summer for thirty years: that fact was of little comfort to Haig, who was now deeply involved in a battle which he could not afford to lose, whatever the weather and the unexpectedly strong German resistance.

It was now all too clear that Gough's assumption that he could capture the Gheluvelt plateau as a subsidiary part of his main thrust had been hopelessly over-confident: he was unable to do so even when it became his main objective. It was therefore allotted to Plumer, who was left in no doubt about its importance. Plumer was no hot-headed optimist like Gough, and responded by saying that the preparations for capturing Gheluvelt, which the Germans had now fortified very strongly, would take three weeks. Three weeks is not a long time to bring an army up to full strength and fighting efficiency, but in a critical battle in which every day is vital to ultimate success it is a very long time indeed. Two Corps,

which had seen endless hard fighting since the days when it had
been commanded by Smith-Dorrien, was now to be transferred
from 5th Army to 2nd Army. However, before that happened it
would be required to capture Glencorse and Inverness woods on
the side of the notorious Menin road. The attack was launched
in pouring rain and gale force winds on 27 August. The battalions
allotted to lead the attack had spent the previous night standing up
to their knees in mud and slime, while being shelled continuously.
When the attack began, the creeping artillery barrage which was
meant to protect their attack moved too quickly and left them
behind and unprotected. The other corps used in the attack, 18 and
19, were no more successful. Most of the troops were withdrawn
to their original start line after suffering heavy casualties, and the
vital objective still remained in German hands.

At the end of August, 5th Army received an order from GHQ
which was signed by Lieutenant General Kiggell, Haig's Chief of
Staff. Kiggell had risen to his high rank without ever having
served in anything but staff and administrative appointments. In
the order the following remarks appeared:

> The Commander-in-Chief considers it inadvisable that you
> should attempt any operation on a great scale before the 2nd
> Army is ready to co-operate. He therefore desires that in
> present circumstances your operations may be limited to
> gaining a line including Inverness Copse and Glencorse and
> Nonne Boschen Woods and to securing possession by
> methodical and well-combined attacks on such farms and other
> tactical features in front of your line further north as will
> facilitate the delivery of a general attack later in combination
> with the 2nd Army. Proceeding on this principle he trusts you
> will be able to arrange for reliefs, and for the rest and training of
> your divisions, so as to ensure having a thoroughly efficient
> force available for the severe and sustained fighting to be
> expected later. He considers these questions of relief, rest and
> training to be of great importance.

The wretched soldiers had already tried desperately, yet failed to take the objectives so glibly described by Kiggell, and although this fatuous statement would have been seen by very senior officers only, most of them on the staff, Haig cannot escape censure for having chosen such a man as Kiggell for his Chief of Staff. Kiggell was later said to have burst into tears when subsequently he went by car to the edges of the battlefield and asked, 'Did we really send men to fight in this?' He received the reply: 'It's worse further in.'

Soldiers were only too well aware that the term 'rest and relief' meant nothing of the sort. Having emerged from the horrors of the battlefield, they would collapse into an all-too-short sleep. They would then be 'smartened up' in a mixture of parades, inspections and training exercises, most of the latter being conducted by NCOs with little, if any, experience of the front line. They assumed, not without reason, that the object of the authorities was to make life so unpleasant behind the lines that they would return to the front with a sense of relief at being removed from pettifogging restrictions.

Conditions on the German side of the line were no better. General H. von Kuhl, a distinguished German historian and former Chief of the German General Staff, considered that Passchendaele was their worst battle, worse in fact than Verdun and the Somme. He wrote:

> The sufferings, privations and exertions which the soldiers had to bear were inexpressible. Terrible was the spiritual burden on the lonely man in the shellhole and terrible the strain on the nerves during the bombardments which continued day and night . . . No division could last more than a fortnight in this hell. Then it had to be relieved by new troops. Looking back it seems that what was borne here was superhuman. With respect and thankfulness the German people will always remember the heroes of Flanders.

There is a view widely held by members of the general public and some writers that Haig was based far behind the battlefield in complete ignorance of the conditions in which the attacks were made. Nevertheless, although he was undoubtedly misled by Charteris and flattered by others around him, who encouraged him to believe that a Commander-in-Chief should distance himself from everyday events, he was well acquainted with the conditions of the front line from his many visits there and talks with his staff.

There might perhaps be an alternative explanation. Haig's inflexibility over the Passchendaele battle may have been based on deliberate policy, not optimistic ignorance. Once again, he was isolated. Lloyd George, who had supported him earlier in the year, had now changed his mind again. In spite of the lesson he had learnt from the disastrous Nivelle offensive, the British Prime Minister once again favoured subordinating British plans to French views. Foch, who might have been expected to support Haig, had joined the Lloyd George school of thought which believed that the war could never be won on the Western Front. Foch therefore wished to strengthen the Italians by sending one hundred guns from Anthoine's 1st Army, contending that they were really surplus to requirements in the Passchendaele battle and could be used more effectively elsewhere. Haig did not agree that the guns were no longer required in France, but reluctantly accepted that fifty could go if politically necessary. Lloyd George approached Haig personally, pointing out that if Foch wanted to send one hundred guns and Britain refused, the French would accuse the British of not wanting to help their Italian ally. That Lloyd George could put this point to Haig while at the same time trying to undermine his military position shows a remarkable flexibility of mind, even if not a particularly creditable one.

Among the thoughts running through Haig's mind at this moment, three were particularly important, and he mentioned them in his despatches. The first was that if the Allies did not secure victory in the West soon, at whatever cost, the Germans would be reinforced by troops returning from the Russian front, and perhaps from Italy, and then an Allied victory would become impossible. By the time the Americans arrived on the scene, the Germans would have won. The second thought was the one which had been nagging away at him since the beginning of the

French mutiny: would morale in the French Army collapse again? If it did, it would almost certainly be as a result of seeing a British defeat. His third, even gloomier, thought was whether Lloyd George would now spare any efforts to undermine his authority and make his position impossible.

In the circumstances, although the Passchendaele battle was clearly horrific, Haig felt there was no alternative but to press on and win it. Like Macbeth, he could have said:

> I am in blood
> Stepped in so far that, should I wade no more
> Returning were as tedious as go o'er.

The operational plan to capture the Gheluvelt plateau had been designed by Plumer himself, who had been a general when Haig was still a captain. Plumer spent some time considering the lessons to be learnt from his previous, hard-won success over the Germans at Messines and now decided that the Gheluvelt project would require four separate attacks at intervals of six days. The intervals would be occupied in bringing up all the necessary supplies and ammunition for the next phase. Three and a half million shells were allocated to the preliminary barrage. German counter-attacks would be met by concentrated artillery fire and by fresh infantry, rather than those who had already been engaged in the battle. Haig had suggested attacking on a frontage of six thousand yards: Plumer shortened it to three thousand. Every unit taking part in the attack was carefully briefed. Thirty-four tanks would be used, but there was no real expectation that they would achieve much progress owing to the torn-up nature of the ground: in the event only one reached its allotted objective. When the first attack went in on 20 September the rain had begun again, but an advance of a mile was made over the whole front. At the same time, 5th Army made a determined attack and achieved an equal success.

On the 26th the offensive was renewed and similar gains were made. The first attack had cost twenty thousand casualties, nearly two-thirds of them being in 2nd Army; the second added another fifteen thousand.* The next attack went in after a slightly longer interval and began on 4 October. The brunt was borne by 2nd Army, but both armies made gains at a cost of a further twenty thousand casualties. The German losses in this battle were extremely high, and in addition nearly five thousand were taken prisoner. It seemed as if, with another thrust, the final break-through might now be made, but Plumer was not in a mood to risk losing his hard-won gains by going into a hastily convened attack against such stubborn opponents as the Germans. In consequence the next phase began on 9 October, after continuous rain. The surface of the battlefield was at this stage a greater obstacle to progress than the Germans, but, of course, the misery it inflicted was common to both sides. The British Army was now in the worst part of the battlefield and had suffered another twenty thousand casualties getting there. But whatever happened they could not stay in such an appalling area, and in consequence orders were issued for the attack to begin again on 12 October.

The British were reaching an area which the Germans had fortified at leisure with considerable attention to detail. Some of the pillboxes are still there today, looking formidable – but not as formidable as they looked when bristling with guns, surrounded by acres of particularly strong wire, and only approachable through a lake of mud. Neither the attack on the 12th nor the more carefully prepared one on the 26th made much progress. Casualties mounted quickly and steadily. Nevertheless the British were doggedly inching forward towards their objective. Among the 'British' troops, the Australians and New Zealanders were showing the ability to withstand prolonged bombardment, an experience which many had previously thought would be too much for them. Although the troops from the old Dominions were held in high esteem for their attacking qualities, their ability to withstand conditions such as the Passchendaele battlefield had been felt open to question. But that question had now been answered.

Conditions all over the battlefield had become so appalling that

* In addition to these there were, of course, a steady stream of casualties from disease, among which trench foot was prominent.

it seemed a nightmare rather than a piece of territory. There were huge pools of water, some a mile wide, in between which were stretches of liquid mud straddled by duckboards and log roads. Any man who fell off a duckboard or from a temporary road was liable to drown in slimy mud before he could be rescued; the same was true of horses and mules. The whole area reeked of mustard and other gases, decomposed bodies, and the foul smell of mud which had been churned over and over. The shell-holes were full of water and pieces of bodies, and were mostly covered with green slime.

By this time the Canadian Corps had come up from the south and joined in the battle. Being fresh to this battlefield, though veterans in experience, they made further inroads on the Germans, though at heavy cost. Meanwhile 5th Army was continuing its slow and bloody progress and, one by one, objectives which should have been reached three months earlier were now captured.

The final assault on the ridge was left to Plumer's 2nd Army, and on 6 November Passchendaele village, by then a ruined heap of stones, was occupied by the Canadians. It was not the end of the battle. Experience suggested that the Germans would counter-attack, and experience proved right. The area north of the village also had to be cleared and the Germans clung to it to the last with stubborn machine gun and artillery fire. But on 10 November it was all over. The ridge was in Allied hands, the Canadian Corps had sustained thirteen thousand casualties in the brief but vital time they had been in the battle, and the entire butcher's bill for the campaign was two hundred and fifty thousand. German losses, although admitted reluctantly, were eventually quoted as being nearly four hundred thousand. In fact nobody knew the exact figures for either side, for there were so many missing, no doubt lying in the depths of the liquid mud. A balance was struck by saying that at least half a million German and Allied casualties had been incurred, a figure less than half that for the battle of the Somme. As Stalin is reputed to have said: 'The death of one man is a tragedy; the death of a million a statistic.'

By the time the battle of Passchendaele was won it was too late in the year to continue the campaign, and the Belgian ports remained in German hands. The following April, on St George's Day, an attempt would be made to put the one at Zeebrugge out of action by a daring raid, but by then the U-boat war was being won by the convoy system, so long resisted by the diehards in the Admiralty.

The defences of Roulers were never tested. Haig's dream of pushing ahead fast into German-held Belgium and liberating it with cavalry sweeps faded as the rain-sodden Belgian autumn drifted into what would undoubtedly be an even worse winter. However, Passchendaele was not fought in vain. French morale certainly recovered and German strength had undoubtedly been sapped, while the attention of the German Army was diverted away from those parts of the French forces where morale and discipline were being slowly rebuilt. All this, though, had been bought at an appalling price in death and misery.

Haig has subsequently been blamed for the high cost of the Passchendaele campaign, but has never been given credit for securing victory against a firmly entrenched enemy with greater resources of artillery and manpower. Ironically, though military Commander-in-Chief, on this occasion he was fighting a battle for political reasons. Although he believed that the northern end of the front offered the greatest chance of ultimate success, he would not have chosen to continue the battle after mid-August if so much had not depended on securing a victory. Until victory was won, slowly or quickly, the offensive must be continued, if only to enable the French to recover. In the closing stages of Passchendaele he was handicapped by losing two divisions because of a disaster on one of the 'second fronts'. On 24 October the Germans had routed the Italians at Caporetto: 265,000 Italians had been taken prisoner and the survivors fell back fifty miles. The British Cabinet decided that the Italians must be helped and, without regard to the fact that Haig was desperately trying to finish off the four-month-long battle of Passchendaele, ordered him to send two divisions to Italy at the earliest possible moment. Shortly afterwards he was instructed to send another three, and then received the unwelcome news that Plumer was being sent to take command of the British forces in Italy.

14

Unexpected Hazards

AMONG THE MANY errors of which Haig is accused, two of the less plausible complaints are that he neglected aircraft and tanks. As seen earlier, he had good reason to respect the value of aircraft for observation, and he would have used tanks earlier than September 1916 if they had been available. There were a number of theories about the correct use of tanks in 1916 and 1917. Some commanders thought that they should be used instead of an artillery bombardment because they would leave the area under attack in a less ruinous condition; others believed they should stay behind with the infantry. Some sceptics believed that once the initial effect of their appearance had worn off their limitations would be exposed and they would be relegated to a secondary rôle. These doubts about the value of tanks on the battlefield persisted all through the 1920s and 1930s, and not until the German Panzers sliced through the Allied armies in France in 1940 did the War Office wake up to the fact that here was a new weapon waging an old form of warfare – that of cavalry – in devastating style.

Curiously enough, the Panzer blitzkrieg tactics owed their existence to the experience gained by the Germans in the battle of Cambrai, which Haig was planning even while Passchendaele was drawing to its bloody close. Haig realised the potential of this new weapon, slow and unreliable though it then was, but he also appreciated that that potential could only be utilised when tanks were available in sufficient number on the battlefield. In late 1917 that moment seemed to have arrived, although it was useless to employ tanks in any number around Passchendaele, which was a graveyard for the new weapon. Tanks required dry, flat ground, and the the most suitable terrain seemed to be the area west of Picardy.

The German General Staff had been extremely perturbed when tanks had appeared at the battle of the Somme but, after assessing the results and noting the tank's proclivity to drop out of the battle for mechanical or other reasons, were not apprehensive about further such attacks. They calculated that planning a battle around tanks might be so complicated that the innovation might in fact be counter-productive.

Just before the Cambrai offensive was due to begin, the Germans captured an Irish prisoner who told them all they wanted to know about British plans for a forthcoming attack using tanks. In view of the conclusions they had already drawn, and suspicious of the fact that the prisoner might be engaged in some ingenious deceptive exercise, they discounted the possibility of any danger from this source. On 20 November, ten days from the end of the battle of Passchendaele, they were therefore dis-agreeably surprised when 381 tanks, followed by small numbers of infantry, attacked them without warning on a fifteen-mile front between Moeuvres, three miles to the north of Cambrai, and Banteux, twelve miles to the south. The pattern of First World War battles had seemed to develop into a convention that no attack would ever begin without a preliminary bombardment, sometimes lasting a few days, sometimes longer. If the Germans had played the more eccentric English games, they would prob-ably have described the unconventional attack as 'not cricket'.

Before approving of the tank battle of Cambrai, Haig had had long discussions with the experts – Brigadier General Hugh Elles, Lieutenant Colonel J. F. C. Fuller and General Sir Julian Byng, commander of 3rd Army in whose area the attack would be made. Byng had a highly creditable record as the victor of Vimy, among other battles, and when he said that there should be no preliminary bombardment his views were accepted.

Byng was well aware that the area in front of his 3rd Army had been well fortified by the Germans, and that the beginning of any bombardment would serve as a warning to all the forward defences to be fully manned. He also knew that, though tanks might make an initial breakthrough while the Germans were too surprised to know what was happening, the enemy would soon rally to the counter-attack. It was therefore necessary to have heavy artillery in reserve to destroy the second and third line of the German defences and also inflict heavy casualties among their reinforcements. One thousand heavy guns were allotted for this purpose. Seven infantry divisions would follow the 381 tanks; and there were four cavalry divisions ready behind the infantry, waiting for an opportunity to pour through any large breach in the German line.

The opening stages were a dramatic success. The Germans were astonished to be confronted by this mass of landship firepower and gave up their first line without making much resistance. The cavalry was ordered forward but made little progress: 5th Cavalry Division could not advance against the concentrated machine gun fire of the German second line, and 1st Cavalry Division was held up by a bridge which one of the tanks had accidentally destroyed at Masnières. Both incidents seemed to show that there was no place for cavalry on the modern battlefield. However, there were four more cavalry divisions in reserve and Haig, who did not seem to have been fully informed of the circumstances of the first checks, was anxious to use them.

Unfortunately, Haig had two handicaps in assessing the progress of this battle. The first was lack of up-to-date information about the events in the front line; this was a problem which in the past might have been solved by 'gallopers' – hard-riding horsemen who could travel quickly around the battlefield – and in the future would be handled by radio communication from specialised units. The second handicap was the information he received from the over-optimistic and misguided Charteris, who failed to emphasise that the Germans were already transferring divisions rapidly from the Russian front and had already brought fresh troops into the area. A specific example was the 107th German Division, which had now arrived in the Cambrai sector.

Charteris's account of the events of this time, as given in his biography of Haig, seems somewhat evasive: 'Haig's own Intelligence Service calculated that no large hostile reinforcements were likely to reach the scene of battle within forty-eight hours; after that they could arrive at the rate of two divisions a day up to a total of thirteen divisions.'

In fact twenty-three divisions had already arrived, but Charteris considered that the attack was a justifiable risk and did not wish to deter Haig from taking it. His motives were undoubtedly good; he wished Haig to take the chance of a certain victory, but felt that if the chances were too narrowly balanced Haig might exercise his normal caution and let the opportunity slip. Charteris knew that by this stage in the war Haig was in no mood to take risks.

Cambrai is a famous battle because it was the first occasion on which tanks were used on a large scale to introduce a new method of warfare. However, it did nothing to change the status quo on the Western Front. The British troops were held up on the second line of the German defences and were then counter-attacked with great vigour. A major factor in the German success in the counter-attack was their use of low-flying aircraft to harass the British infantry. If the British had used their own aircraft to assist the advance of their tanks into the German second line, Cambrai would have been a preview of the 1940 blitzkrieg, in which the Germans used dive-bombers for that purpose.

And, of course, there were not enough tanks. Of the original 381, 179 were out of action by the end of the first day; this was almost half the total British tank strength and, although some of the casualties might have come back into action after repairs, a good proportion had been completely destroyed. Nevertheless, the remainder rallied for the second attack on the German position, which was now manned by fresh troops from 107th Division. Haig relieved his own troops progressively as the fighting continued, but no further progress was made against the larger numbers in the heavily fortified area ahead of them.

On 30 November the Germans delivered a determined counter-attack, using gas. The battle swung back and forth, with the Germans gradually gaining the upper hand. This battle, which had been begun with modern tanks, now became an occasion for old-fashioned cavalry. The 2nd and 5th Cavalry Divisions fought as infantry in a desperate but successful counter-attack; the 4th tried a mounted charge, but made little headway against machine guns. When the battle ended on 5 December, Byng's 3rd Army had sustained forty-seven thousand casualties; the Germans sub-sequently admitted losses of forty-one thousand, although this figure is considered by military historians to be too conservative.

An unexpected effect of the Cambrai battle was the misleading of the British public. Although the press correspondents had been warned not to be too enthusiastic in their first reports, the North-cliffe press, which included *The Times*, decided that any spec-tacular success must be heavily trumpeted to cheer up the public, who were now pondering the appalling casualties and reports of Passchendaele. *The Times* ran a huge headline, simply saying 'The Victory', and underneath talked about 'bewildering success' and 'a glorious battle'. Other papers followed suit, and in consequence the British public behaved as if the war was now won. Church bells were rung, and people danced in the streets.

Two days later, the news of the German counter-attack was published. Northcliffe, instead of feeling contrite, was furious. He considered he had been deceived and vented his feelings by attacking both the Army and the government. The War Cabinet, dismayed at the course of events, set up a Court of Inquiry to ascertain what had gone wrong at Cambrai and why. It did not take long to pin much of the blame on the faulty intelligence supplied by Charteris. Lord Derby, the Secretary of State for War, then wrote to Haig and informed him that the War Cabinet considered Charteris to be quite unfit for his post as Director of Military Intelligence.

Haig's reaction was to send for Charteris, inform him of the War Cabinet's view, and to say that he personally did not blame Charteris as he himself had relied on many other sources of information apart from his Director of Military Intelligence, among them the War Office's own regular reports. In view of Charteris's record, apart from Cambrai, this was an extraordinarily generous, or perhaps foolish, attitude to take. But even when told by Kiggell that Charteris was extremely unpopular in both corps and armies, Haig was reluctant to let him go. Eventually, however, realising that to cling obstinately to such a liability would weaken his ability to stand up to Lloyd George, he decided to part company. Charteris's replacement seems to have been almost as unsuitable – the Hon. Herbert Lawrence, who had resigned his commission in 1903 when Haig had been promoted over his head to command the 17th Lancers. However, Haig continued to ask Charteris's advice for the short period in which Lawrence held the post (he became Chief of the General Staff in January in place of Kiggell) and even afterwards.

Charteris wrote of these events in a very restrained way:

> The effect on the relations between General Headquarters and the government was instantaneous and Haig, under strong pressure from home and with deep reluctance, deemed it advisable to reorganise his Staff who had been with him almost without change throughout his command.
>
> The health of the Chief of the General Staff [Kiggell] had suffered severely under the prolonged strain, and on medical grounds his resignation of his office was inevitable, although Haig would have wished to give him a period of leave of absence in the hope his health might be restored. In addition to this change Haig replaced his Quartermaster-General [Maxwell] (who was transferred to an appointment at home) and the Head of his Intelligence Service [Charteris himself] (who was given another post at General Headquarters).

Haig was, of course, fully aware that Lloyd George's principal wish was to replace him as Commander-in-Chief, but knew that if this was done abruptly it would produce a public outcry. The Prime Minister therefore planned to undermine Haig's position by removing his closest supporters and friends. Charteris was an obvious candidate and had paved the way for his own dismissal. Lloyd George's next target was Robertson, who would be more difficult to move, despite the fact that, not surprisingly, the CIGS was by now tired of the political and military intrigues which surrounded him.

The first step to remove Robertson had been taken even when the Passcher.daele battle was in its final stages. The Italian defeat at Caporetto during October, and the hasty despatch of British troops and a British general to boost resistance in that area, had convinced the Allies that a better co-ordinated joint policy was needed. British, French and Italian representatives therefore met at Rapallo on 5 November and without hesitation decided to establish a Supreme War Council to meet this need. The meeting was convened with Foch as the Chairman and Henry Wilson as the British representative; Robertson immediately objected to this arrangement as it appeared to undermine his own authority as the British CIGS. He suspected, correctly, that it was a scheme hatched by Wilson with the approval of Lloyd George, something which would not have surprised Haig, who had long ago decided that Wilson was a master of underhand dealing.* However, in November Haig was too busy considering the Cambrai project to be able to spare much time looking over his shoulder at the manoeuvres of politicians and intriguers. Although he was still extremely concerned about the weakness of the French Army, he was encouraged when there was another government upheaval in France and Clemenceau emerged as joint Prime Minister and Minister for War. The seventy-six-year-old Clemenceau promptly proclaimed that his aim was 'to be entirely in unity with the soldier, to live, suffer and fight with him; to renounce all that does not directly further our country's interest'.

These stirring word convinced Haig that there might now be a resurgence of French morale. In order to give that time to take effect, he decided to make a somewhat rash gesture of goodwill by taking over an additional sector of the French line. He assumed that this would enable the French to reorganise their forces and

---

* Wilson subsequently rose to the rank of field marshal, but left the Army after the war and become a Conservative MP for an Ulster constituency. He was assassinated by two members of the IRA outside his house in London in June 1922.

deploy the best of them in their front line. However, as he knew that the Germans had fresh troops coming in steadily from Russia, and that he himself had already had to relinquish five divisions to Italy, one wonders whether he had not become too obsessed with the needs of the French. The French Army tended to be unpredictable, though some parts of it fought with the most impressive tenacity and dedication.

On 21 January Haig was gratified to receive a visit from General Smuts, once an enemy in the Boer War and now a valued friend, and Sir Maurice Hankey. They gave the impression that they were touring army units in order to find out what they could do to help. In fact they had been sent to France by Lloyd George, as he mentions in his memoirs, in order to ascertain whether there was a suitable replacement for Haig as Commander-in-Chief. Such a man they were unable to find, which Lloyd George considered 'very disappointing'. However, although Lloyd George could not oust Haig, he was determined to restrain him from planning any further offensives. He therefore ensured that the despatch of reinforcements to France was slowed down – a move which could have contributed substantially to a German victory.

Lloyd George's attitude to Haig is understandable. All his contacts with Haig had left him with the impression that here was a man of military competence much ahead of his contemporaries. On the other hand, he felt that Haig and his entourage were almost entirely devoid of imagination and at the same time were stoically indifferent to the fact that the youth of the nation was being sacrificed without any alternative plans being considered. He suspected that Haig and his generals saw the youth, and therefore the future, of the nation, not as human beings, but as so many companies, battalions, brigades or divisions. He doubted if Haig had any concept of the fact that if the war went on much longer there would be no one left to fight, and that even before that happened, a revolution could break out in Britain.* There

---

* There was an under-current of feeling against the war owing to the huge losses, but it fell far short of anything remotely resembling a revolution.

must, he reasoned to himself, be a better way than Haig's. The Gallipoli landings had been a costly disaster, but that did not mean that the lessons learnt from that experience could not help to make another landing elsewhere a success. With the exception of Wilson, the Higher Command seemed to Lloyd George to consist of elderly, unenterprising diehards who had failed so often that they no longer thought of their disasters as failures at all. The majority had been well advanced in rank even before the outbreak of war. It was no argument, he felt, to say that the German Army was run on identical lines: the aim of Britain should be to beat the German Army, not merely to imitate its policies. On 9 February the axe fell on Robertson, who had been steadfastly loyal to Haig. He was replaced by Wilson; Wilson's job with French GHQ was filled by Rawlinson.

Meanwhile the Germans were steadily reinforcing the Western Front and by mid-February had 177 divisions confronting 165 of the Allies'; more were coming up to join the Germans every day. Two German armies were positioned to attack between Ypres and La Bassée, and five more were deployed between Arras and Reims; these would presumably thrust south-west in the direction of Paris. Apart from the right flank, which was held by the French 6th Army, the Germans would be opposed by British armies: the 3rd and 5th in the south, and the 2nd in the north. These British armies, which had already been thinned out in order to cover a wider area, were outnumbered by nearly three to one – in both numbers and guns. Although Lloyd George and his colleagues had decided that the war could not be won on the Western Front, their views would have found no support among the Germans. Ludendorff had pre-empted the strategy of the Second World War in which the British Army would be separated from the French, and both would be encircled by flanking movements. The German intentions were well enough known to the Allies; the only doubt was where the main blow would fall.

On 21 March these doubts were resolved. After a massive bombardment, using a high proportion of gas shells, the German infantry attacked under cover of dense fog. During that day they drove a deep wedge into Gough's 5th Army and reached Péronne.

Territory which had taken the British Army weeks of bitter fighting to gain was now lost in hours. Byng's 3rd Army was stronger than Gough's, for it was holding a shorter front, but it had to give up ground in order not to leave its flank exposed as 5th Army fell back. The German planners had not expected such a tenacious resistance by 3rd Army; they therefore had to modify their original strategy which had been to turn sharply north after making a deep penetration into the 5th Army position. This would have brought them up behind 1st and 2nd Armies and set them on their way to capturing Calais and Boulogne. On the basis of never redeeming failure but only reinforcing success, Ludendorff ordered the main German effort now to be concentrated on exploiting the gains made against 5th Army. Three days later the Germans had reached a line running from Bapaume to Nesle, with Péronne well inside it. Haig, puzzled and disturbed by the fact that 5th Army should have been pushed back so far without being able to offer much resistance, visited Gough.

Pétain now appeared, full of fight and firmly convinced that the British and French Armies should remain in close touch. The following morning, however, he appeared again with a very different story. He now expected to be attacked in a massive German drive through Champagne. He did not expect to be able to hold it, and he was therefore in the process of creating a reserve army which could fall back and help protect Paris. Pétain, although 'the hero of Verdun', had lost his nerve just as he would do in the Second World War, and was prepared to leave the right flank of 5th Army completely exposed.

On receiving this news, Haig decided that he must take the initiative, even if it meant appearing to put the British Army under French supreme control. Pétain was clearly a broken reed; he must be replaced by someone who could and would fight. Haig felt it should be Foch.

The news of the staggering defeat of 5th Army had vigorous repercussions in London. Lloyd George decided that the French held the key to reversing the situation, as they had so far not been attacked, and he therefore sent Milner, a member of his War Cabinet, to Paris to consult the French government. By this time,

24 March, Wilson had received a telegram from Foch, and another from Haig; both suggested that Wilson should come to British GHQ immediately. Wilson met Haig at Montreuil and suggested that Foch was the man to co-ordinate the joint effort. Haig, who had already made up his mind on this point, had no difficulty in agreeing.

A conference then took place at Doullens. It was attended by Haig, Milner, Wilson, Lawrence, Pétain, Foch, Weygand, Poincaré★ and Clemenceau. There was an immediate clash between Pétain and Haig when the former explained that he had had to order the French to cover Paris because the British were now unable to do so. Haig pointed out that this move was not necessary, and that a far more important point to hold at that moment was Amiens. This was agreed. The conference ended harmoniously with the agreement that Foch should be appointed co-ordinator of the Allied Armies.

Five days later this bland statement was found to be inadequate. The agreement was therefore strengthened and, at a further conference where Lloyd George was also present, Foch's authority was extended to the 'strategic direction of military operations'. However, the respective Commanders-in-Chief, British, French and American, would continue to be responsible for the 'tactical employment of their forces'. Ten days later, this compromise was found to be unworkable and Foch was appointed Commander-in-Chief by agreement with the governments of Britain, France and the USA.

Meanwhile the Germans were pressing hard and the British Army was fighting desperately to retain what ground it could. Losses in the first fortnight of the battle had amounted to 177,739, but only 14,823 had been killed: a large number, some seventy thousand, had been taken prisoner and their positions had been over-run. However, the Germans had paid dearly for their success, having had 250,000 casualties, a higher than usual proportion of which had been killed. These unexpectedly high losses

★ Weygand was Foch's Chief of Staff. Poincaré was a former French Prime Minister, and later President.

caused them to change their strategy and reduce the number of divisions they had planned to use in the northern sector.

The fact that 5th Army had inflicted heavy losses on the Germans did not suffice to save Gough. Lloyd George insisted that he was a failure and should be removed. Haig pointed out that Gough had had a long front to cover and had only recently taken it over from the French, but Lloyd George was not impressed; he may well have remembered that Gough had not been markedly successful either on the Somme or at Passchendaele. Haig then refused to dismiss Gough without a direct order. He received one the next day in a telegram from Lord Derby, the Secretary of State for War. Gough was thereupon sent home and replaced by Rawlinson; 5th Army was now renamed 4th Army, reviving the name of Rawlinson's former command.

Foch had begun briskly in his new appointment. He had curtly informed Gough that there must be no further retreat – an order easier to give than to obey. The Germans continued to press on, but more slowly now. British Intelligence reported – and this was subsequently borne out by German Intelligence – that the Germans began to lose heart and cohesion when they saw the quality of the British equipment and supplies. So far from being elated by its capture the German troops felt that any success against such a well-equipped enemy could only be temporary. Looting and drunkenness also helped to slow them down. Meanwhile, Pétain was ordered to cancel his plans to withdraw his troops and was told to stand firm. French divisions were sent from the reserve army to cover the approaches to Amiens; other troops were sent to take over a section of the line from 5th Army.

Haig was well aware that if a similar blow fell on the sector held by 2nd Army it would be impossible to repel it. He therefore asked Foch to send French troops to reinforce the area around Ypres; Foch refused. Instead, he offered to send four divisions to the Arras sector. This manoeuvre would do nothing to help 2nd Army, but would place a wedge of French troops between the British 2nd and 4th Armies. Before this unsatisfactory compromise could be implemented, the Germans began their attack in that sector. Once again they used gas shells in their initial bombardment and pushed forward their infantry under cover of fog. In manpower they had fourteen divisions to oppose six, and the British were forced back, though only for a short distance. The Germans were clearly aiming for the famous Messines Ridge, and beyond that Hazebrouck, which was a railway junction of critical importance. A breakthrough here would put them twenty-two miles from the Channel.

Haig then sent out an Order of the Day to all the troops under his command. Such orders are only issued in desperate situations, and nothing could be more desperate than this:

Three weeks ago today the Enemy began his terrific attacks against us on a 50-mile front. His objects are to separate us from the French, to take the Channel ports, and destroy the British Army.

In spite of throwing already 106 divisions into the battle and enduring the most reckless sacrifice of human life, he has as yet made little progress towards his goals.

We owe this to the determined fighting and self-sacrifice of our troops. Words fail me to express the admiration which I feel for the splendid resistance offered by all ranks of our Army under the most trying circumstances.

Many amongst us now are tired. To those I would say that victory will belong to the side which holds out the longest. The French Army is moving rapidly and in great force to our support.

There is no other course open to us but to fight it out! Every position must be held to the last man: there must be no retirement. With our backs to the wall and believing in the justice of our cause, each one of us must fight on to the end. The safety of our homes and the freedom of mankind alike depend on the conduct of each one of us at this critical moment.

D. Haig
F.M.

Thursday 11 April 1918

The Germans, realising that they had let their offensive in the south lose momentum and finally halt, were resolved that there must be no repetition of that mistake. They pressed on relentlessly towards Hazebrouck. Fortunately Foch was now alert to the seriousness of the situation and was beginning to send reinforcements north. Even so, they were far from sufficient, amounting merely to five divisions of which only two were infantry and the rest cavalry. Haig pressed for more, suggesting at least eight divisions. Foch was willing to help but felt constrained by Pétain's unwillingness to see any part of his force removed from his own area, where it was blocking the main German thrust towards Paris; Pétain seemed unaware that the German drive for the Channel ports presented an even greater threat.

The crisis was resolved when Foch was formally appointed Commander-in-Chief of the Allied Armies. However, even as he announced his intention of supporting the British armies by despatching a reserve of fifteen French divisions, the situation still remained critical. The Germans made a powerful attack on the village of Villers-Bretonneux, using fourteen tanks; they captured it but lost it again in the British counter-attack. At the end of April the Germans made their final desperate attacks in the northern sector. They made headway, but failed to reach the objectives they so desperately required. Both the huge German offensives had now been halted for the time being.

Although the French Army had recovered from the traumas of the previous year, the brunt of the German attack had been held by the British. The cost had been high – 259,779 casualties, of which 22,741 had been killed. German losses had been greater, amounting to 348,300, with an even higher percentage killed.

Although there was a lull in the fighting during May, it was due to exhaustion rather than lack of intention. Ludendorff realised that time was running out for Germany. In spite of having incorporated the divisions which had returned from the Russian Front, his forces had now declined dangerously in quantity and quality. On the other hand, the Allies, though sorely battered by the recent battle, could look forward to receiving large reinforcements from America. Ludendorff realised that he must strike again quickly or his last chance of success would have gone. He decided that the weakest place in the Allied line was now on the French sector: he knew the French reserves had been sent to help reinforce the hard-pressed British. His objective was the famous Notre Dame de Lorette Ridge, which Haig had cause to remember from 1914. Although this was now a French sector, the British 9 Corps had been sent to the eastern end on the grounds that it was a quiet area, unlikely to be attacked, and therefore the five divisions in it could rest and recover after their earlier heavy fighting. Haig had informed Foch that these divisions were in no condition to be used again as front-line troops.

However, on 27 May that is what they became. Ludendorff opened the offensive with the usual devastating bombardment and followed it up with massed infantry attacks. Within five days the Germans had reached Château Thierry on the River Marne. History was repeating itself in a manner which the Allies had never anticipated. The British divisions suffered a further 28,703 casualties, the French over three times as many with 98,634. However, Haig was not entirely happy that the French had fought to the best of their ability, a view which was confirmed by both Foch and Weygand: they suspected that many had been taken prisoner too easily.

Meanwhile, the arrival of American troops in France had brightened the outlook for the Allies. Unfortunately mobilising, equipping, transporting* and training American troops had taken time. In the spring of 1918 many American units were attached to British units to learn the techniques of trench warfare. Foch would have preferred them to acquire experience by plugging gaps in the French sector. Haig objected: he thought that to put raw troops into a critical battle at this stage would be ruinous to them and militarily useless. General Pershing, not surprisingly, was strongly opposed to American troops being separated and distributed over the front; he wanted them to go into action as an army, and was stubbornly insistent on the point even when it was suggested that this might not be in the best interests of the Allies as a whole.

Foch's interpretation of the extent of his new powers soon

---

* Over 50 per cent were brought to Europe in British ships.

alarmed his allies. Having decided that the French sector had priority, he began moving both French and British divisions from the north to the south. News of these moves so alarmed Lloyd George that he called a conference to discuss the matter. Foch emphasised that he had the authority to move any troops, British or French or American, at short notice, to where they were most needed. Haig argued that he did not feel this should be done without his being consulted. Clemenceau, while supporting Foch's right to move troops as he thought fit, forbade him to move troops from Haig's area of command without first stating his intention.

In the middle of these discussions the Germans pushed forward once again. This time the French 3rd Army received the brunt of the attack, which came in between Montdidier and Noyon and reached a point a mere eleven miles from Compiègne. As it was continuing, there was another massive assault on the French 4th and 5th Armies in the sector running east from Château Thierry towards Reims, and beyond. Apart from a small penetration near Château Thierry, this later attack was a complete failure. There was then a lull in the battle while both sides reviewed the situation and wondered what action to take next.

Haig was the first to move. He decided that Le Hamel, a village on a hilltop some fifteen miles east of Amiens, would be an important acquisition, and at the end of the month assigned it to Rawlinson's 4th Army. The mainspring of this assault was the Australian Corps, commanded by the redoubtable General Sir John Monash. He had sixty of the latest Mark V tanks, from which much was hoped although they could only manage 4½ miles an hour. In spite of strong objections from Pershing, four companies of Americans were attached to the Australians and acquitted themselves well, although sustaining 134 casualties. The Australians advanced some two miles and took 1472 prisoners for losses of only 775.

Foch now took the initiative. The recent German offensive had left their troops in a highly vulnerable position south of the Aisne. A surprise assault by the French 10th Army, which used two hundred of the new Schneider tanks, inflicted heavy casualties and captured nearly thirty thousand prisoners as well as a large number of guns. Then the front settled down once more. It was known that Ludendorff was contemplating an offensive, but less well known that he had insufficient troops to make this more than a threat until he dug more deeply into his reserves. Haig was now approaching the point at which, at long last, he would be able to demonstrate the strategic and tactical skills for which his military life had been one long preparation.

The chosen date was 8 August, and the direction of the attack was along the Somme, east of Amiens, after which this battle was named. The main assault would come from 4th Army under Rawlinson, who was familiar with the area from hard experience. Rawlinson was allotted the Australian Corps which was commanded by Monash and contained five divisions, and the Canadian Corps, commanded by General Sir Arthur Currie, which contained four. While 4th Army attacked in the south, there was to be a diversionary attack further north by the British 3 Corps, which had not yet fully recovered from the mauling it had received five months earlier but which was still strong enough to confuse the Germans over the principal British intention. Again there would be no preliminary bombardment to warn the Germans what was coming, but instead an advance by infantry and 324 Mark V tanks. The Mark Vs were too slow to expand any gap made in the German defence, so Haig had also allotted ninety-six Whippets which, though lightly armed, had a top speed of 8 miles an hour. Supplementing the Whippets were three divisions of horsed cavalry.

The attack went in under cover of morning mist and reached all its objectives by noon, an advance of five miles. Fourteen thousand prisoners and three hundred guns were captured; casualties in 4th Army amounted to three thousand five hundred. Exploiting the victory was more difficult: two-thirds of the tanks were knocked out, and the cavalry could make no headway against concentrated machine gun fire. Even so, of the end of this phase of the battle Ludendorff wrote in his book *My War Memories* in 1919: 'August 8th was the black day of the German Army in the history of this war. This was the worst experience I had to go through.'

The attack was continued on the 9th and 10th, but progress was slow; the Germans knew what to expect now and were defending stubbornly. Haig took note of this, and when Foch visited him on the 10th and put forward a plan for Rawlinson to continue his attacks while the French 1st and 3rd Armies launched others further south, Haig was distinctly lukewarm. He thought that 4th Army had done enough for the time being and should be given time to recover and regroup; he felt that the best policy would be to allow the momentum to be kept up by Byng attacking with 3rd Army in the Arras–La Bassée sector.

Foch would have none of it. He wanted 4th Army to continue attacking as part of his overall plan, and gave Haig an order to this effect. Haig thereupon went to Rawlinson and passed on the order. Not surprisingly, Rawlinson was furious. 'Are you commanding the British Army or is Foch?' he asked indignantly. It was a delicate situation. Foch was Commander-in-Chief, but that did not necessarily empower him to give components of the British Army direct orders against the wishes of its Commander-in-Chief. Haig then agreed that Rawlinson need not be involved in this attack, which in 4th Army's present exhausted state was likely to bring heavy casualties with few gains. Needless to say, Foch was enraged at this defiance of his newly acquired authority. He repeated the order for 4th Army to join in the general attack.

On 14 August Haig, having discussed Foch's plan with Rawlinson and his corps commanders, went to Foch's headquarters. He was greeted somewhat brusquely with the question, 'When is 4th Army going to attack?' Haig replied with patient firmness that, although Foch was responsible for the overall strategy, he himself was responsible to the British government and people for the handling of the British forces. To his surprise and gratification, Foch's response was quite mild. All he required, said Foch, was information about British intentions so that he might co-ordinate his plans with the other armies. He agreed that Haig was quite right to take the stand he had.

Perhaps it was mere coincidence that four days later Clemenceau came to Haig at Amiens and conferred on him the Médaille Militaire. The episode also reflects credit on Foch, who, realising he had overstepped his authority as GOC-in-C, gracefully conceded the point. In the event, the mere presence of Rawlinson's army confronting them caused the Germans to divert reserves to that sector in preparation for the next attack. The chief beneficiary was the French 10th Army, which then put in a successful attack on a thinly held sector of the German line.

The attack which Haig had proposed for Byng's 3rd Army began at dawn on 21 August. It advanced nearly five miles, taking five thousand prisoners. Two days later 4th Army came into the attack again, making substantial gains. This was followed by a successful attack by 1st Army. Haig was determined that the Germans should not have a chance to recover, and planned to hit them with one massive blow after another. He suggested to Foch that the Americans should now be brought into the attack, a proposal with which Foch readily agreed. Pershing was at first prepared to co-operate, but when Foch proposed that the Americans should be put under a French army command, he objected strongly. There was no budging Pershing, but when the planned attack – between the Meuse and Aisne – was launched under American commanders it failed badly; the American Army, potentially good, lacked the experience necessary and incurred heavy losses.

At this point Haig was roused to fury by what he felt was quite unjustified interference by his old enemy Wilson, who sent him a telegram. It ran: 'Just a word of caution in regard to incurring heavy losses in attack on Hindenburg Line [the Siegfried Stellung] as opposed to losses when driving the enemy back to that line. I do not mean you have incurred such losses, but I know the War Cabinet would become anxious if we received heavy punishment in attacking the Hindenburg Line, without success.'

Haig was so infuriated by this patronising communication that he went to the War Office as soon as he could clear himself from his most urgent commitments in France. He saw Milner, and recorded the interview as follows:

I stated that *the object* of my visit was to explain how greatly the situation in the field has changed to the advantage of the Allies. I considered it to be of the first importance that the Cabinet should realise how all our plans and methods are affected by the change. Within the last four weeks we had captured seventy-seven thousand prisoners and nearly eight hundred guns. There has never been such a victory in the annals of Britain and its effects are not yet apparent. The German prisoners now taken will not obey their officers or NCO's. The same story is told me of the prisoners from our hospitals. The discipline of the German army is quickly going, and the German officer is no longer what he was. *It seems to me the beginning of the end.* From these and other facts I draw the conclusion that the enemy troops will not await our attacks in even the strongest positions. Briefly, in my opinion, the character of the war has changed. What is wanted now at once is to provide the means to exploit our recent successes to the full. Reserves in England should be regarded as Reserves for the French front, and all Yeomanry, cyclists and other troops now kept for civil defence should be sent to France *at once*. If we act with energy now, a decision can be obtained *in the very near future*.

Unfortunately his appeal fell on stony ground. Milner, supported by Wilson, thought that Haig was overstepping the mark and was about to embark on a campaign which would invite losses on the scale of the first day of the Somme; he warned Haig to be careful. The army he was now commanding, said Milner, was the last one Britain would be able to produce. There was no longer a source of reinforcements. Haig realised that this was really the voice of Lloyd George speaking and that it showed a complete misunderstanding of the military realities: German morale was breaking and this was the time to press home the final attacks. There was, of course, a considerable element of risk. The Germans had been laboriously and skilfully building their fortifications for over two years. They would not give them up without a struggle.

On 18 September, 1st, 3rd and 4th British Armies swept forward to the core of the Siegfried Stellung. In doing so they captured another 116,000 prisoners, but not without heavy losses to themselves. Everything now depended on the final assault. It was to be in the shape of a huge pincer movement, with the northern claw being the Belgian Army and the British 2nd Army, and the southern claw Pershing's American Army. The centre of the pincer would be 1st, 3rd and 4th Armies, and on their right would be the French 4th Army.

The final assault to break the Siegfried Stellung began on 22 September, but in order to deceive the Germans it did not go in in one wave but sector by sector. The Americans began, with the difficult assignment of the Argonne forest; the French quickly followed; and then the British armies triumphantly smashed their way through to Bourlon Wood and Cambrai. The northern claw recaptured Gheluvelt and pressed on along the Lys Valley to Roulers. Rawlinson's 4th Army was the last to join in the battle, but eventually the most successful. By 5 October he was through the third line of the complex German fortifications.

On the 6th Germany asked for an armistice but did not offer to surrender. The war was by no means over: although their main defence had been broken, the German Army in France had not given up the struggle. Foch thought that it should return to the Rhine as evidence of good faith before negotiations should begin, but this it was not prepared to do.

Now, at long last, all the infantry and cavalry training of the pre-war armies came into its own in the pursuit that followed. The Germans clung tenaciously to their positions as they retreated, and this final, long-drawn-out rearguard action gave credence to later German belief that their armies had never been finally defeated in the field, but only driven back before accepting an armistice in good faith. In fact they had been fairly and squarely beaten in a four-year war in which they had fought with courage, skill and resolution, but had eventually lost mainly due to a British army which had remained steadfast when its allies were falling away. The credit for that fact is certainly Haig's, yet instead of it being freely accorded to him he is remembered wrongly as the man responsible for the slaughter of so much of British youth.

> Time hath, my lord, a wallet at his back,
> Wherein he puts alms for oblivion,
> A great-size'd monster of ingratitudes:
> Those scraps are good deeds past; which are devour'd
> As fast as they are made, forgot as soon
> As done.
>
> *Troilus and Cressida*

15

Public Service

THE GERMANS HAD first asked for an armistice on 6 October. On the 9th Haig received a guarded message of congratulation from Lloyd George: ' . . . have just heard from Marshal Foch of the brilliant victories won by the First, Third and Fourth Armies, and I wish to express to yourself, Generals Horne, Byng, and all the officers and men under your command my sincerest congratulations on the great and significant success which the British armies, with their American brothers-in-arms, have gained during the past two days.'

Haig understood exactly what Lloyd George was saying: Foch was the architect of victory, and the British and the Americans were backing him up well. Haig thanked the Prime Minster politely. A more welcome message came from his former colleague, now Field Marshal French, who had been one of his severest critics: 'You will be tired of congratulations, but let me say that as you approach the scene of our former exploits together my heart and thoughts are with you. Don't reply. French.'

The German request for an armistice had been sent to Woodrow Wilson, the American President, who had now produced four principles and Fourteen Points which he felt were necessary conditions for world peace. Since Lloyd George had just won an election on the basis of 'Make Germany pay', Poincaré wished to erase Germany from the map, and most of the other belligerents were hoping for a reward for whatever efforts they had made, the situation did not look auspicious. Clemenceau summed up the general opinion of Wilson: 'The American President has fourteen Commandments: the Good Lord Himself has only ten!'

Not until 18 October was Haig formally asked for his views about possible terms for an armistice. Foch had already submitted his views, which were for compliance with a very harsh ultimatum. Haig disagreed totally. He thought that to try to impose severe and humiliating terms on the Germans would merely cause them to fight to the end, however bitter. He felt that this might involve the Allies in a highly dangerous situation in which all might still be lost.

He pointed out that the French Army had lost all will to continue fighting, in spite of what Foch might be saying, and that the American Army lacked experienced officers and NCOs and was dependent on the Allies for most of its equipment and supplies. The British Army was extremely efficient, but it lacked reinforcements; however, if the war was to be continued into Germany the British Army would have to bear the brunt of the fighting and would be sacrificing British lives for no sensible reason. In spite of having fought the Germans for four long years, Haig felt no bitterness towards them and had no wish to humiliate them. He suspected that the French wished to continue the war in order to revenge themselves for the heavy defeat in 1871, and the devastation of French territory since 1914, and he did not think that British lives should be sacrificed for that purpose. He therefore suggested surrender terms which were much less harsh than those put forward by Foch.

Nevertheless, the ensuing compromise, the armistice signed on 11 November, leaned more in favour of Foch than Haig. In the event Haig had overestimated Germany's ability to continue the fight: when the Kaiser had abdicated and revolution seemed in prospect, with Austria and Turkey already out of the war, the Germans were ready to accept peace at almost any price. However, Haig was sufficiently a student of history to know that the peace treaty of one war has often sown the seeds of the next, and hoped it would not happen this time. He was not consulted about the peace treaties: this was a subject which the politicians felt they could best settle themselves. Haig was not perturbed; he had plenty of other matters to occupy his mind.

The first was demobilisation. The War Office, prompted by the government, had suggested that, in order to restart industry as quickly as possible, trained technicians and skilled workers should be demobilised first. This idea optimistically presumed that several million men who had survived the hardships and dangers of war would be prepared to sit calmly in camps, at a time when army discipline had become very frail, while their ranks were picked over for men to be demobilised first and given the best jobs. Haig pointed out that to demobilise men out of turn, and hence unfairly, would produce uncontrollable unrest, not to mention bribery and corruption. He was ignored, the inevitable occurred, and there were mutinies even in élite regiments where such occurrences would previously have been thought impossible. Fortunately, the selective demobilisation plan was changed to one establishing length of service with an overseas force. When Winston Churchill succeeded Milner as Secretary for War in July 1919 he was astonished to find papers showing that Haig had long before made an accurate prophecy of what would happen if the now discarded demobilisation scheme was introduced; this had, of course, been ignored.

Haig now had time to visit some of those who had suffered badly in the war. Duff Cooper quotes an occasion when he had tea with seventy Belgians who had spied and sabotaged for the Allies. 'One woman was the last of a family: the Germans had shot the rest of them. "It was pathetic," wrote a witness, "to see how their faces lit up as he spoke words of comfort and sympathy to them." Driving away in the motor afterwards, the Field Marshal was visibly upset.'

Haig was less at ease when trying to sympathise with his own countrymen. It is, of course, a formidable task to try to say something comforting to someone who has lost their sight or a limb or been otherwise badly disabled, but it was particularly difficult for Haig, for he lacked small talk at the best of times. In any case, confronted with the hardships caused by the war he felt that words were totally inadequate. In consequence he often seemed abrupt, and spoke in the stilted, formal manner which people sometimes use to prevent their emotions getting out of control. For this reason he acquired the reputation of being hasty and unfeeling.

The facts were, of course, different. He considered that the government and the Army Council were making a totally inadequate response to the problems of the war disabled. He was already receiving a steady stream of letters, not always from the individuals themselves, pointing out how badly many of the war disabled were being treated. The pensions which they had been granted were insufficient even for subsistence, let alone to provide for the extra needs which their disabilities necessitated. Many, in fact, had not received any pension at all, and even those who had had often experienced long delays. Haig was in fact seeing at first hand the injustice which apathetic bureaucracy fosters; similar stories would be told after the Second World War. He suggested that a scheme should be set up by which men who were partially disabled should be found employment in government service; after the Second World War a much improved version was brought in.

The government was not particularly grateful for reminders of its deficiencies and that the speed at which it began to remedy these left something to be desired. That Haig's relations with the Prime Minister had not improved in the mellow glow of peace became evident when he was offered a viscountcy: this was the title which had been offered to, and accepted by, Sir John French after he had failed in the battle of Loos. It was a calculated belittling of Haig's achievement as Commander-in-Chief and he refused it, not because he thought it unworthy – although he cannot have failed to do so – but because he felt that before he could accept an honour the men who had fought under him must be provided for adequately. To have accepted a title when many were still waiting for their pensions would have seemed a betrayal. 'I am well satisfied with the rank and honours already conferred on me,' he said. 'If the government at this time wish to make a grant of money I could not accept it until the new Pensions Ministry have really accomplished something. Reports of very many sad cases still reach me.'

The government's reaction was predictable. They thought their bluff was being called and that it would be politically dangerous for them to have their offer thrown back into their faces. Lloyd George therefore offered him an earldom with a grant of £100,000.* Haig was still inclined to refuse, but accepted when it was pointed out that honours were being conferred on others all round him, and continued refusal would require a public statement and publicity of the kind he did not relish. He therefore became Earl Haig, Viscount Dawick, and Baron Haig of Bemersyde.

There were receptions, processions and an official drive. At this stage he was still being treated as the conquering hero: the criticism would come much later. A public subscription was launched to purchase and present to him Bemersyde, which was now owned by Arthur Balfour Haig, the 28th Laird, and therefore seemed an appropriate gift.†

From 15 April 1919 he held the appointment of Commander-in-Chief of the Army in Britain, Plumer having succeeded him as C-in-C the BEF. In February 1920, he retired from the active list.

It seemed possible that he would be appointed to one of the élite posts in the British Empire – Governor-General of Canada, or Viceroy of India – but he intimated that he did not wish to be considered for either. His task, he felt, lay with the welfare of the soldiers he had commanded. He was particularly relieved when his active appointment had come to an end, for he dreaded having to order troops to suppress any civil disobedience which might develop. The 'disobedient' civilians of the early 1920s included many who had served under Haig's command during the war, and were disaffected by the lack of jobs.

Civilian life did not provide the rest and pleasurable leisure Haig had expected. Inevitably he was in great demand as a public speaker, partly when unveiling war memorials, partly in order to

* Wellington had received a dukedom with £500,000, even before Waterloo.
† It needed much restoration before he could move in, three years later. He spent £30,000 on it between 1920 and 1924.

raise funds for ex-servicemen's organisations and partly to please associations which expected him to address their members. Since he was well aware that he was ill-equipped to be an impromptu speaker, each talk he gave required long and careful preparation. As his speaking engagements multiplied he acquired a certain expertise, but never developed into the type of speaker who can rise to his feet at a moment's notice, deliver a few acceptable sentiments, tell a few stories, sit down again and forget all about it.

In June 1919, the Principal and Fellows of Brasenose gave a dinner in Oxford Town Hall so that members of the College could meet Haig; the College dining hall was too small for this purpose. The Principal, Dr C. B. Heberden, who had been Haig's tutor when he was an undergraduate, spoke of his wartime career: 'He was always the same, absolutely imperturbable. He bore the almost intolerable strains of the Commander-in-Chief for four years with infinite patience, endurance, strength and skill. He never for a moment lost heart or allowed others to lose heart.'

In his reply, Haig said:

It is one of my firmest and most pleasant convictions that the great struggle through which we have passed has justified our faith in University education. Wherever I have gone – and of late I have become something of a pluralist in the matter of Universities – I have found the same splendid record among University men. I have had the opportunity, too, to judge the real value of that record from close at hand, and I know that it is well deserved.

It is here in Oxford that is found the main stronghold of the opinion that the highest and most important object of education is the formation of character. Believing as I do that our national character is chiefly due to our success in battle, and being aware of the criticisms that from time to time have been levelled against University education, it is only natural that I should seek to turn an occasion such as this to profit, by telling you how convinced I am you are right . . .

He continued:

Self-forgetfulness, self-sacrifice, the belief in right for right's sake, and the spirit of comradeship which springs from such beliefs held in common, steeled the resolution of our Armies, and enabled them to endure to the end . . .

In order fully to comprehend the wonderful performance of our Armies last year, one must seek in other directions than merely the material. The decisive factor which held up at last the enemy's attacks, and then carried our troops forward to victory, was British stubborn determination, British comradeship, British spirit, British moral.

Reporting the event, the College magazine, *The Brazen Nose*, added: 'At conclusion of the dinner the guests returned to the college where a bonfire had been lit and many of the Vice-Principals of the past must have turned in their graves as the Brasenose men, unchecked and unreported, fed the fire with various assortments of fuel, not unassisted, so scandal reports, by an old member of the College whose name is world famous.'

Many of Haig's post-war speeches were for the purpose of assisting ex-servicemen, some of whom were disabled, others out of work. At Liverpool in 1922 he said:

To my mind, it is one of the most pathetic sights to see a man who has fought for his country genuinely anxious to find work and finding it impossible to do so. It is even more pathetic to see the maimed man still waiting after all these years for the job suitable to his physical capacity. I think it is wonderful the way these men, both the fit and the maimed, remain as cheerful as they do under the circumstances. Nor have I any patience with the callous individual who shrugs his shoulders and says that the ex-serviceman does not work, or that if work is found for him, will trade upon the preference which has been granted because of his war service and be a slacker. There are wasters in every class of the community and there are wasters, of course, amongst ex-servicemen, but taken generally, the men who fought and saved England are the pick and flower of England, and it is a bad day for the country when that flower is allowed to wither because of neglect and apathy . . .

Business is not a charitable undertaking and Managing Directors are bound to see that the work they do is efficiently performed but, Ladies and Gentlemen, something must be done for the half million ex-servicemen eking out a miserable existence on the fifteen shillings per week dole.

When made a freeman of the City of Oxford, Haig spoke to a wider audience than the university:

We have spent nearly five years in the active destruction of wealth. The stream of our national prosperity has been directed deliberately, though not of our own choice, into the bottomless abyss of war. We have now got to create. The wealth that we have lost has got to be built anew, and that can only be done by work. Moreover, it is not work alone that is needed but corporate work, combination in effort and comradeship in striving.

Haig's speeches contain much information about his character and philosophy. He saw the First World War as a crusade against a very dangerous and amoral nation. 'We were doing duty for a higher form of civilisation, in which man's duty to his neighbour finds a place more important than his duty to himself, against an Empire built up and made great by the sword, efficient indeed, but with an efficiency unredeemed by any sense of chivalry or of moral responsibility to the weak.' Defeating this powerful enemy required a very high degree of morale. He respected the military ability of the Germans, but did not trust them: the subsequent birth and growth of the Nazi party, with all its attendant horrors, would not have surprised him.

When not preparing or giving speeches, Haig was heavily involved in correspondence. The letters he received, from former soldiers or their widows, often required him to take some action on their behalf or that of others. Each, he felt, merited a personal reply. He always answered letters in his own hand. When it was suggested he would save himself much trouble if he merely dictated and then signed his letters, he refused: people expected a personal reply, he said, and it was only fair that he should give one. Correspondence soon became a huge burden in conjunction with speechmaking; he was warned by his doctors that he was overdoing it. He listened to their advice, and neglected it.

Secrett considered that Haig worked harder than ever in retirement. He had a constant stream of callers, often up to thirty a day, usually without making an appointment. He managed to interview most of them but, if he had previous engagements, a few would be disappointed. Most of them brought along huge bundles of correspondence with the War Office or other official body. Sometimes applicants asked him if he could tide them over with a small loan, but Haig was adamant in his refusal: he said that if he once became known for handing out 'loans' his number of callers would increase greatly.

Since 1918, several organisations had come into being with the aim of improving the lot of the ex-serviceman. Each felt it was the best for that particular purpose, and inevitably a jealous and undignified rivalry began to grow up. Haig was concerned that their parochial attitudes were inefficient, wasteful, and unworthy of the cause to which all avowed they were dedicated. He felt that the answer was to create one central organisation. The fact that he had already influenced the House of Commons to review the previous pension scheme and improve it gave his argument an authority which it would not have had if it had relied solely on his former appointment as C-in-C. In consequence, in June 1921 the British Legion came into existence. It was formed by the amalgamation of the National Federation, the Comrades of the Great War, the Officers' Association and the National Association. The essential characteristic of the British Legion was that it was completely democratic. But as it was likely that control of the branches of the Legion would almost inevitably fall into the hands of ex-officers, Haig felt that active steps must be taken to prevent this happening. He wrote in a letter to Colonel Crosfield on 14 March 1922: 'There *ought* to be no question of "rank" in the Legion – we are all "comrades". That however is not possible and so we must legislate to ensure that the "other ranks" are adequately represented.'

It would have been easy for Haig to conclude that, once the British Legion had been established, his task was done and he could fade out of the picture. However, he did not do this. Large organisations, he realised, can easily become bureaucratic and fossilised. He felt that it was likely that those dealing with applications for assistance could all too easily begin to treat their work as routine administration, and lose sight of the fact that they were dealing with problems in which a kindly, sympathetic approach was of paramount importance. He suggested that interviewers should serve for short periods only, and be replaced regularly by people who had had personal experience of the conditions which the applicants were explaining.

Haig knew, of course, that the problems which the British Legion was tackling at home were mirrored in overseas countries which had supplied troops to the BEF. The first one of these that he visited, in 1921, was South Africa, where there were already four rival associations in existence. At first none wished to amalgamate: however, by reasoning and persuasion they were induced to resolve their differences and to join together as the British Empire Service League.

After an interval of four years, Haig visited Canada on the same mission. This time he encountered fourteen separate organisations, all of which had had time to consolidate their differing views. The fact that Byng, the former commander of 3rd Army, was now Governor-General of Canada, undoubtedly helped Haig in his formidable task of persuading the different organisations that the unity offered by amalgamation represented strength which could be nothing but beneficial to the ex-servicemen whom they were all dedicated to assisting.

However, as time went on and the organisation which he had helped bring into being settled down, he was able to spend more time at Bemersyde and with his family and friends. Although many of the latter were military men, he also had others in the literary, musical and artistic worlds. Among these were Sir William Orpen, Maurice Baring and F. S. Oliver. Haig had shown some talent as an artist in his early days in the Army, but had neglected it in order to pursue his career. It comes as no surprise, therefore, to find that his son, the present Earl, who was born in March 1918, is a painter, a former member of the Royal Fine Art Commission for Scotland, a present member of the Scottish Arts Council, a Trustee of the National Galleries of Scotland, President of the Scottish Craft Centre and an Associate of the Royal Scottish Academy. Haig's niece, Emily Haig, was also a talented sculptor and painter.

Haig divided his leisure time between riding, fishing, tennis and golf, becoming President of the St Andrew's Royal and Ancient Golf Club. He was keenly interested in rugby football which is, of course, played with vigour and strong rivalry in the Border counties. He was Colonel of four regiments, one of which was the Royal Horse Guards, 'The Blues'. He was presented with the freedom of a number of cities and attended the ceremonial presentations. He unveiled many war memorials. He became Rector and then Chancellor of St Andrews University. There were commercial interests, too. He was on the board of a number of companies and enterprises, including the Royal Bank of Scotland, the Fife Coal Company, the Distillers' Company and the London and North Eastern Railway. He was also Chairman of John Haig and Company. He took considerable trouble to ensure that he was well informed about world events, none of which suggested that the 1914–18 war had been, as had once been optimistically forecast, 'the war to end all wars'. He read widely.

All this was against a background of declining health, but he had no intention of sparing himself. He had never completely shaken off the malaria which he had contracted in India, and more recently had been diagnosed as having mild angina. His stamina and resilience when he held posts of awesome responsibility had been phenomenal, but the strain had taken its toll. It would have been understandable if he had imposed a rigid limitation on his commitments in the post-war years, but all he insisted on was having some time to spend with his family, with whom he lived a very simple life at Bemersyde. He knew that he was unlikely to live to a great age, but had no intention of prolonging his life by adopting a dull lifestyle, which might perhaps have made that possible.

The end came sooner than he, or anyone, expected. On 27 January 1928 he went to London, to stay with Henrietta at Prince's Gate prior to taking a holiday in France. On the 28th he went to Richmond to attend a Scout rally at which a new troop was being formed. It was to be called the Haig Troop, and would be filled with the sons of disabled ex-servicemen. He could not have refused either to go, or to make a short speech, although it was observed that in the middle of that speech he paused and went very white. After a few moments he continued, telling the boys to try to realise what citizenship and public spirit meant, to remember that they belonged to a great Empire, and that if people spoke disrespectfully of England they should stand up and defend their country.

Apparently none the worse for the experience, he returned to Prince's Gate and wrote a letter making arrangements for the following Tuesday. The next day was Sunday and he spent it quietly; he played cards after dinner and went to bed early. Shortly afterwards, his brother John, who was also staying in the house, went upstairs; as he passed Haig's room, he heard sounds indicating that something was amiss. Haig was conscious, but gasping for breath. It was all over in minutes. Haig's life had ended on 29th January 1928; he was sixty-seven.

He had already chosen his own burial place, in Dryburgh Abbey. At the state funeral in Westminster Abbey, the royal princes walked behind the gun carriage and Foch and Pétain were both pall-bearers. From Westminster the coffin was taken to St Giles' Cathedral, Edinburgh, where his body lay in state. It made the final journey to Dryburgh on a plain farm cart, drawn by four farm horses. His headstone, at his request, was identical to those in the cemeteries in France.

16

Some Judgements

FOR NEARLY TEN years after the end of the First World War there was little adverse comment on the way it had been conducted; attention was strongly focused on other matters. During the war, soldiers had been 'beloved Tommies'. Over a million from Britain and the Empire had died, while thousands had been disabled, physically and mentally. Britain had taken on huge financial burdens during the war, and now the bill had come in. There were huge numbers of ex-servicemen looking for jobs in a country which was still trying to convert its industry back to peacetime requirements and to recapture its previous position in world trade. The spoils of victory were noticeably absent. Ex-soldiers, including officers, were reduced to doing jobs which were so menial that in some cases they seemed akin to licensed begging, though there were plenty of people who had done very well out of munitions and contracts and made enormous profits.

The upper classes seemed to have shrugged off the war quickly and resumed their former lifestyle. However, many penniless ex-servicemen were no longer prepared to return to their position at the bottom of the heap, and resentment against money and privilege fermented, stimulated by political activists who spoke glowingly of the earthly paradise of equality of opportunity which had been created in Russia by the revolution there. A major attraction of their new form of government, which had an almost religious appeal, was that it forecast a world freed from war by the universal brotherhood of Communism. Not surprisingly, the disabled or jobless ex-soldier began to wonder why Britain's war leaders had continued fighting the war at appalling cost when the Russians had made an early peace and established such a sensible form of government.

There was, of course, plenty to criticise in Britain in the 1920s. The politicians, who had made so many promises during the war, 'a land fit for heroes', votes for women and other peacetime benefits, had failed to deliver. There was worse to come. When the great slump hit Britain at the end of the decade, many of the attempts that soldiers had made to rebuild their lives and livelihoods would once more be destroyed. But, until 1929, over ten years after the Armistice, little was said against the conduct of the war itself.* In general, the British people thought it had been so horrific that it was best forgotten, except on Remembrance Day when everyone bought a poppy in aid of Earl Haig's Fund for the Disabled.

It could not be expected to last, and in 1929 this particular armistice ended and the flood gates were opened. Suddenly the probing searchlights were turned on the men who had been in authority during the war – mainly generals, but others too. There had been a hint of what was coming when C. E. Montague had published his memoirs, *Disenchantment*, in 1924, but now it was claimed by many writers that the whole military system was absurdly inefficient, that much of the hardship and many of the deaths had been totally unnecessary. And, even if it had all been a model of efficiency, would the war have been worth the effort? As people looked around them in the late 1920s, they wondered what the war had achieved. Novelists and poets, such as Siegfried Sassoon, Robert Graves, Richard Aldington and Cecil Roberts, implied that it had lasted so long and been so horrific because of the incompetence of those who were directing it. The futility of war appeared to be shown perfectly in R. C. Sherriff's new play *Journey's End*, in which the whole of the company, officers and men, are wiped out in the final scene. Women who had preferred

---

* Although Lord Beaverbrook never missed an opportunity to criticise Haig, even after his death.

not to know the exact circumstances in which their husbands and lovers, sons and brothers had died, now had the appalling facts pushed into their faces by books, films, poems and plays. 'Official versions' of events were branded as a bunch of lies. There were over a million women in Britain whose husbands, or potential husbands, had been killed in the war, and their sadness turned to bitterness and anger.

Haig was dead by the time the literature of disillusionment was released on to the public, but there was no question of 'de mortuis nil nisi bonum'. Suddenly he was no longer the deeply respected Commander-in-Chief who had won the war for the Allies. Instead he was seen as an aloof, callous figurehead, who had sent men to their deaths in thousands without knowing or even caring what he was doing. There were plenty of others to share the blame, not least Churchill and Ian Hamilton, the C-in-C Mediterranean, for the failure at Gallipoli. But Haig was not there to defend himself, nor did it seem likely that he would have tried to do so if he had still been alive.

The critics were not limited to writers and widows – there were plenty in the Army itself. Analysed in the cold clinical atmosphere of the Staff College or conference room, the mistakes were easy to identify: they always are. Analysts at post-war conferences tend to overlook the fact that men do not always behave rationally if they are deafened, wet, too hot or too cold, hungry, apprehensive and tired. Whatever else a man may be experiencing when he is in a battle zone, it may be reliably assumed that he is tired – very, very tired. Haig would not have been tired as men in the trenches were tired, but he must have felt drained of energy most of the time. There was no rest for him from 1914 to 1918, for even when he was on leave his mind was occupied by thoughts of his responsibilities. There must have been numerous occasions when he made decisions which he would not have made if he had been relaxed and rested.

During the 1930s, when there were strong anti-war movements in France and Britain, and many people believed that the best defence against Hitler's rearmed Germany was to pretend it did not exist, gradually Haig's name became generally associated with all the worst features of war. Strangely enough Kitchener, whose face on the famous poster bearing the slogan 'Your Country Needs You' had induced thousands to join up, was cleared of all responsibility for what happened to them afterwards. French, Plumer, Gough, Smith-Dorrien and Rawlinson were not even known: the nearest reference made to them in the press was that the 1914–18 war had been fought by 'cavalry generals', any one of whom might have been the subject of the joke, 'There was once a cavalry officer who was so stupid that his brother officers noticed it.' The villain of the piece, the fallen idol, was Haig. Even the fact that Lloyd George retracted some of his former criticism of Haig made no difference.* There was a feeling of relief on the outbreak of the Second World War that Haig was no longer in charge. There were some doubts about Viscount Gort, who was appointed Commander-in-Chief of the BEF in 1939, but it was assumed that, though he had been old enough to have fought with distinction in the First World War, he was too young at the time to have been tainted by the medieval ideas of its generals. Gort knew an irretrievably lost battle when he saw one, and for that reason suggested a swift evacuation of 338,000 men at Dunkirk. A month later, this total was increased to some five hundred thousand by other evacuations. Gort had won a VC in the First World War and would have preferred to stay and try to fight it out with the Germans, but he knew that the task was impossible, and he had been warned about the danger of incurring casualties on the scale of the 1914–18 war.

This attitude continued throughout the Second World War. Soon after the fall of France, Greece and Crete were evacuated – admittedly after some hard fighting. Singapore, which had lasted twice the time that France had, and without the benefit of an air force, navy or tanks, was surrendered to save civilian casualties. There was still a hope that victories could be virtually bloodless, even though the North African, Sicilian and Italian campaigns

* 'There was no conspicuous officer in the Army who seemed to be better qualified for the Highest Command than Haig.' (Lloyd George, *Memoirs*, Vol. 2, 1936.)

took a toll of lives. But anything was better, it was felt, than reverting to the trench warfare associated with Haig. There was, of course, some trench warfare, particularly in Italy, and some of the battles were as unpleasant as those in the First World War, but they were recognised as the exception. There was hard fighting in the North West Europe campaign, but the general view was that the war could be won at a lower cost in casualties by using bombing raids. The fact that the number of aircrew killed was greater than that of the subalterns in the First World War was conveniently ignored.

The Allies, pleased with their successes in North Africa, Italy and France, failed to appreciate that these were really sideshows in relation to the main effort, which was taking place in Russia, and that the war which was being fought there was closely akin to the war which Haig had fought. The Germans were eventually beaten by mass infantry (and tank) attacks which were not unlike those of the Somme and Passchendaele. Similarly, the Japanese were beaten and driven out of Burma by infantry attacks which cost thousands of lives. Even in the Pacific, where the Americans used more high explosive than in any other theatre, the essential gains were made by infantry. The Japanese had to be removed from the lands they had over-run by hard infantry and artillery battles, and the Germans had to be forced back out of Russia by continuous ground attacks.

Seven years later, the North Koreans and Chinese were pushed out of South Korea by infantry attacks, and in the next decade American troops in South Vietnam were driven out by infantry attacks. Wars, it became clear, could only be won by sacrificing lives. The assumption that Haig was an archaic survival of earlier conflicts who fought the First World War by a needless sacrifice of infantrymen, and that afterwards easier and less costly methods of winning wars were used, is an illusion. There is no quick, easy or bloodless way to remove well-armed, unwelcome invaders of one's country. Haig knew that to be true, and it is as true now as it was then.

Haig has been criticised, notably by Winston Churchill in *The World Crisis*, Vol. III, (1927) for continuing the Passchendaele offensive too long. It was one of the first attacks on Haig's tactics, and he was still alive to refute it: 'It is impossible for Winston to know that the possibility of the French army breaking up in 1917 *compelled me to go on attacking*. It was impossible to change sooner from the Ypres front to Cambrai without Pétain coming to press me not to leave the Germans alone for a week, on account of the awful state of the French troops.'

In 1952, when there was trench warfare in Korea not unlike that on the Western Front in 1917, Robert (later Lord) Blake, the Oxford historian, published an edited edition of the Haig diaries and papers, entitled *Private Papers of Douglas Haig 1914–1918* (Eyre and Spottiswoode). This was a digestible collection of the most relevant portion of the papers, and had the additional benefit of shrewd summaries and wise comments at the beginning of each chapter.

In 1963 John Terraine's study, *Douglas Haig: the Educated Soldier*, appeared. Although one might quibble at the use of the word 'educated' in the title, it is the best and most comprehensive study of Haig so far and is likely to remain so for a long time to come. This is a book for the serious reader, but is clearly written and free from jargon. The research is impeccable and the judgements are sound, though Terraine has been accused by Haig's critics of idolising his subject.

Among the subsequent books, one, *Douglas Haig, 1861–1928*, was written by a young American, Gerard de Groot. It is comprehensive and interesting but contains some remarkable generalisations about Haig, such as: 'His ultimate rejection of the Oxford life is itself a clue to the man he became', and concludes with the statement: 'It was Haig's ironic fate that, he, an eminent Edwardian, eventually came to be judged according to the very different standards of another age.' Haig was not, of course, an Edwardian. He spent forty years of his life under Queen Victoria, nine under Edward VII, and seventeen under George V.

Tim Travers, of the University of Calgary, takes a critical view of Haig in his book *The Killing Ground*. He concludes:

The British army's reaction to the emergence of machine

warfare was therefore a conservative reflex, perhaps because full accommodation to modern warfare would have required social and hierarchical changes with unforeseen consequences. In this the British army was not unique, being similar to the French army, while the German army embarked on an entirely new conception of war and ideology that was soon to have grave results in the reorganisation of German society.

Professor Travers arrived at this conclusion by stages:

By far the greatest problem was the way in which the late nineteenth-century paradigm failed to come to grips with the twentieth-century paradigm – one set of ideas simply did not engage the other emerging set of ideas because the act of conversion to a fundamentally different kind of war was essentially an emotional one that was extremely difficult to make.

Haig's personality revolved around an almost obsessive need for order. His structured interior and exterior life due, it can be argued, to an early developed inner-directed character, meant that he was simply not receptive to basic changes in ideas and life style.

But, it seems, in 1918 – when, incidentally, Haig was winning his first victories – there were signs of a change:

Perhaps even more important was the way in which the proponents of the human battlefield paradigm were starting mentally to engage the technological paradigm, although fundamental conceptions of war were naturally hard to change ... In contrast to Ludendorff and the OHL [German High Command], Haig and his GHQ tried to adapt resources, men and technology to the traditional paradigm of war rather than the other way round.

In a wide spectrum of conflicting opinions, perhaps the final word should come from someone who knew Haig well and had experienced at first-hand the conditions under which and for which Haig's decisions were made. General Sir James Marshall-Cornwall was a veteran of both World Wars. In the first he won a DSO and an MC and was mentioned five times in despatches; in the second he commanded III Corps in France and was GOC British Troops in Egypt and later in Western Command, and was mentioned twice more in despatches. He assesses Haig's place in history thus:

Germany's spirit of resistance was broken, mainly by the courage and resolution of Haig's armies, which had complete confidence in the leadership of their Commander. They were inspired by his foresight and determination, for he never wavered from his fixed purpose of breaking down the powers of resistance of his enemy, both morally and physically. Had Haig not had the moral courage to shoulder the main burden of the struggle in the Somme battles of 1916 and the Flanders fighting in the previous year, French resistance would have crumbled and our principle Ally might have thrown up the sponge before a single American soldier landed in Europe. Haig was one of the main architects of the Allied victory.

17
The Jury Is Out

THE ESSENTIAL FACT about Haig is that he commanded the largest army Britain had ever put into the field and achieved victory with it, even on the occasions when his allies were unable to be of much assistance. He had reached his eminent position by hard work, driving ambition and the ability to use influence. His appearance suggested unruffled efficiency and self-confidence. His predecessor, Sir John French, had never looked like a commander-in-chief, and Plumer, although probably a more talented soldier than Haig, also lacked the presence necessary for supreme command. Allenby and Byng both looked the part and possessed good qualifications, but were not noticeably superior to Haig.

Critics of Haig seem more concerned with his deficiencies than his assets, and look for reasons to blame him for the vast death toll of the First World War. It was not Haig, however, but the Germans who killed the men who lie in the cemeteries of France. When Haig became C-in-C of the BEF he was confronted with a German army that was well dug in and intended to achieve victory whatever the cost; he defeated it, but such a victory could not be achieved without hideous losses on both sides. Unlike Napoleon, Haig was not indifferent to battle casualties, but he realised that the Germans could not be defeated and pushed out of France without an enormous cost in lives.

In the seventy-three years which have elapsed since the First World War ended there have been many criticisms of Haig – but very, very few have suggested alternative tactics or strategy. Haig has been condemned for achieving with men what his critics think should have been done with metal. But it was the Germans who had the material superiority for the first part of the war, and even at the end they were equal, not inferior. Haig, no doubt, would have liked to be in the enviable position of Montgomery at Alamein, able to wait until he outnumbered his opponents by two to one in airpower, tanks, guns and men. But Haig always had time against him. At any moment after 1916 the French Army could have collapsed entirely, allowing the Germans to walk through to victory. He was also in the absurd but nevertheless frustrating position of being under a Prime Minister who was always trying to hinder him when, in spite of lack of political support, he was winning victories.

It is Haig's misfortune to be remembered by posterity not for his victories, but for the cost of them. He defeated what was until then the most powerful army in the world. He did so because, whatever the circumstances, he never lost his nerve.

Professor Charles Carrington, who fought from beginning to end of the First World War, should have the last word: 'The nerve of the German Higher Command failed at the decisive point. The allies were better soldiers and Foch and Haig were better generals than their adversaries. It is nerve that wins battles and the last battle is the one that matters.'

Select Bibliography

Arthur, Sir George, *Lord Haig*, Heinemann, 1928.

Bean, C. E. W., *The Official History of Australia in the War of 1914–1918*, Angus and Robertson, 1942.

Blake, Robert (ed.), *The Private Papers of Douglas Haig 1914–1918*, Eyre and Spottiswoode, 1952.

Blunden, Edmund, *Undertones of War*, Putnam, 1932.

Bond, Brian, *The Victorian Army and the Staff College*, Eyre Methuen, 1972.

Boraston, J. H., *Sir Douglas Haig's Despatches December 1915–April 1919*, Dent, 1919.

Bülow, Prince von, *Memoirs*, Putnam, 1932.

Carrington, Charles, *Soldier from the Wars Returning*, Hutchinson, 1965.

Chapman, Guy, *A Passionate Prodigality*, MacGibbon and Kee, 1965.

Charteris, Brigadier General J., *Field Marshal Earl Haig*, Cassell, 1929.

Charteris, Brigadier General J., *Haig*, Duckworth, 1933.

Clark, Alan, *The Donkeys*, Hutchinson, 1961.

Coombs, R. E. B., *Before Endeavours Fade*, After the Battle Publications, 1983.

Cooper, Duff, *Haig* (two vols), Faber and Faber, 1936.

Davidson, Major General Sir John, *Haig: Master of the Field*, Peter Nevill, 1953.

Dewar, G. A. B. and Boraston, J. H., *Sir Douglas Haig's Command* (two vols), Constable, 1922.

Duncan, G. S., *Douglas Haig as I Knew Him*, Allen and Unwin, 1966.

Edmonds, Brigadier General, *Military Operations in France and Belgium (Official History 1914–1918)*, HMSO.

Falls, Cyril, *The First World War*, OUP, 1960.

Farrar-Hockley, A. H., *The Somme*, Batsford, 1954.

German Official History, *Der Weltkrieg 1914 bis 1918* (4 vols), Mitler and Sohn, Berlin, 1929–36.

Glubb, Lieutenant General Sir John, *Into Battle*, Cassell, 1978.

Gough, Sir Hubert, *Fifth Army*, Hodder and Stoughton, 1931.

Graves, Robert, *Goodbye to All That*, Cassell, 1957.

Gristwood, A. D., *The Somme*, Cape, 1927.

Haig, The Countess, *Douglas Haig: His Letters and Diaries* (unpublished), Moray Press, 1934.

Select Bibliography

Haig, The Countess, *The Man I Knew*, Moray Press, 1936.

Haig, Major General Douglas, *Cavalry Studies*, Hugh Rees, 1907.

Hankey, Lord, *The Supreme Command 1914–1918*, Allen and Unwin, 1961.

Hindenburg, Field Marshal von, *Out of My Life*, Cassell, 1920.

Holmes, Richard, *The Little Field Marshal: Sir John French*, Cape, 1981.

Jünger, Ernst, *Storm of Steel*, Chatto and Windus, 1929.

Kuhl, H. von, *Der Weltkrieg 1914–18*, Weller, Berlin, n.d.

Liddell-Hart, B. H., *History of the First World War*, Cassell, 1934.

Lloyd George, D., *War Memoirs* (revised), Odhams, 1938.

Ludendorff, Erich, *My War Memories*, Hutchinson, 1919.

Marshall-Cornwall, James, *Haig: As Military Commander*, Batsford, 1973.

Masefield, John, *The Old Front Line*, Heinemann, 1919.

Maurice, F. D., *The Life of General Lord Rawlinson*, Cassell, 1928.

Montgomery, Major General Sir A., *The Story of the Fourth Army in the Battle of the Hundred Days, August 8th to November 11th 1918*, Hodder and Stoughton, 1950.

Parsons, I. M., *Men Who March Away*, Chatto and Windus, 1966.

Pershing, John F., *My Experiences in the World War*, Hodder and Stoughton, 1931.

Pitt, Barrie, *1918 The Last Act*, Cassell, 1962.

Repington, Colonel, *The First World War*, Constable, 1920.

Robertson, Field Marshal Sir William, *Soldiers and Statesmen 1914–18*, Cassell, 1926.

Robinson, H. Perry, *The Turning Point*, Heinemann, 1917.

Russell, John, *The Haigs of Bemersyde*, Blackwood, 1881.

Secrett, T., *Twenty-Five Years with Earl Haig*, Jarrolds, 1929.

Sixsmith, E. K. G., *Douglas Haig*, Weidenfeld and Nicolson, 1976.

Spears, Sir Edward, *Prelude to Victory*, Cape, 1939.

Taylor, A. J. P., *The Course of German History*, Hamish Hamilton, 1945.

Terraine, John, *Douglas Haig: The Educated Soldier*, Hutchinson, 1963.

Terraine, John, *To Win a War: 1918, the Year of Victory*, Sidgwick and Jackson, 1978.

Travers, Tim, *The Killing Ground*, Allen and Unwin, 1987.

Tschuppik, Karl, *Ludendorff: The Tragedy of a Specialist*, Allen and Unwin, 1932.

Wilhelm, Crown Prince, *My War Memories*, Thornton Butterworth, 1922.

Wilson, Keith (ed.), *The Rasp of War: The Letters of H. A. Gwynne to the Countess Bathurst 1914–1918*, Sidgwick and Jackson, 1988.

Winterbottom, Derek, *Henry Newbolt and the Spirit of Clifton*, Redcliffe, 1986.

Woodward, David R. (ed.), *The Military Correspondence of Field Marshal Sir William Robertson: Chief of the Imperial General Staff, December 1915–February 1918*, Bodley Head for Army Records Society, 1989.

Index